MINUTES OF THE VESTRY

OF

ST. HELENA'S PARISH,

SOUTH CAROLINA

1726-1812

Edited by

A. S. SALLEY, JR.

Secretary of the Historical Commission of South Carolina

Southern Historical Press, Inc.

Greenville, South Carolina

This volume was reproduced from
A personal copy located in the
Publisher's private Library

Please direct all correspondence and orders to:

www.southernhistoricalpress.com
or
SOUTHERN HISTORICAL PRESS, Inc.
PO Box 1267
375 West Broad Street
Greenville, SC 29601
southernhistoricalpress@gmail.com

Originally published: Columbia, SC, 1919
ISBN #0-89308-295-3

Printed in the United States of America

INTRODUCTION

St. Helena's Parish was established by an act of the General Assembly of South Carolina, ratified June 7, 1712. It was bounded on the east by St. Helena Sound and Combahee River, on the north by a line from the head of Combahee River to the Savannah River and to the south on the ocean. A rector was obtained soon after, but no church was built until 1724, the rector, in the meantime, holding services at the houses of the planters in various parts of the parish. If there was an earlier book of minutes its whereabouts is not generally known, and only by a rare bit of good fortune has this book been rescued from oblivion. During the war between the United States and the Confederate States this book disappeared. In 1902 Theodore Hawley wrote from New Canaan, Connecticut, to the editor hereof, who was then secretary of the South Carolina Historical Society, in Charleston, sent him this book and offered to sell it to the Society, stating that he had purchased it at an auction sale in the North. After some negotiations between officers of the church, in Beaufort, and the holder of the book, the latter was purchased by Mr. Charles M. Barnwell and returned to its rightful owners. Before it was returned to Beaufort, however, the editor hereof secured permission to copy it.

[1[1]]

The Parish of St.
Helena's Vestry
Book Anno Dom
1726

(3[2])

An Order drawn Upon Collo. Alexr. Parris Esqr. Treasurer to pay to John De: La: Bere Esqr. and Mr. Thomas Stanyarne Churchwardens for the parish of St.. Helina the sum of fforty pounds being Parochial Charges due for the Year 1725.

An Order drawn Upon Collo. Alexr. Parris Esqr. Treasurer to pay John De: La: Bere Esqr. and Mr. Thomas Stanyarne Churchwards. for the parish of St.. Helina fforty pounds being Parochial Charges due for the Year 1726

An Order drawn On Collo. Alexr. Parris Esqr. Treasurer to pay John De: La: Bere Esqr. & Mr. Thomas Stanyarne Churchwds. for the parish of St. Helina One hundred pounds being Money Appropriated for repairing or hireing a House for the Minister.

An Order drawn On Collo. Alexr. Parris Esqr. Treasurer to Pay John De: La: Bere Esqr. & Mr. Thos. Stanyarne Churchwds. for the parish of St. Helina One hundred pounds being Money Appropriated for repairing or hireing a House for the Minister.

(4)

At a Vestry held at the Parish Church of St. Helina
Decemr. ye: 28th: 1726

Present.

The Revd: Mr. Lewis Jones Rectr.
Willm. Hazzard Esqr.
Mr. Nathll. Barnwell,
Mr. Alexr. Parris Junr.

Ordered That Certificates be Made ready to Give each person a Title to the Pew they have purchased wch. Certificates are to be Sign'd by the Vestry and Churchwardens.

1The first page is not numbered.
2The second page is blank.

The Inhabitants of the Parish of S^{t}. Helina Mett at the parish Church Aprill y^{e}: 9th. 1727. and Choose Vestry Men as ffolloweth

Present

The Rev^{d}. M^{r}. Lewis Jones Rect^{r}.
Willm.. Hazzard Esqr.
M^{r}. Rich^{d}. Wigg Senr
Capt. Thomas Inns
M^{r}. James Hatcher
M^{r}. Thos. Burton
Capt. Barnabas Gillbart
M^{r}. Rich^{d}. Ricketts--

(5)

The Vestry being Elected and Quallified Choose
M^{r}. Thomas Stanyarne and M^{r}. Nath^{ll}. Barnwell } Churchw^{ds}.

At a Vestry held at the Parish Church of S^{t}. Helina April y^{e}. 25.. 1727.

Present

The Rev^{d}. M^{r}. Lewis Jones Rect^{r}
Willm. Hazzard Esqr.
M^{r}. Richd Wigg Senr.
Capt. Barnabas Gillbart
M^{r}. James Hatcher
M^{r}. Thomas Burton
M^{r}. Rich^{d}. Ricketts
M^{r}. Thomas Stanyarne and M^{r}. Nath^{ll}. Barnwell } Churchw^{ds}.

M^{r}. Thomas Stanyarne Chuchwarden Delivered In his Acco^{t}. for the Year 1726 their being Due to parish ffive pounds ffive Shillings.

(6)

The Same day John De: La: Bere Esqr.. Churchward^{n}. Delivered in his Acco^{t}. for the Year 1726.

At the Same time Mr. Thos. Stanyarne................ Delivered In the Accot. of John Woodward Esqr. Deced. their being due to him from the Parish of St. Helina £103...18..6

Ordered by the Vestry that Sixteen foot of the West end of the Church on both Sides be disposed off for building of Pews for the Parishoners at ffive pounds ℔ foot Provided they build the Pews not Exceeding five foot in Breadth and Eight in length wch. sd. Pews are to be of the same height of those at the East End and to be built with Cedar.

Mr. James Dunlop delivered in his Accot. and their is due to him by Work for the Church £11..7..6 Wch. was Accordingly payd.

Ordered That the Churchwardens do Agree wth. Some Workman to Make Air Holes through the Church Wall to preserve the ffloor.

Ordered That the Churchwardens do Get the Church Tarred and get more Sounding Bords and further repairs as required.

(7)

Ordered That the Churchwardens do Use Means to get fforty pounds from Joseph Cockram being Money Disbursed by the parish for a Cure done On the Body of the sd. Cockram by Doctr. Richd. Handcock.

June ye: 25th: 1727

The Vestry Mett at the parish Church of St.. Helina And Drew an Order Upon Collo. Alexr. Parris Esqr. Treasurer to pay Unto the Revd. Mr. Lewis Jones two hundred And ffifty pounds being due the 25th. of March Last

November ye: 2d. 1727

The Vestry Mett At the parish Church of St. Helina and Drew an Order Upon Collo. Alexr. Parris Esqr. Treasurer to pay the Revd. Mr. Lewis Jones two hundred and ffifty pounds Due the 29th. of September.

The Inhabitants of the Parish of St. Helina Mett at the parish Church Aprill ye. 22d. 1728 and Choose Vestry Men as followeth.

Present

The Revd. Mr. Lewis Jones Rectr.
William Hazzard Esqr.
John De: La: Bere Esqr.
Capt. Thomas Juns
Capt. Thomas Inns
Mr. James Hatcher
Mr. Thos. Burton
Mr. Richd. Ricketts
Mr. Thos. Stone

(8)

The Vestry being Elected and Quallified Choose
Alexr. Trench Esqr. and Mr. Edward Scott } Churchwardens

Ordered That Alexr. Trench Esqr. and Mr. Edward Scott, Churchwardens for the parish of St. Helina do receive from Collo. Alexr. Parris Esqr. Treasurer fforty pounds being Parochial Charges Due for the Year 1727.

Ordered That the Churchwardens pay Unto Rowland Serjeant Clerk of the Parish Church of St. Helina fforty pounds being his Sallary Due March ye: 1st. 1727.

Ordered That Alexr. Trench Esqr. and Mr Edward Scott Churchwardens for the parish of St. Helina Settle the parish Accots. wth. Mr. Thomas Stanyarne Late Churchwarden And receive the Ballance due to the parish.

Ordered by the Vestry That Collo. Alexr Parris Esqr. Treasurer pay Unto the Revd. Mr. Lewis Jones Two hundred and ffifty pounds Due the 25th. of March 1728.

(9)

Ordered That the Churchwardens do Agree with some person to White Wash the Church Tarr it and what else is Necessary.

Ordered That the Churchwardens do Search into the Law that Obliges persons to Build on there Lotts in Beaufort Town According to the time therein limitted for Default of which to prosecute Such person or persons as the Law Directs and If any Amendment be Wanting to put that Law in force That Application be Made to the representatives for Granvil County to have the Opinion of the Assembly in that Case.

Ordered That Mr. Thos. Burton do build the Vacant North Side at the West End of the Church with Pews the Ground being Equally Devided for the following persons (Vizt.) The Revd. Mr. Lewis Jones or his Successors, Alexander Trench Esqr. Capt. Edward Scott, Edmond Ellis and Allen Mc.Lane, The Ministers Pew to be payd for by the parish the Others at the rate of Twenty two Shillings & Six pence ℘r. Yard Square for the fframe Work, The Benches at ffifteen Shillings ℘. Yard, ffooring Three pounds Ten Shillings ℘. Square.
That the Charges of the parish Metting be payd by the Church-wardens being £5,,0,,—

(10)

Ordered That the Churchwards. do Agree with Mr. Thos. Burton to build as Many Seats as can be Conveniently put in the middle Ile two foot Eight Inches Each to be payd for by the parish.

The Inhabitants of the parish of St. Helina Mett at the parish Church Aprill ye: 7th.. 1729 and Choose Vestry Men as followeth

Present

The Revd. Mr. Lewis Jones Rectr.	Mr. Alexr. Parris Junr.
John De: La: Bere Esqr.	Mr. Thos. Hardwick
Willm. Hazard Esqr.	Mr. James Hatcher
Capt. Barnabas Gillbart	Mr Thos. Stone

The Vestry being Elected and Quallified Choose

Mr. Edwd. Scott and Mr. Thos. Wigg } Church wardens

At the same time Rowd. Serjeant & Richd. Ricketts being put Up for Clerk of the Church the said Rowd. Serjeant was Accordingly Choose Clerk.

(11)

Ordered by the Vestry that the Churchwardens pay Unto William Haynes Twenty pounds for Copying out the Laws of the Church.

Ordered That the Churchwardens pay to Rowd. Serjeant and Richd. Ricketts each of them Twenty pounds for Officiating as Clerk's of the Church half a Year Each from March 25th. 1728 To Mar 25th. 1729
An Order Drawn Upon Collo. Alexr. Parris Esqr. Treasurer to pay Mr. Edwd. Scott or Mr. Thos. Wigg Churchwds. for the parish of St. Helina fforty pounds being Parochial-Charges due for the Year 1728

The Vestry Drew an Order Upon Collo.. Alexr. Parris Esqr Treasurer to pay to the Revd. Mr. Lewis Jones or Order Two hundred and ffifty pounds Due the 25th. of March 1729
At the same time William Haynes was Sworn Register and Clerk of the Vestry.

(12)

At a Vestry held at the parish Church of St. Helina August ye: 5th. 1729

Present

The Revd. Mr. Lewis Jones Rectr.
John De: La: Bere Esqr.
Willm. Hazard Esqr.
Capt. Barnabas Gillbart
Mr. Jas. Hatcher
Mr. Thos. Hardwick
Mr. Thos. Stone

Ordered By the Vestry that Mr. Thos. Stanyarne Late Churchwarden Accot. be passed and Audited.
Ordered By the Vestry that Mr. Edward Scott the present Churchwarden Accot. be passed and Audited.

(13)

Ordered By the Vestry That Alexander Trench Esqr. Collo. John Beamore Esqr. and Mr. John Fripp be Appointed to Assess One hundred pounds Currt. Money On the parishoners of the parish of St. Helina for parochial Charges
Ordered By the Vestry That the Vacant South Side of the Church be built with Pews four feet & half Wide Eight foot long At ffive pound ℔ foot the Ground being Equally Devided for the following persons (Vizt.) The Pew Next the Wall for Capt. Thos. Inns & Mr. Rowd. Serjeant, The Next for Mr. Thos. Stone, and Mr. James Hatcher, The Other for Mr. Edward Scott, & Mr. Thos. Wigg, all to be built wth. Cedar At there Own Cost and

Charges. the other Next the South Door for M^{r}. Rich^{d}. Reynolds and Mr James Reynolds.

Agreed By the Vestry That the Rev^{d}. M^{r}. Lewis Jones be payd Thirty pounds p^{r}: Ann for ye time he hath been Curate for the parish of S^{t}. Helina and Yearly & every Year Untill the Parsonage House be built.

(14)

1726		Dr.. The Parish of St.. Helina to Thomas		
Decebr.	18	To: 2: Bottles Clarett.........	£.1,,10,,–	
May:	14	To: 1: Do....................	,,15,,–	
		To Cash paid Mr. Serjeant.....	47,, 2,,6	
		To Cash paid Dunlop for Iron Work	11,, ,,–	
		To Cash paid Drayton for Making Air holes	3,, ,,–	
1727/8 Janr.	26	To Cash paid Mr. De:La:Bere John Gwinups Accot. Iron Work	6,, ,,–	
		To Thos. Burton's Accot.......	6,,15,,–	
		To Do. pd. Capt. Scott for: 300: 10d Nails	1,, 2,,6	
		To Cash for White Washing the Church	25,, ,,–	102,,5,,0
		Cash pd. John Woodward ℘ Order......		105,, ,,–
				207,,5,,0
		To Capt. Edward Scott..................		42,,2,,6
				£249,,7,,6

Errors Excepted
℘ Thos: Stanyarne
1729

(15)

Stanyarne & Na: Barnwell Contra Cr.

1726				
Decr.	26	By Offerings	£2,,17,,6	
Apll.	6	By Do.	3,,17,,6	
		By Do.	2,,12,,6	
		By Parochial Charges	40,,—,,-	
		By Cash for a Parsonage House and Building...	200,,—,,-	£249,,17,,6

By A Note of Parochial Charges payable by Collo. Alexr. Parris for forty pounds wch. I have Now in My hands as Yett not being paid As Witness.

James Island July: 12th: 1729 Thos Stanyarne

1729

(16)

Dr.. The Parrish of St.. Helina To Edwd. Scott		
To Mr. Burton for ye Parsonage Pew	£11,, 4,, 4½	
To a Lock for the Door and Hinges	2,, 0,, 0	
To Nales Glew and hinges..	1,,17,, 6	
To: 5: Bottles of Wine for the Sacrament	1,,11,, 3	
To Mr. De:La:Bere for: 2 Bottles of Do. at ye Vestry	0,,12,, 6	
To Mr. Serjeant for 30 Bushells of Lime	3,,15,, 0	
To Salt for the White Wash	0,,10,, 0	
To: 12lb: of Paint @ 6/3 ℔r.	3,,15,, 0	
To a Gallon of Oyle.......	2,, 0,, 0	
To Mr. Burton for Setting Up the Glass	0,, 7,, 6	
To a Vestry Book..........	4,, 0,, 0	
To Sundry times raising the Ladder	1,, 0,, 0	
To the Painter	1,,10,, 0	
To Collo. Hazard for his Negro Man: 14: Days @ 7/6 ℔r Day	5,, 5,, 0	
		£39,, 8,, 1½
Monday Augst. 4th 1729	Ball Due from Capt Scott To the parish	110:18: 1½
		150: 6: 3

(17)

Pr. Contra Cr..

By Offerings at Xmas	£ 3,, 8,,9	
By Do at Easter	2,,16,,3	
By Do. at Whitsuntide......	1,,18,,9	
By Mr. Trench for his Ground	20,, 0,,0	
By Mr. Gillbart for Do......	20,, 0,,0	
By Mr. Ellis & Mr. M".Lane..	20,, 0,,0	
By Mr. Stanyarne...........	42,, 2,,6	
By an Order in Mr. Stanyarne hand	40,, 0,,0	
		$150,, 6,,3
Errors Excepted By me Edward Scott	Ball—	110,,18,,1½
		39: 8: 1½

(18)

Brougt. Over from ye other Side	£39,, 8,,1½
To: a: Bell Rope	15,,0—
To a Bottle of Wine..................	6,,3
	£40,, 9,,4½

(19)

Pr Contra Cr,,

By Sundrys from the other Side.........	£150,, 6,,3
By offerings at Easter	2,, 1,,3
	152,, 7,,6
Balance Due from Capt. Edwd. Scott To the parish of St. Helina	40,, 9,,4½
	£111,,18,,1½

Which Said Sum of One hundred and Eleven pound Eighteen Shillings and a penny half penny Was Order'd to be paid to The Revd. Mr. Lewis Jones and Wm Haynes

(20)

The Inhabitants of the parish of St.. Helina Mett at the parish Church March the 30th. 1730. And Choose Vestrymen. (Vizt.)

Present.

The Revd. Mr. Lewis Jones Rectr.
John De: La: Bere Esqr
Capt. Edwd. Scott
Capt. Barnabas Gillbart

Mr. Thos. Wigg
Mr. Rowd. Evans
Mr. Thos. Burton
Mr. Richd Ricketts

The Vestry being Elected & Qualified Choose

Collo. Wm. Hazard Esqr.
and } Churchwardens
Capt.. Thos.. Inns

An Order Drawn Upon Collo. Alexr. Parris Esqr. Treasurer to pay Wm.. Hazard Esqr. or Capt. Thos. Inns Churchwardens for the Parish of St.. Helina fforty pounds being Parochial Charges Due for the Year 1729.

Then Adjourn'd to Aprill the Seventh

(21)

Aprill ye.. 7th.. 1730

The Vestry and Churchwds. Mett According to Adjournment.

Present

The Revd. Mr.. Lewis Jones Rectr.
John De: La: Bere Esqr.
Capt. Edwd. Scott
Capt. Barnbs. Gillbart

Mr. Thos: Wigg
Mr. Thos. Burton
Mr. Richd. Ricketts

Collo. Wm.. Hazard Esqr
and } Churchwds.
Capt. Thos. Inns

Ordered By the Vestry and Churchwardens that Lt.. James Watt, and Ensign Thos. Farrington, pay Each of them Twenty ffive pounds to the present Churchwds. for Breaking Ground in the Chancel and every person that shall have Ground Broke Up in any part of the Said Church for the future Shall pay ffifty pounds.

Ordered By the Vestry that Collo. Wm.. Hazard Esqr. or Capt. Thos. Inns the present Churchwds. do gett the parish Accots. wch. are Now in the Custody of Mr. Thos. Stanyarne and either of their rects. Shall be a Discharge for the same.

(22)

Ordered By the Vestry and Churchwds.. That Wm.. Haynes have Twenty pounds ℘r Ann for being Clerk of the Vestry &c.

An Order Drawn By the Vestry & Churchwds. Upon Collo. Alexr.. Parris Esqr. Treasurer to pay Unto the Revd. Mr. Lewis Jones or Order Two hundred and ffifty pounds being due the 25th. March 1730.

Ordered By the Vestry and Churchwards. That Rowland Serjeant have Twenty pounds ℘r Ann for Officiating the place of Sexton.

An Order By the Vestry and Churchwds. Upon Capt. Edwd. Scott for the Sum of Seventy One pounds Eighteen Shillings and a penny half penny being part of the Ballance due from the Said Capt Edwd. Scott to the parish of St.. Helina Wch. Order was Given to the Revd. Mr. Lewis Jones in part of paymt. of One hundred and Twenty pounds Due to the sd. Mr. Jones for four Years House rent the: 10th: March 1729/30

An Order Drawn by the Vestry & Churchwds. Upon Capt. Edwd. Scott to pay Unto Wm Haynes forty pounds being the other part of the Balla. Due from the sd. Capt. Scott to the Abovesd. parish Twenty pound's for coppying ye Church Laws & Twenty pounds being Clerk of the Vestry for the Year 1729.

(23)

Ordered By the Vestry and Churchwds. That the Pew No. (4) be for the Minister of the Within Menconed parish and his Successors.

At The Same time Certificates was Drawn out and Sign'd to Give each and every person a Title To their Pew that have payd for the Same.

At a Vestry held at the parish Church of St. helina Octor. 6th. 1730.

Present

The Revd.. Mr. Lewis Jones Rectr:
Mr. Thos: Wigg
Capt. Rowd. Evans
Capt. Barnbs: Gillbart
Mr. Richd Ricketts

Wm.. Hazard Esqr.
&
Capt. Thos Inns
} Churchwds:

An Order Drawn By the Vestry and Churchw^{ds}. Upon Coll^{o}: Alex^{r}. Parris Esqr. Treasurer to pay Unto the Rev^{d}. M^{r}. Lewis Jones or order Two hundred & Fifty pounds being Due the 29th. of Sep^{t}. 1730.

Ordered That W^{m}. Haynes do gett the Tax of the Inhabitants on Ladys Island In the room of Alex^{r}. Trench Esqr. when assess'd.

(24)

The Inhabitants of the Parish of S^{t}.. Helina Mett at the parish Church May.. 3^{d}.. 1731 And Choose Vestry Men (Viz^{t}.)

Present

The Rev^{d}. M^{r}. Lewis Jones Rect^{r}.	M^{r}.. Nath^{ll}. Barnwell
John De: La: Bere Esq	Capt^{t}. Edwd. Scott
M^{r}. Thomas Wigg	M^{r}. Thomas Burton
Mr Thomas Stone	M^{r}. Rich^{d}. Ricketts

The Vestry being Elected and Qualified Choose

M^{r}.. Richard Reynolds and Mr James Hatcher } Churchwardens

An Order Drawn on Coll^{o}.. Alex^{r} Parris Esqr. Treasurer to pay M^{r}. Richard Reynolds or M^{r}. James Hatcher Churchw^{ds}.. for the parish of S^{t}.. helina Forty pounds being Parochial Due for the Year 1730.

(25)

At a vestry held at the parish Church of S^{t}. Helina October the 13th 1731

Present

Edward Scott	
Thomas Wigg Lewis Jones Rect^{r}	Thomas Stone
Thomas Burton	Richard Rickets

Ordered that Coll^{o}. W^{m}. Hazzard and Capt.. Thos. Inns Late Church Wardens Do pay to Tho Burton the Sum of three pounds

& five Shillings & to James Dunlop the Sum of Thirty Shillings for work Done to the Church.
Ordered that the late Church wardens Do pay to M^{r}. W^{m}. Haynes the Sum of nineteen £ Three Shilling & nine pence for Sallery Due to him
Ordered that Capt Rowland Evans pay m^{r}. Serjeant Clark the Sum of Twenty pounds being his Sallery
Ordered that Coll^{o}. Alex^{r}. Parris pay to the Rev^{d}. Lewis Jones the Sum of Two Hundred & fifty pounds being for his Six months Sallery to the 29th. of September Last
The Inhabitants of the parish of St Helina met at the parish Church Aprill ye 10th. 1732 and Chose vestry men as followeth viz. -

(26)

Present

The Rever^{d}. M^{r}. Lewis Jones Rect^{r}.	M^{r}. Richd Rickets
M^{r}. John Dela Bere	M^{r}. Nath^{ll} Barnwell
M^{r}. Thomas Wigg	M^{r}. Thomas Stone
Capt. Thomas Inns	Mr Rich^{d}. Franklin

The Vestry being chosen & Qualify'd Chose
Mr Richard Reynolds and Thomas Burton } Church wardons

Ordered that Coll^{o}. Alex^{r}. Parris pay to the Rever^{d}. mr. Lewis Jones the sum of Two Hundred & fifty pounds due to him for supplying ye Cure of S^{t}. Helina due the 25 day of march last

Ordered that Coll^{o}. Alex^{r}. Parris pay the parochial Charges being forty pounds due the 25th of march last to Richard Reynolds & Thomas Burton Church wardons

Certificates was given to & signed for y^{e}. Pews to each person

To {
M^{r}. Rich^{d}. Reynolds & James Reynolds — N°. 11
M^{r}. Thomas Wigg — N°. 12
M^{r}. Thomas Stone & M^{r}. James Hatcher — N°. 13
M^{r}. Rowl^{d}. serjeant & Capt. Thos. Inns — N°. 14

27

Ordered by the vestry that Richard Reynolds & Tho. Burton pay unto m^{r} Rowland Serjeant Clark the Sum of Twenty Pounds for Officiating ye place of Sexton———————

Ordered that m^r^. Richd Reynolds & Tho. Burton pay unto m^rs^ Deborah Haynes the Sum of fifteen pounds for her Deceased husband's Officiating Clark of ye vestry for Ten months

Ordered by the vestry & Church wardens that m^r^. Richard Reynolds & Thomas Burton pay unto m^r^. Lavis the sum of twenty six pounds & thirteen shillings for keeping of Charles Purdy's Childe to the 10th. of April 1732

Ordered that Thomas Burton have one pound two Shillings & six pence for work done at ye Church

Ordered that ye owners of the four Pews of the South side at the West End pay unto m^r^. Richard Reynolds & Thomas Burton for the Ground the sum of ninety pounds

Att a vestry mett on whitsun monday may y^e^. 29th 1732

Present

The Rever^d^ Mr Lewis Jones Mr Na^th^ Barnwell Mr Rich. Franklin M^r^. Thomas Inns Mr Thos. Wigg Mr Rich. Rickets	vestry	Mr Richard Reynolds Tho Burton Church ward^ons^—

(28)

Ordered that five of ye vestry & ye two Church wardons Do Rase y^e^. Sum of Eighty four pounds on y^e^. Parish rateing them according to y^e^. Generall Tax of this Parish at five Shillings in the Pound

At a meeting of the vestry att the parish Church of St Hellena on the 14th august

1732

Present

The Rev^d^. Mr Lewis Jones Mr John Dela Bere Esqr: Capt Tho. Inns Mr Richard Franklin Mr Tho. Stone Mr Tho Wigg	vestry	Thos Burton Church Wardon.

Ordered y^{t} ye former Order of y^{e}. last vestry for raiseiing ye Sum of Eighty four pounds on the parish at the rate of five shillings in y^{e}. pound according to what Tax they Paid, to be paid to M^{r}. Richard Reynold or Tho. Burton Church wardons on or before ye Last day of September next ensuing

(29)

Easter Munday 1733

Mett According to Notiss the Inhabitants of St Hellena and made Choice of the Fallowing Gentelmen for the ensuing Year, and Quallified According to Law. Viz

Lewis Jones
Major Barnwell
John De La Bere
Tho Wigg.
Tho: Inns.
Tho Burton
Rich: Reynolds
Rich: Franklin
} Vestrey

Thos. Stone
Rich: Ricketts
Church=Wardens

Ordred that Coll: Alexander Parris Treasurer pay the Rev,^{d} M^{r}. Jones the sum of two houndred and fifty pounds

Order;d that Mrs Levis be paid at the rate of 40^{s} p^{r}. month and one week from the first of March 1731½ to the 6th of November 1732 —

Order'd that Charles Purdy be bound to Mrs Levis Planter until he is of the age of 21 years and that the Parish pay her ten pounds in Consideration of her giving him a years Schooling

(30)

Order'd that the Indentures be draw'n for the Binding of Charles Purdy to the Said Mrs Levis.

Order'd that Coll: Allexander Parris pay the Parochial Charges being forty pounds to the Church Wardens

Order'd that the Church Wardens pay Mr Rowland Sarjeant the Sum of twenty Pounds Currency

1734.—

The Parishoners of St. Helen's Mett on Easter Monday, & chose Vestry-Men as followeth; & qualify'd According to Law.

Lewis Jones Wm. Hazzard Senr. Wm. Hazzard Junr. John Mc. Gilvery Thos. Burton Thos. Inns Richd. Ricketts Allen Mc.Lane	Vestry	At the Same time they made choice of —————— John Frip Senr. } Church= Philip Jevins } Wardens.

Order'd that an order be Drawn on Coll. Alexdr. Parris Treasurer for two hundred & fifty Pounds Payable to Mr. Lewis Jones.
Order'd that Coll. Alexr. Parris Pay the Church-Wardens 40£= Parochial Charges.
Order'd that Mr Jones go to St. Helena Island to perform Divine Service once in 6 weeks for Six Months.—
Order'd that the Vestry reimburse themselves the 40 pounds laid out in the Cure of Joseph Cockram, out of ye Money Levy'd on the Parish for the use of the poor.—

(31)

Order'd, that Mr. Burton pay Mr. Sergeant twenty Pounds as Sexton for the year 1733.
Order'd that Mr. Burton be paid 20 Shills. for Drawing the Indentures for binding out Chas. Purdy.
Order'd that the Church-Wardens Settle Accts. with Mr. Burton And receive the Ballance remaining in his hands.
Order'd that Mr. Wigg pay the Church-Wardens twenty two pounds ten Shills. for his Pew Ground.
October Mett then According to Notice

1st. 1734.	Lewis Jones, Rectr. Coll. Wm. Hazzard Capt. Thos. Inns Mr Thos. Burton Mr. Rich'd Ricketts Mr Wm. Hazzard, Junr.	the Vestry

Agreed, that thanks be return'd to Capt. John Bull, for his Generous Donation of 100£,, Currency to this Church of St. Helen's towards the Purchasing a Piece of Plate for the Use of the Communion table.

Agreed

that Mr. Jones Send to England, by the first convenient Opportunity, to Purchase a Cup for the Communion table with the aboves'd money; and that ye following words be Engraven upon it, viz: The Gift of Capt John Bull to the Parish of St Helena.

Agreed

that an Order be Drawn on Coll. Alexander Parris Treasurer to Pay the Revd Mr. Lewis Jones the Sum of two Hundred & fifty Pounds Currency — — — — — — — — — — — — — — —

Agreed

that the Church-Wardens take up Catharine Thomas, who is reported to be with Child, & bring her before a Magistrate there to declare upon Oath the father of the Child; and upon Such an Oath taken, they are to oblige ye father to Give Security to the Parish for the Maintenance of ye sd. child.

(32)

Decbr. 26th.

1734.

Mett then According to notice, Philip Jeffeins } Church= Warden

Lewis Jones
Coll. Wm. Hazzard
Wm. Hazzard Junr.
Thos. Burton
Richard Ricketts } Vestry

Order'd that Expences of James Smithers, a poor Sick Stranger, be paid by Mr. Lewis Jones out of ye Sacramnt.-Money lying in his hands.

The Inhabitants of the Parish of St. Helen's Mett on Easter Monday 1735, and chose vestry men & Ch. Wardens, as followeth. vizt.

Lewis Jones, rector
Coll. Wm. Hazzard
Mr. Richd. Reynolds
Wm. Hazzard Junr.
Mr. Ricketts
Mr. Mc.Gilvery
Mr. Burton
Mr. James Hatcher. } Vestry

James Reynolds
Allen Mc.Lean } Church-Wardens.

The Above said Gentlemen being not Qualify'd According to law, the former Vestry & Ch. Wardens pass'd y[e] following Orders, viz[t]:
Order'd that the Publick treasurer pay M[r]. Jones £250.. Currency.
Order'd that the Publick treasurer pay 40£.. parochial Charges to the Ch. Wardens.

(33)

Order'd/
that the new Vestry & Ch. Wardens meet & qualify on the 15th. of May next.
Mett then According to Order, & qualify'd According to Law.

Lewis Jones, Rector.
Coll. W[m]. Hazzard.
Cap[t]. James Hatcher
M[r]. W[m]. Hazzard, Jun[r].
M[r] Rich[d]. Ricketts.
} Vestry

Order'd
that James Reynolds be fin'd ten Pounds for not Appearing & qualifying According to Law.
Order'd/
that Capt Jemmitt Cobley & Allen M[c].Lean Serve as Ch. Wardens for the Ensuing Year; who both qualify'd According to Law.—
Order'd
that M[r]. Burton Pay Cap[t]. Jemmitt Cobley Ch. Warden the Sum of 31£,,6.,3. lying in his hands for the Use of the Parish.
Order'd/
that M[r]. Ricketts Pay Cap[t]. Jemmitt Cobley Ch. Warden the Sum of 19£,,10.,00. it being for M[r]. Wigg's pew-ground, lying in his hands for the use of the Parish.

The Inhabitants of the Parish of S[t]. Helen's mett on Easter Monday 1736, and chose vestrymen and Ch. Wardens, as followeth viz[t].

M[r]. Lewis Jones
Coll. W[m]. Hazzard
M[r]. Tho[s]. Wigg—
M[r] W[m].. Hazzard Jun[r].
M[r] Tho[s]. Burton—
M[r]. Rich[d]. Ricketts
M[r] Tho[s]. Stone
M[r] James Hatcher
} Vestry

M[r]. R. Woodward
M[r]. J. Barnwell
Ch. Wardens.

(34)

Then Order'd by the former Vestry, that the New Vestry & Ch. Wardens meet on the 17th. of May to qualify According to Law.

May 17th. Mett then and qualify'd According to notice, vizt.

1736.	M^{r}. Lewis Jones Coll. W^{m}. Hazzard M^{r}. W^{m}. Hazzard Capt. James Hatcher M^{r}. Thos. Burton	Vestry-men.

August 4th. 1736. The Parishioners met an chose M^{r}. James Reynolds & M^{r}: Simon Jones Church-Wardens in the room of M^{r}. Rich^{d}. Woodward & M^{r}. John Barnwell who refus'd to qualify.

The Inhabitants of the Parish of S^{t}. Helen's Met on Easter Monday 1737; And Chose Vestry-men and Church-Wardens as followeth, who qualify'd according to Law.

Lewis Jones, rector Coll. W^{m}. Hazzard M^{r}. Thos. Wigg M^{r}. Rich^{d}. Wigg M^{r}. W^{m}. Hazzard M^{r}. Thos. Stone M^{r}. Rich^{d}. Ricketts M^{r}. Allen M^{c}.Lean.	Vestry	M^{r}. James Reynolds M^{r}. Simon Jones Ch. Wardens.

Order'd by the Vestry that M^{r}. Hugh Bryan, M^{r}. Rich^{d}, Reynolds, Coll. Nath. Barnwell be Appointed Assessors to Rate the Parish for 100£ Currency for the Support of the Poor.
Order'd that Mathew Hicks be bound Apprentice to George Hogg until he Arrives at the Age of 21 Years; and that proper Indentures be prepar'd for the Same.

(35)

Order'd at the Same time that the Ch. Wardens do Demand of M^{r}. Rich^{d}. Woodward & M^{r}. John Barnwell a fine of 10£ Each for refusing to Serve as Church-Wardens for the Year 1736.——
An Order then Drawn upon M^{r}. Gabriel Manigault for 40£. Parochial Charges Due March 25th. for the Preceding Year.——

Order'd that the Ch. Wardens assign over the abovesd. Order to Mr. Rowland Sergeant for officiating as Clark of the Church the Preceding Year. ¬¬

Order'd/

That the Ch. Wardens do agree with a Carpenter to repair the Steeple & get the Bell hung, as Soon as Conveniently it may be Done.

Ordered/

That the Ch. Wardens do agree with a Carpenter to Build 6 Pews, vizt 3 Pews to the East End of the Church & 3 to the West End for the Following Persons, Mrs. Dawley, Mr. Mikel Mr. Simon Jones, Mr. Ricketts, Mr. Burton, Mr. Richd. Stevens.¬⌐

Lewis Jones
Thos Wigg
William Hazzard
Richard Wigg
his
Alen A McClen
mark
William Hazzard Jur-
Richard Ricketts[1]

(36)

On Easter Monday, April 3d. 1738.¬⌐

The Inhabitants of the Parish of St. Helena Mett as usual And Chose Vestry-men & Church- Wardens, as followeth ¬⌐

Lewis Jones, Rectr. Capt. Hugh Bryan Mr. Ambrose Reeve Mr. John Barnwell Coll. Wm. Hazzard Mr. Richd. Ricketts Mr. Thos. Stone Mr. Allen Mc.Lean	Vestry.
Mr. Jonathan Bryan Mr. Wm. Hazzard	Church= Wardens.

[1]Autograph signatures

August 7th.. 1738.

The Inhabitants of the Parish of St. Helena met according to notice & made choice of John De La Bere and Thos. Wigg Esqrs. Vestrymen who qualify'd according to Law, In the Room of Coll. Wm. Hazzard who refus'd to qualify, And Thos. Stone lately Deceas'd.¬⌐

At the Same time Stephen Bull Esqr: was chosen Church-Warden for the present year in the Room of Mr. Wm. Hazzard Junr., who refus'd to Qualify.¬⌐

Order'd by the Vestry that an Order be Drawn on the Publick Treasurer for forty Pounds Parochial Charges Payable to the Church-Wardens, and that the Sd. Order be assign'd to Mrs. Serjeant for her husband's Salary as Church-Clark for the Year 1737. ¬⌐ ¬⌐

Order'd that Mr Thos. Burton be Establish'd as Church-Clark & Sexton.

Order'd that Hugh Bryan Esqr., Coll. Nathaniel Barnwell, And Mr. John Barnwell be Appointed to Assess this Parish five Shills. in the Pound according to the Tax on Land & Slaves for this Present Year.

Present

Lewis Jones, Rectr.
Hugh Bryan Esqr
John De La Bere Esqr.
Thos. Wigg Esqr.
Mr John Barnwell
Mr Ambrose Reeve
Mr Richd. Ricketts } Vestry.

Steven Bull Esqr.
Mr. Jonathan Bryan
Church-Wardens.¬⌐

(37)

On Easter Monday, April 23d. 1738./

The Inhabitants of the Parish of St. Helena Met as Usual & chose Vestry Men & Church Wardens as ffolloweth.

Lewis Jones, Rectr.
Capt. Hugh Bryan
Natl. Barnwell
John Barnwell
Step. Bull
Amb: Reeve
Tho: Wigg..
Allein McLaine } Vestry

John Frip Junr.
Edward Wigg. }
Church Wardens.

April 23d. 1739 Recd: of Hugh Bryan forty Pounds part of the Poors Rate & of John Barnwell forty three Pounds Ninteen Shills: & 6 pence which is deliver'd to the Revrd: Lewis Jones for the use of the Poor.—

Capt Jemmitt Cobley brought in An Acct., the ballance in his favour being 24-18-3- was Allow'd of, & paid Accordingly.⌐—

Mr. Richd. Reynold's Acct. of 6£= was laid before ye Vestry And Allow'd.

⌐—Order'd at the Same time that Advertisemts. be immediately fix'd at proper places to Inform the Inhabitants on the Island of Port-Royal that they pay the Poor's Rate in a month's time at furthest into the hands of Mr. Edwd. Wigg Church-Warden; or Executions will be Issu'd out, witht. any further Notice.

⌐—Order'd that the Church-Wardens do Demand of Rich'd Woodward Esqr. & Mr. William Hazzard Junr. 10£= a piece being their fine for refusing to Serve as Church-Wardens; And In Case they do not Comply with this Demand, that Warrants may be Issu'd out agst. them witht. further Notice.

⌐—at the Same time there was an Order, Drawn on the Treasurer, for 40£= Parochial Charges Payable to Messrs. Edwd. Wigg & John Frip Junr. Ch. Wardens.⌐—

⌐—Order'd that the Abovesd. Order of 40£= parochial Charges be Assign'd over to Mr. Thos. Burton for officiating as Church Clark for the Year 1738.⌐—

38 August 28th. 1739. (St. Helena Parish.)

Mett then According to Notice the Inhabitants & Chose Mr. Andrew Deveaux As Ch. Warden, who qualify'd accordingly. Mett According to Notice the Vestry as followeth, vizt.

Lewis Jones
Hugh Bryan
Stephen Bull
Ambrose Reeve
John Barnwell⌐—
Thos. Wigg⌐—
} Vestry

Agreed at the Same time, to Issue out Warrants agst. the Defaulters for not paying the Poor's rate.

Agreed that an Order be Sent by the Vestry to John Frip to Qualify forthwith, or to pay his fine.⌐—

Recd of Mr. Hugh Bryan the Sum of Six & Twenty Pounds In full for Six Months boarding and Nursing of Lydia Jones; by me

Her
Elisabeth X Griffiths¬–
Mark

Agreed that the Sum of Thirty Three Pounds Nine shillings be paid to Messrs Woodward & Flowers for Victualling and Transporting Poor Seamen lately Prisoners at the Havana, to Charlestown

On Easter Monday 1740.¬–

Then Mett the Inhabitants of St. Helena Parish, And Chose Vestry men & Ch. Wardens as follows, who Qualify'd accordingly. vizt;

Mr. George Livingstone
Mr. James Deveaux
Church-Wardens.¬–

Vestry:
Lewis Jones, Rectr.
Thos. Wigg Esqr.
Mr Richd. Wigg
Mr. Hugh Bryan
Mr. John Barnwell
Mr. Am. Reeve¬–
Mr. Edward Wigg¬–
Mr. Allen Mc.Lane

39

1740. Easter Monday. ¬– ¬– ¬– ¬– ¬– ¬– ¬–
An Order Drawn by the Vestry Payable to the Ch. Wardens for 40£= Parochial Charges Due 25th of March 1739, In the room of the former Order Drawn for the same sum. ¬– ¬– ¬– ¬– ¬– ¬– An Order Drawn by the Vestry Payable to the Ch. Wardens for 40£= Parochial Charges Due 25th. of March 1740, ¬– ¬– ¬– Agreed that the two abovesaid Orders be Assign'd over by the Ch. Wardens to Mr. Burton for his two Last Years Salary as Ch. Clark. ¬– ¬– ¬– ¬– ¬– ¬– ¬– ¬– ¬– ¬–Agreed that Mr. Edw'd. Wigg do pay Mrs. Griffiths wt. remains Due to her for Boarding & Lodging Lydia Jones.¬– ¬– ¬–Accepted of Simon Jones's Order of 67£= Due to him for boarding & Lodging Lydia Jones, Payable to Mr. Thos. Hepworth.¬–

¬–On Easter Monday 1741.¬– ¬– ¬– ¬– ¬– ¬– ¬–
Then Met the Inhabitants of St. Helena Parish & Chose Vestry

Men & Church-Wardens as followeth, who Qualify'd not According to Law, vizt.

Chas. Purry / Rich^{d}. Capers } Church= Wardens }

Lewis Jones ~ ~
Amb. Reeve ~ ~
Joseph Edwd. Flowers
Nath. Barnwell ~
Rich^{d}. Ricketts ~
Thos. Wigg ~ ~
Edwd. Wigg. ~ ~
Rich^{d}. Wigg ~ ~ } Vestry-Men ~

~On Easter Monday. April 18th.— ~1742.~

Then Met the Inhabitants of S^{t}. Helena Parish & Chose Vestry-Men & Church-Wardens as followeth, Viz^{t}.,

Ch. Wardens-
Chas. Purry
Rich^{d}. Capers ~ }

Vestry }
Lewis Jones ~
Amb. Reeve~
Coll. Nath. Barnwell
Coll W^{m}. Hazzard
Capt- Rich^{d}. Wigg~
M^{r}. Edwd. Wigg — —
Rich^{d}. Ricketts
John Barnwell

All then Qualify'd according to Law Except M^{r}. Ambrose Reeve, & M^{r}. John Barnwell ~ ~ ~

40

1742. Drew two orders at the Same time for Parochial Charges on M^{r}. Manigault Publick Treasurer, One for forty pounds Due at Easter 1741, the other Due at Easter 1742. ~

~Agreed that the afores^{d}. orders be assign'd over by the Church-Wardens for the payment of M^{r}. Burton as Church-Clark, and they were assign'd accordingly.~

April 4th.. 1743 Easter Monday~

Att a metting of the Parrishioners of St Helena the under mencioned Persons were Chossen As Vestry Men and Church wardens for the Ensueing Yeare~

Church Wardens
M^{r}.. Chas: Purry .... }
Coll^{o} Nath^{ll} Barnwell }

The Revd Lewis Jones
Edwd Wigg
Richd Ricketts
Richd Wigg
Rich^{d}. Capers
Benj^{a}: Lloyd
Simmon Jones
Coll Willm: Hazzard } Vestry Men

Ordered that the abovesaid Vestry and Church Wardens Do meet on the 10th Day of this Instant Aprill to Qualifie themselves According to Law—

41

Met According to Order the following Persons, & Qualify'd according to Law, vizt.,

Col Nathaniel Barnwell M^{r}. Charles Purry Church-Wardens.		Lewis Jones—. Col. W^{m}. Hazzard Edward Wigg Rich^{d}. Wigg Rich^{d}. Ricketts Benjamin Lloyd Simon Jones	Vestry-Men

Mett according to appointment this 19th April 1743 and Orderd that M^{r}. James Deveaux Coll^{o}. William Hazzard and Mr Richard Capers be appointed to assess this Parrish one shilling & six pence on every pound according the last Tax on land and slaves.–

and Drew an order on Gabriel Manigault Esqr Publick treasurer for Forty pounds Parochial Charges payable to the Church Wardens, & the said order was then assigned to Mr Thos. Burton as his Salary as Church Clark for the year 1742.

This day the Rev^{d}. Mr Lewis Jones D^{d}. in his acco^{t}. & the ball^{ce}. Due in his favour is £138..2..10. Exclusive of his house Rent. which house Rent together wth. the above Ball^{ce}. will make next March £168,,2,,10—which money we shall Indeavour to raise by Subscription,

There still remains in Mr Jones hand £92..15..10 Curren^{y}. money belongin to the Church, which Sum he may make use off, until the above sum of £168,,2,,10 be paid him

Natha^{l}. Barnwell. Chas. Purry.—	Church W^{den}—	Lewis Jones William Hazzard Richd Capers Ben Lloyd Simon Jones Richard Ricketts	Vestry- men.—

42
Dec 26th. 1743

Mett then according to Notice.

Collo Nathl Barnwell } Church
Charles Purry } Wardens.

Lewis Jones.
Collo Willm Hazzard.
Richd Capers
Richard Ricketts
Edward Wigg—
} Vestry

Ordered that those persons that do not pay their poors rate by the first day of February next, Warrants to be Issued out against them, and that Collo Hazzard Richard Capers, ℘ James Duvax put advertisements up for that purpose:—

March 26th: 1744 Easter Monday

Att Meeting the Parrissioners of St. Helena Parrish, the Under mentioned Persons where Chosen as Vestry men and Church Wardens for the Ensuing Year

Church Wardens

Nathl. Barnwell
Robert Williams

The Revd. Mr Lewis Jones
Charles Purry
Edwd. Wigg
Richd. Ricketts
Ben Lloyd
Richd. Capers
Collo. Wm. Hazzard
Richd Wigg
} Vestry Men

43

April 10: 1743[1]

Mett then according to Notice

Nathl. Barnwell Church Warden

Lewis Jones
Wm. Hazzard
Richd. Richetts
Chas. Purry
Edwd Wigg
Ben Lloyd
Richd. Wigg
} Vestry

[1]Should be 1744.

M^{r}Edwd Wigg Delivered his acco^{t}. in for the Yeare 1739 as follows on acco^{t} of Goods Ball^{ce}. £21,, 9,, 4¾
for Simon Jones order pay to T Hepworth........ 67,,—,,—

£88,, 9,, 4¾

out of which he has rece^{d} for Poors Rates....
for 1743 60,, 9,,10½

paid Mr Edwd. Wigg this Day in full £27,,19,, 6¼
out of the Poors Rates for 1743——

M^{r}. James Deveaux paid in the Poors Rates for 1743.£58,, 6,,—
out of wch. money was paid W^{m}. Wainswrights Nursing .... 22,,—,,—

£36,, 6,,—

Paid Mr Wigg out this ball^{ce} £28,,—,,—
Paid Mr Burton................ 6,,—,,—
34,,—,,—

Remains out the Poors Money £.. 2,, 6,,—
M^{r}. Chas. Purry deliverd in his acco^{t}. the ball^{ce}.
due from him Church-Money................ 17,,—,, 9

Remains wth. Nath Barnwell £19,, 6,, 9.

Orderd that the Church Warden to pay Mr Thos. Burton as fast as he receives the Church Money One hund^{d}. Pound Currencey for building the Steple
Drew one Ord^{r} att the same time for Parochial Charges on Mr Motte Publick Treasurer for Forty pounds Due at Easter 1744: Agreed that the aforesaid Ord^{r} be assigned over by the Church Wardens for the pay^{t} of Mr Burton as Church Clark: And it was assigned over accordingly.—

44.
Ordered that Warrants be Issued againts all the Defaulters that have not paid their last years assessment for supporting the Poor

Lewis Jones
William Hazzard.
Ben Lloyd
Natha. Barnwell Richard Ricketts
Church Wardens. Ed Wigg.
Chas^{s}. Purry.

April 15th. 1745 Easter Munday

At Meeting of the Parrissioners of St Hellena Parrish. the under mentiond Persons, where Chosen as Vestery Men & Church Wardens, for the Ensueing Year.

Robert Williams }
D^{r}. Ambrose Reeves } Church Wardens.

Coll^{o} Wm Hazzard.
Coll^{o} Thomas Wigg.
Charles Purry.
Nathl Barnwell.
Richard Ricketts
Edward Wigg:
Benjamin Lloyd.

Drew at same time one Order for Parochial Charges on Mr Motte Publick Treasurer for Forty pounds dues at Easter 1745. Agreed at same time that the aforesaid ord^{r} be assignd over by the Church Wardens for the pay^{t} of M Burton as Church Clarck. And it was assignd over Accordingly.——
same day the Vestry Men acepting B Lloyd. was Qualifyed according to Law:—

April 22^{d}. 1745—

The Vestry meet according to Notice. Doct Reeves refuses to serve as C. W. findable Ten pounds. same time Choise Coll^{o} Jno Mullryn as Church Warden in his Room & sev^{l} Acco^{ts} Del^{d} in—

45.

Monday. Augt. 5th. 1745—

Meet then according to Law.

Coll^{o} Wm Hazzard
Coll^{o} Nath Barnwell
Charles Purry.
Edward Wigg.
Richard Ricketts.
} Vestry men.

Coll^{o} John Mullryn who was appointed att the last meeting of the Vestry was Choisen Church Warden. who refuses to act: Fineable Ten pounds. and in his Room Isaac Weatherly is appointed Church Warden:—
Agreed at same time, to allow Thomas McFarley Thirty pounds Curr^{y} to be paid in a twelve Month towards finding him in Cloths:—

March 31. 1746. Easter Munday.

At meeting of the Parrissioners of S[t] Hellena Parish. the under mentioned Persons, where Chosen as Vestry men & Church Wardens, for the Ensueing Year.

Church Wardens	Vestry Men
Isaac Weatherly—	Coll[o] W[m] Hazzard.
William Harvey	Thomas Wigg.
	Nath[l] Barnwell.
	Robert Williams
	Edward Wigg—
	Charles Purry.
	Richard Ricketts

Order[d]. that the sum of Eighty pounds be Raised on the Inhabitants of this parrish for the support of the Poor and that the Church Wardens do Collect the same

Drew at the same time an order for the Parochial Charges on M[r]. Motte Public Treasurer for Forty pounds, due at Easter 1746. agreed at the same time that the affores[d]. order be assigned over by the Church Wardens. for the payment of M[r]. Burton as Church Clerk. and it was assigned Accordingly. order[d] that the Churchwardens to apply to Doctor Reeves for his Fine of Ten pounds. and that the order for Coll[o]. John Mullryne to be Fined is now Canceled it appearing that he did not Refuse to Serve

46.

March 30th. 1746 Settled Robert Williamss. accot. vizt.

Dr.		Cr.	
Deliverd. Greaves for a Sailor	1.13. 9	By Cash Recd. of Mr. Jones Sacrament money	19,, 2..10
To paid Henry Orr for Do	20. 0	By Saml. Hastings fine	1 .. ..
To Stephen Greves for Do	4.. 0	By Jo: Butlers Tax.	3,,17. 3.
To Delagayeys. Accot.	9,, 8,, 9	By Capt. Mc.Phearsons Do	2,,17.10
To paid for a Solders Pass	15....	By Churchmoney Recd. of Mr. Purry	10,,17,, 6
	35,,17,, 6	By Fines Recd. of George Ellison.	20,, 0....
To paid Capt. Nortons ballce.	.. 4,,11		
To Expence for Burying an old Dutchwoman ..	1,, 2,, 6		
To so much paid Ambros. Barr for carrying back. a poor man to Georgia.	2,, 0,, 0		
To Cash pd. Capt. Norton For the mentinance of an old woman.	17. 5. 0		
Ballce... due.......	1,, 5,, 6		
	£57,,15 5—		£57,,15,, 5

Janry. 8th. 1746 at a meeting of the Vestry and Churchwardens of this Parrish. was present.

William Harvey, Ch. Warden

Vestrymen

Collo. Natha. Barnwell
Collo. William Hazard
Chas. Purry——
Richd. Ricketts
Edwd. Wigg——
Robert Williams

When it was agreed that the Parrish be Taxed with Eighteen pence in the pound According to the Rate that Each paid for the Public Tax in the year 1745: and that Mr. William Harvey do Receive the Same for the use of the Poor of the Parrish which money is to be Raised in a month from this date

47

And that the Sum of Thirty pounds be paid by the Churchwardens out of the poor Rate to Thomas MacFarling as before——— Appointed. Orderd. for the Future that the Church Wardens shall Lay out their money Appointed for the Poor in Such necessaries as they shall think proper

April 20. 1747. Settled William Harveys Accot. Vizt.

Dr.		Cr.	
To paid Mr. Wigg for Mcfarling	£1.15.0	By Poor Rate recd of Sundry Persons .	£26–17–1
To do. pd. Mr. Purry for do	28– 5–0		
To do. pd. Mr. Purry for 2 Blankets for Mrs. Wamsley . .	9–10–0	By Balla. from the parrish due to W: H	18–2–11
To pd. Mr. Wigg for Sundrys, do. a poor Sailor which died in Beaufort	5–10–0		
	£45– 0–0		£45– 0–0

1747

Apl 20.—Balla due Mr Harvey on above Accot - - - -	£18,,2,,11.
due to Robert Williams for Sundrys for a poor man	11,,5—0

& Wo-. ℘ Accot..————

Deduct 25/6 for so much due the Parrish from R. Williams on a former Accot————

48

April: 20. 1747. Easter Munday÷

At Meeting of the Parishoners of St Hellena Parrish. the under mentiond Persons were Chosen as Vestry Men & Church Wardens— for the Ensueing Year.—

John Delegaye & } Church
John Cattell. } Wardens.

Coll° Wm Hazzard—
Coll° Nath Barnwell—
Robert Williams
Charles Purry—
Edward Wigg.
Richard Ricketts—
Thomas Wigg—
} Vestrymen—

Drew at same time an Order for the Parochial Char^s^. on Mr Motte Publick Treasurer for Forty Pounds Due At Easter 1747—Agreed at same time that the aforesaid Order be Assignd over by the Church Wardens, for the payment of Mr Burton as Church Clark. and it was Assignd Accordingly & Swore the above Vestry Men, for the Ensuing year.—
& the New Church Wardens shall pay the former Church Wardens Acco^t^. & Robert Williams the first Money they get:¬¬

49

May 25th. 1747

At a meeting of the Churchwardens and Vestry of this Parrish at the desire of the Rev^d^. M^r^. Orr who laid before us a letter Coppy underneath

London Charter house Octo^r^. 20th. 1746

Worthy Gentlemen

I most heartily Condole with you on the Death of your worthy Pastor M^r^. Jones, and the Society for Propogation of the Gospel for Forreign parts (M^r^. Hugh Jones the Nephew being Settled to his Satisfaction in these parts, have given the Rev^d^. M^r^. Orr of S^t^. Pauls Parrish if he thinks proper to be their missionary to your Parrish of S^t^. Hellens and thereby as they hope and believe have provided you with such a Pastor as you desire in your Letter of march the 25th 1745 to them, and then they expect y^t^. you on your parts will do every thing in your Power to Encourage and Support him in the good work of his mission and Elect him after a years Tryal the Rector of the Parrish and god Grant, if he comes among you he may prove a worthy one. but if by the vestry of S[t]. Pauls haveing Chosen him Rector of their Parrish or by any other Cause M[r] Orr Sho[d]. be hinder[d]. from being missionary to you, the Society on proper notice will provide you with another Recomending you to gods blessing. I am—

Gentlemen your very Obedient
Serv[t]. in Christ.
Phillip Bearcroft
Secretary

This is a Second Letter

50

Aug[t]. 3[d]. 1747

At a meeting of the Church Wardens and Vestry of this parrish mett according to Law

Present

John Delagayey
Church Warden

William Hazzard
Nath[ll]. Barnwell
Tho[s]. Wigg——
Edw[d]. Wigg
Robert Williams
Cha[s]. Purry
Rich[d]. Ricketts
} Vestry men

It is agreed that the sum of thirty pounds Curr[t]. money be paid in Clouthing for one year to John Morgan for the support of himself and that the Church Wardens do send a Letter to M[rs]. Fripp to order a poor man now at her house to Return to the parrish he belongs to and that the following Letter be wrote to M[r]. Manigault

Port Royall aug[t] 3[d]. 1747

Sir.

The Church Wardens & Vestry of this Parrish. being now mett have applyed to M[r] Ch[s] Purry being one of the Exors of M[r] Lewis Jones Dec[d]. for a Legacy left by him, towards the Education of poor Child[n]. of this Parrish. he Informs us the sum of £50 stg now Lyes in y[r] hands & desires that the same may be p[d] to the Church Wardens & Vestry of this Parrish in part of said Legacy to be app[d] as aforesaid. we desire y[r] answer which will much oblige

S[r] Y[r] Most h Ser[ts].

Jn° Delegaye Church Warden

To
Gab. Manigault Esq
In Ch[s] Town

W[m] Hazzard
Nath Barnwell
Tho[s] Wigg—
Ch[s] Purry
Rich[d] Ricketts
R Williams
E Wigg.
} Vestry Men

51

Order[d]. also that Warrants be Imediately Issued Out against the Defaulters for not paying their poor Tax and agreed that the sum of Fifteen pounds be paid to Tho[s]. Item towards the support of a Deserted Child named John Sims left at his House

Dec. 7th. 1747—

At a Meeting of the Church Wardens & Vestry of this Parrish.

Present—

John Delegaye
Church Warden

Nath[l] Barnwell.
Thomas Wigg—
Edward Wigg—
Robert Williams
Charles Purry-
Richard Ricketts—
} Vestry Men

At same time Chose Hill Wigg to be Vestry Man in the room of M[r] Rich[d] Ricketts:-
also att same time The Rev[d] M[r] S[t] John. produced a Letter from Doct Bear Croft & The Rev[d] M[r] Garden. & wrote a Letter to M[r] Garden, At same time Voited thet the Land Vacant in the Church for three Pews; to the Eastward to be built for Rob[t]. Williams John DeLagaye & upon the same terms as y[e] other Pews in this Church in Stead of Tho[s]. Burton. Rich[d] Rickets & M[rs]. Daly

Febr[y]. 16th. 1747/8

At a meeting of the Church wardens & Vestry of this Parish.

Present

The Rev[d]. M[r]. S[t] John

John Delagayé
Church Warden

Edward Wigg
Thomas Wigg
Hill: Wigg
Robert Williams
Charles Purry
} Vestry men

Sworn Mr. Hill: Wigg in as Vestry Man this day
Order'd that Doctor Reeves attend George Buncle at the Expence of Prince William Parish

52

April,, 11th,, 1748

At a Meeting of the Vestry and Churchwardins of the parrish of St Helena for Easter 1748—

Present

John Delagaye, John Cattell — Church Warden's	The Revt.. Mr Richd: St John	Vestry
	Edward Wigg	
	Collo: Wm: Hazzard	
	Robt: Williams	
	Thos Wigg.	
	Hill Wigg	
	Nathl. Barnwell	
	Chas. Purry—	

Setteld. the Churchwardens Accots. vizt. . . . .

	£ s d		
To Paid to the poor as ℔ acct.	124,,2,, 6	By Cash Recd. for Poor Tax	36.15.3
To Paid R: Williams ballce.	10,,0,, 0	By Ditto from Richd Capers	30. 0..
To Do. to William Harvey.	18.2.11	By Due to Jno Delageyey.	85,,10,,2.
	£152,,5,, 5		£152,,5,,5

Dr.			Cr
To Cambrick and mending the Surpless	5.13.9	By Sacamt. money at Xmas	22. 3..
To wine.	2,, 5.0	By Do. march 6th. . .	14.16.3
To Ballce. Lent Mr Legeyey till he can Receive the above	61..17.6	By Do. at Easter . . .	32..17..
	£69,,16,,3		£..69.16.3

at the Same time An Order was Drawn, payable to the Rev^{t} Mr Richd St John for his Six Month's Sallary to the 25th March 1748– as also One other Order for Forty pounds payable to the Church Wardens for the Parochal Charges
An Answare to a Letter was wrote to the vestry & Church Wardens of prince williams parish relateing to Mr George Buncle

53

April 11th. 1748 Continued

At the afores^{d}. meeting Choose for Vestry & Churchwardens

The Rev^{d}. M^{r}. S^{t}. John Coll^{o}. Nath^{ll}. Barnwell Coll^{o}. Hazzard——— Coll^{o}. Thos. Wigg M^{r}. Chas. Purrey——— M^{r}. John Delegaye. Robert Williams Edwd. Wigg.	Vestry men	Hill Wigg John Stone	church warden's

Ordered that the Church warden's Do. Imediately assess the several parrishioners for the poor rate at the rate of Two Shillings for Every Twenty Shill^{gs}: they shall pay in the General Tax of this province and the mony arising by Such an assesment to be Imediately collected in. by the Said church wardens—
Ordered that Mr George Buncle bee Imediately removed from M^{rs}: Searles, Unto M^{r}: Michael Moores whom it is Agreed with to take care of him at fifty Shillings p^{r} week Until be Shal be removed by the Vestry & Church wardens of Prince williams Parash or otherways Ordered by the vestry of this parrish &^{ce}—

54

June 22^{d}. 1748.

At a meeting of the Vestry & Church Wardens of the Parrish of St Hellena—

Present.

John Stone Church Warden	The Revd Mr St John. Robert Williams Thomas Wigg. Charles Purry. John Delegaye. Edward Wigg.	Vestry Men.

At same time. Drew an Order on Mr Robert Thorpe in Favour of the Church Wardens for Forty two pounds. Ten Shillings. for his promice to pay for the Maintance of George Buncle, to the 11th April past: Agreed att same time, that Mr William Gough School Master. shall Learn as many Children from this Date. any Four Chilldren as either of the Church Wardens shall send. att the rate of Ten pounds Each ꝑ annum. ¬¬

Its orderd that the Church Wardens shall pay to Mrs Searles the sum of Fifteen pounds. Ten Shillings when in Cash for the order on Mr Thorpe.—being the Ballance due her, for the Maintance of George Bundle—

Extract of ye. late Revd. Doctr. Lewis Jones's last Will.

I give and bequeath ye. sum of one hundred pounds sterln. for ye. support of a School at Beaufort to be putt out at interest for ye. said use, which interrest shall be for ye. payment of a Schooll Master for instructing and teaching as many poor Children as ye. interrest of ye. said sum will allow of.—

I will also that when ye. Children to be taught by this Charity can read well in ye. Bible and are thoroughly instructed in ye. principles of ye. Christian faith according to ye. Church of England and are taught to write a fair hand and Cast Account, the Minister and Vestry and Church-Wardens—for ye. time being, whom I do hereby appoint as Trustees of this Legacy, shall from time to time recommend such poor Children whose Parents are not Capable to pay for their Schooling; and above all others I will that such poor Children be preferred who are Orphans and—are left poor & Destitue.—

55

Aug. 1st: 1748¬¬

At a Meeting of the Vestry & Church Wardens of the Parrish Of St Hellena———— Present—

Church Wardens	Vestry Men
Hill Wigg	The Revd Mr St John
John Stone	William Hazzard.
	Thomas Wigg.
	Nathl Barnwell.
	Charles Purry
	Robt Williams¬¬
	John Delegayee
	Edward Wigg.

Sep 14. 1748—

At a Meeting of the Vestry & Church Wardens of the Parrish of St Hellena——

Present

Hill Wigg Church Warden.

The Rev^{d} M^{r} S^{t}. John
Nathl Barnwell.
Robert Williams
Thos Wigg⌐⌐
John Delegaye—
Edward Wigg.
Charles Purry.—

} Vestry Men

ordered that M^{r}. Robt Thorpe pay Directly the sum of £42.10/ Curr^{y} for an order Drawn on him the 22^{d} June 1748 in fav^{r} of the Church Wardens, or to Issue out a Warr^{t}. against him for the same. also agreed that the sum of Two hundred and Forty-pounds be Raised Imediatly by Subscription to make good the Dificiency of the Society and for House Rent for the Present year Ending the 25th. of Octo^{r}. next to the Reverend M^{r}. S^{t}: John. also that the Said M^{r}. S^{t}. John agrees to Receive from the s^{d}. Parrish what they can conveniently Raise by Subscription for Future years towards making good the said Deficiency and House-Rent.

56

Nov 16. 1748.

At a Meeting of the Vestry & Church Wardens of the Parrish of St Hellena—

Present.

Hill Wigg. Church Warden.

The Revd Mr Richd St John
Thomas Wigg
Robert Williams
Charles Purry
John Delegaye
Edward Wigg

} Vestry men.

At same time Drew an Order on the Publick Treasurer pay^{a} to the Rev^{d} M^{r} S^{t}. John for his Six Months Sallary due to 25 Sepr past. also drew an order in fav of the Church Wardens, for the Money allow'd by the Gena^{l} Assembly out of the present Tax. towards Building a Parsonage house. for the minister of the Parrish:⌐⌐

Orderd that Ten pounds Curry to be paid to Mr Rattary for a fee in Regard to George Buncle being sent from Prince William Parrish :¬¬

Orderd that the Church Wardens do Imeadiatly Asses the severall Parishioners for the poor rate att the rate of Two Shillings & six pence for every Twenty Shillgs they shall pay in the Gennerall Tax of this province¬

March 27. 1749. Easter Munday.

At a meeting of the Inhabts of St Hellena Parrish. the under mentiond persons were Chosen Vestry Men & Church Wardens for this parish for the Insuing year.——

Church wardens:
John Green
Danll Howard

Vestrymen.:
Collo Wm Hazzard
Collo Nathl Barnwell
John Barnwell
Thomas Burton
Thos Wigg.¬
Charles Purry¬
John Delegaye

57

Easter Munday 27th March 1749

at the same time Drew an order for the Parochial charges payable to the Church wardens¬¬

as also gave the Church Wardens Orders to pay Mr. William Gough the Sum of Forty pounds Out of the Intrest mony. now Due on that part of the Revd Mr Lewis Jones Legacy paid into the Said parish by the Executrs for his Teaching six poore Children for the yeare past

———— . . . . ————

Ordered that the church wardens Do Assess the Parish at the rate of Eighteen pence for Every Twenty Shillg Each Inhabitant has paid towds the General Tax to Defray the maintainance of the poore of this parish for the yeare past

———— . . ————

Mr. Danll. Howard Refused to Serve as Churchwarden has paid his Fine of Ten pounds Currcy. which money was paid to Robert Williams on Accot. of Cash he paid Mr. Thos. Burton for Two Coffins and and money paid Mrs. Searls for a man that Died at her House.———

and Mr. Isaac Waites was duly Choosen in his Stead——

58

August 7th.. 1749

Att a Vestry held this Day it was Ordered that the assessment made by a former Order Last Vestry Day be Imediately raised & a return made of the Same On the first Monday in October next, at the Same time Coll^{o} Nath^{ll} Barnwell undertook to receive the assessment for Port royal & that part of the Indian Land that belongs to this parish & that Mr Isaac Waites was to receive the same from St Helena— — — — — — — — — — — —

August,, 28th.. 1749

at a Vestry held this Day there being ꝑsent

Coll^{o} Nath^{ll}: Barnwell..¬ — The Rv^{t} M^{r}. Rich^{d} S^{t}. John
Coll^{o} Willm Hazzard ⌐ ⌐
Mr John Barnwell ¬ ¬
M^{r}: John DeLeGaye ⌐ ⌐ ⌐
Mr Chas Purry ¬ „ ¬ „ ¬
Mr Thomas Burton ¬
Mr Thomas Wigg ¬ ¬ ¬

At the Same time the Rev^{t} Mr Richd St John had Liberty to be absent to go for Europe for his health; & Carried with him a Letter from the Vestry to the Secret^{y} of the Hon^{able} Society

And at the same time Drew Two Orders for Eleven Month's Salary in favour of M^{r}. St John—

---

att the Meeting of the Vestry On the Second Day of October 1749. Settled the Acco^{t} of Mr Hill^{d} Wigg as p^{r} the other Side

59

D^{r}. the Parish of St Hellena to Hill Wigg................D^{r}.

1748

May 29.	cash p^{d} for a Bottle Clarrett.............	£ 0–15–0
	ans^{d} to Mich^{l} Moore in Part of George Buncle Board	26,, 7,,6
	Sundrys goods Del^{d} Ann Wamsley..........	16,, 5–0
	Cash paid John Morgan....................	9–15–0
	Sundry goods D^{d} Geo Buncle...............	13– 0–0
	Ditto to Old M^{c}farley	30– 0–0
	Cash p^{d} Thos Iten for Board^{g} Jno Simes a Little boy	8..10..0
	Cash p^{d} Pat: OBrien for 5 M^{os} of Ditto......	12-.10..0
		£117.,, 2..6

Per Contra Cr.

1748

May 29. By Cash reced from Mr St John S. £16,,13,,0

By Cash reced from sundry People for their Poor Rate............ } 80,, 9,,1

1749 By Mr Delegaye ansd................ 7.. 7..6 £104,,9– 7

Balance due to Hill Wigg Octor. 2d. 1749. £12,,12,,11
for which he Reced the Cash in full.

this 2d Octor. 1749. paid Michl Moore in Part of his Accot the sum of Forty Pounds Twelve Shillings & Nine Pence:
Collo Barnwell pd: Mackfarlg: out of the poore rate's £17,,17,,8 at the Same time paid Mr Isaac Waites Twenty three pounds to be paid On accot. of Mrs Womsly to Mr. John Evans, as also Paid to Mr Waites £14:5:3 for necessry for the said Mrs Womsly

---

At a Vestry held the 16 day of April 1750 being
————Easter Monday————

At which time was chose by the Majority of Inhabitants then Prest. the following Gentlemen as Vestrye for the said year

Coll.............................. Nat: Barnwell
Coll.............................. Willm. Hazzard

Church Wardens
John Fendin
Jemmit Cobley

Mr. { John Delegaye
Cha: Purry
Thos. Burton
Jno Barnwell
Coll Thos. Wigg

Who where all duely Qualified

60

1750—Easter Monday 16 April —

At the same time drew an Order for the Parochial Charges payable to Church Wardens £40 for the year 1749—

---

a Vestry held this 30th Apll: 1750 Present

John Fendin
Jemtt Cobley } churchwardens

Collo Nathll: Barnwell
Collo.. Willm. Hazzard
Mr John Barnwell
Mr John D Legaye
Mr Chas: Purry—
Mr Thos Burton
Mr Thos: Wigg

Gave Orders to the Church Wardens to Pay to Mr William Gough the Sum of Sixty Two pounds Ten Shillings being mony —arising from the Intrest of Mr Jones' Legacy to Easter Last, for Schooling of Sundry poor Children as pr his Accot—

Ordered that the Church Warden's Do— Imediately assess the parish for the poor rate after the rate of Eighteen pence for Every Twenty Shillgs they payd for theire General Tax. Advertising the Same at Diferent parts in this Parrish & to be paid within Three Month's from this Date

---

at the Same time Drew an Order on the Publick Treassr. for Two Hundred & fifty pods: payable to Mr Thos Wigg being mony granted by the General Assembly in the Estamate for the Yeare 1748 towards building a Parsonage house in St Helen's parrish

1750

61

A Vestry held On Monday
the 5th Day of August¬
Present

Church wardens	Vestry
John Fendin	Collo: Nathll Barnwell
Jemtt Cobly.	Collo: Willm: Hazzard
	Mr Jno. Barnwell
	Mr Chas: Purry¬
	Mr Thos Burton
	Mr Thos: Wigg¬

Settled with Thos: Macfarling this Day and there is Due to him £42..2..4..
Ordered that Michall More be Paid of the full of his Accot which is £35..7..6, wch was also paid¬
Recd at Same time of Mr John Fendall being for the poore rates of the Island of St Helena for the Yeare 1749 the sum of £25 wch he is Orderd to pay for the use of Mrs Womsly——..———-
Rec'd at the Same time of Mr Jemitt Cobly for the Poor rates he recd for the Yeare 1749 the Sum of £55:11:7½ at the Same time he was orderd to pay Michell Moore £35..7..6.. as also to pay £5— to Mr Fendall for the use of Mrs Womsly
Ordered that Mr Cobly also pay to Collo Barnwell the Sum of £15:4:1½ On Accot of Mackfarling.

62

Easter Monday Aprill 8th.. 1751

The Inhabitants of St Helena parish being Met Did chuse for Vestry Men & Church¬ Wardens the Following persons (Viz^{t})

Mr Andrew Bell
M^{r} W^{m}. Waight } Church Wardens & Qualifyed accord^{g} to Law

Coll^{o} Barnwell
M^{r}. John Barnwell
Mr Chas Purry
Mr Jon^{a}. Norton
Mr Richd Capers
M^{r} Jno- Mullryne
Mr John Gordon } Vestry

Thursday June 20th. 1751

At a meeting of the Church Wardens, Vestry and Parishioners

M^{r}. Rich^{d}. Capers refusing to Qualify as a Vestry Man Coll Thos. Wigg was chose in his Room.

At the same time the following persons qualified as Vestry Men in pursuance to the choice made on Easter Monday last.

Pres^{t}. } Church Wardens
Mr Andrew Bell
M^{r} W^{m}. Waight }

The Rev^{d}. M^{r}. W^{m}. Peasley
Coll: Barnwell
Coll^{o}. Tho: Wigg
M^{r}. Jno- Barnwell
Cha: Purry
Jona: Norton
Coll: Jno- Mullri[1]

At which time the Vestry Church Wardens & Parishioners made choice of Willm. Gough to be the Clerk of the Parish in the Room of M^{r}. Rich^{d}. Rickets who resigned. the said Gough to allow the said Rickets £20 ℔ anno during his being Clerk & the Life of the said Rickets—

63

At the same time was Read a Letter from D^{r}. Bearcroft Sec^{y}: to the Society for propagating the Gospel in Foreign parts recommending the Rev'd M^{r}. Willm Peasley as Rector for this Parish

An Order was drawn on the Public: Treasurer for £40 payable to the Church Wardens for the Year 1750.

---

[1]Scratched out. Intended for Mullryne.

Order'd, that the Inhabitants of St. Hellens Parish be Assess'd for the support of the Poor at the Rate of fifteen pence in the pound on what mony's they paid towards the general Tax to be advertised to be paid within two months from this day—

Order'd at the same time that Mr. Thos. Wigg pay unto Mr. Andrew Bell and Willm Waight Church Wardens £250,, rec'd by him from the pub: Treasurer granted by the General Assembly for the building a parsonage House in the Parish of St. Helens.

Thursday 27 June 1751—

At a Meeting of the Church Wardens and Vestry—

Church Wardens	
Mr. Andw. Bell Prest.	The Rev'd Mr. Wm. Peasley—
Wm. Waight	Coll Barnwell
	Coll Wigg
	Coll: Mulryne
	Mr. Chas: Purry
	Jona. Norton
	John Gordon

Mr. John Gordon qualified as a Vestry Man Order'd That the Cash above mentioned to be paid by Collo. Wigg to the Church Wardens be by them imediately put to Int: on good Security—

64

Order'd That the Church Wardens do as soon as possible pay the sum of £108,,19,,3 unto Mr. Henry Talbot for the Boarding of Geo: Buncle deceased

---

1751.

At a Vestry held Monday 5 Augst:

Church Wardens	Present
Mr. Andw Bell	The Revd. Mr. Wm. Peasely
Mr Willm. Waight	Collo. Barnwell
	Collo. Wigg
	Mr. Chas. Purry—

Their not being a sufficient Number to make a Vestry
——Adjourned——

Augst. 14th. 1751. At a Vestry then held

Present

Church Warden Mr. And: Bell.

The Rev'd Mr. William Peaseley
Coll Nath: Barnwell
Mr. John Barnwell
Mr. John Gordon
Mr Charles Purry
Coll John Mullryne

The Church Warden, Rec'd Order's to pay William Gough Fifty Six pounds Curry. due on Easter Monday last for teaching Sundry poor Children according to the Legacy left by the late Reverend Mr. Lewis Jones for that purpose—

65

Memorandum, Dec: 20th. 1751, An Order was drawn on the public Treasurer for One Hundred & Eighty three pounds, Six Shillings & 8d, Currency, payable to the Rev'd William Peaseley, for four months Salary, due on Michaelmass past.——

—— Signed ——

Church Warden } Andrew Bell

Vestry { Nath: Barnwell
John Barnwell
Thos. Wigg
Chas. Purry
Jno- Gordon

March 30th. 1752, Easter Monday . . . .

——————At a Vestry then held——————

Present

Mr. Andrew Bell } Church
Wllm. Waight } Wardens

Vestry { Rev'd Willm. Peasely
Coll: Nat: Barnwell
Capt Jno- Gordon
Coll Thos. Wigg
Mr. Chas. Purry
Mr. Jona Norton

Balance from Aug 5. 1750 to this Day due to Mr. Thomas Mcpherling as settled £76..9.10½

Balance due to Mrs. Walmsley deceas'd

66

1751 Mr. Andrew Bell and Mr- William Waight Church Warden

	Dr.——
To Sacrament Money from Mr. Rickets	£ 9,,16.3
Money rec'd from the F Masons— — — — — — — —	13,, 5,,3
Cash from Robt. Williams Esqe for Matthews's Swearing	16,,11,,3
Widow Evan's Estate —— —— —— —— ——	16,,17,,6
Cash rec'd for Poor Tax —— —— —— —— .	103,,11,,-

Church Warden . . . . Dr	
To Cash in hand	7 ,, 3 ,, 3
Cash of HW	10 ,, –
	£7,,13,,3

67

℘ Contra ———————— Cr,	
By Cash pd for Sundries at Graves's Fun:	£ 1,,11,,—
Cash from Widow Evans	14,,14,, 9
for Mcpherling Shoes — — — — — — — —	2,,10,,—
Blue plains — — — — — — — — — — — — —	- 14,,—
for Pickets washing the Surplice— — —	10..—
for Bread & Wine Do— — — — — — — —	1,, 5,,—
paid Dr. Steel	5,,11,, 6
Do. Jno Stone for a Coffin	2,,10,,—
Do. Mr. Morgan for 300 shingles	1,,—,,—
Do. Jno- Smith Tar &c—	3,, 7,, 6
3 day Negro hire	1,,10,,—
Hooks for the Church Yard	1,, 2,, 6
paid Henry Talbot — — — — — — —	108,,19. 3
Wine paper & Quils — — — — — — —	1,, 2,, 6
Coffin &c for Ann Walmsley	6,,10,,—
Ball - - -	7,, 3,, 3
	£160,, 1,, 3

Cr.	
By Cash pd Mr. Bona for Coffin &c— — — — — — — — —	£4,,—,,—
By Cash in full	3.13 3
	£7,,13. 3

68

March 30, 1752-

An Order was drawn on Jacob Motte Esq: for the Parochial Charges being £40 which Order was to be indorsed for the use of the Clerk being his Salary for the Year 1751———

An Order was also given to the Church Wardens to pay unto Willm. Gough Fifty Six pounds for teaching poor Children according to the Legacy of the Rev'd Lewis Jones deceased.

An Order was also drawn on Jacob Motte Esqe. for £275. for 6 Months Salary due to the Rev'd Mr. William peasely.

Andrew Bell
William Waight
Church Wardens

Signed { Nathl. Barnwell, Thos. Wigg, John Gordon, Jona Norton }

Then choice was made of a Vestry for the year 1752 when the following Gentlemen were appointed

For Church Wardens
Mr. John Fripp
Mr. Fra: Stuart

The Rev'd Mr. Willm. Peasely
Collo: Nathaniel Barnwell
Collo- Thomas Wigg
Capt Jno Gordon
Mr. John Barnwell
Mr. { Jona Norton, Chas. Purry, Coll Jno- Mullryne }

69

At a Vestry held July 10th. 1752

Present
The Revd. William Peasely
Coll: Nath: Barnwell
Coll: Thos. Wigg
Coll: Jno- Mullryne
Mr. Jno- Barnwell
Mr. Chas: Purry

Who were all qualified as Gentlemen of the Vestry.

Mr. Francis Stuart, being Nominated Church Warden—would not serve, but paid his Fine Ten Pounds; And Mr. Edward Wigg was appointed in his Room.

Order'd to meet the first Monday in August at 9 of the Clock in the forenoon to do business.

At a Vestry held Augst: 3. 1752.

——— Present ———

Ch: Wardens	Vestry
Mr Edw'd Wigg	Rev^{d}. William Peasely
Mr Jno. Fripp	Coll: Nathl. Barnwell
	Coll: Thomas Wigg
	Coll: John Mullryne
	M^{r}. John Barnwell
	M^{r}. Charles Purry
	M^{r}. Jona: Norton

The two Church Wardens, were this Day Qualified; and M^{r}. Jonathan Norton, as a Vestry Man; and William Gough was Qualified as Register of this Parish—

Due this day to M^{c}.farling........................£86,,16,,6½

One p^{r}. Shoes 50/ blue plains 14/℔ Bell's Acc^{t}. .. 3,, 4,,—

carried over due £83,,12,,6½

69[1]

——— August 3^{d}. 1752 ———

Order'd, that a Subscription be drawn up for another Year's Rent for the Ministers House

Order'd, that a Subscription be also drawn for the building a Personage House of the Dimensions of 20 by 36 with two P H^{s}.

The Parish ....D^{r}.

To Alex^{r}. Grieves, on Acc^{t}. of Mrs Walmsley ℔ Bill £72..10..—

— Jonathan Norton, on......D^{o}- .... 15..12..3

— William Gough, Sacramen^{t}. Wine 15/ Anne May burial £ s d 4..1..3 — 4..16..3

— Thomas M^{c}farling to this day. .... 83..12..6½

£176,,11,,–½

Parish D^{r}. 176,,11,,–½

D^{o}. . . C^{r}. 66,,11,,3

£109,,19,,9½ Parish Debt

[1]Marked 69 in the original, but it should be 70.

⅌ Contra	Cr.
By Mr. Stuart's Fine	£10,,—,,—
— Sacrament Money	52,,18,,—
— Cash of Mr. Bell being the bal of his Acct.	3,,13,, 3
	£66,,11,, 3

Order'd, That, the Parish be assess'd at 3 Shillings in the Pound, according to what they Pay to the General Tax: And that payment be made on or before, the first Day of December next, of which public notice is to be given.

At the same time the Vestry agreed to make good the £20. ⅌ ann paid by William Gough to Richd. Rickets & ordered as a farther favour a Subscription for a Negro for the said Wm. Gough

71

Memorand: Nov: 7th. 1752 An Order was drawn on the Public Treasurer for £275,,— Currency payable to the Rev'd Mr. William Peasely for Six Months Salary—due the 29th September past——

Signed by Nath: Barnwell
Jno. Mullryne
Jno. Gordon
Cha: Purry
Thos. Wigg

Edwd: Wigg Ch: W

Friday January 5th. 1753.

At a Vestry then held————

Present

The Rev'd Wm. Peasely
Coll: Nath: Barnwell
Coll: Tho: Wigg
Coll: John Mullryne

Capt John Gordon
Mr. John Barnwell
Mr. Charles Purry
Mr. Jona: Norton

Mr. Edward Wigg }
Mr. John Fripp } Ch: Wardens.

It was further resolved, That Mr. Thomas Walker and Mr. Ellicott Story, Carpenters, should be consulted concerning the Charge of Building the parsonage House, according to such form, and in such a manner, as was then drawn up, and agreed to, by the said Vestry, and that one of the said Carpenters, should be agreed with to undertake and finish the said Building with the utmost dispatch——

72

Friday January 26th. 1753

Vestry then held

Present

Rev'd Wm. Peasely

Mr. Edward Wigg Ch Warden

Coll: Nath: Barnwell
Thos: Wigg
Jno- Mullryne

Capt Jno- Gordon
Mr. Jno- Barnwell
Chas. Purry

Several Conferences were had concerning the Parsonage House wch. was now agreed to be Built 18 ft by 38 ft and Coll: Mullryne undertook the Sawyers Work.

Vestry held Saturday 17 March 1753

Present

Rev'd Wm. Peasely

Coll: Nath Barnwell
Thos. Wigg
Jno- Mullryne

Capt Jno- Gordon
Mr. Chas: Purry

A Letter was writt, & sign'd by the Vestry, unto the Representatives for this Parish; Requesting them to lay before the Honble: House of assembly, the necessity the Parish is under of desiring the additional Sum of £1000, may be granted, to enable them to finish the Parsonage House———

Resolv'd, If the sum of £500 be granted, that the Vestry will supply the deficiency, They to be repaid by a further Subscription—

73

Easter Monday April 23d. 1753

————At Vestry then held————

Present

Revd. Mr. William Peasely

Mr. Edward Wigg
Mr. John Fripp } Ch: Wardens

Vestry

Coll: Nath: Barnwell	Mr. John Barnwell
Coll: Thos. Wigg	Mr. Charles Purry
Coll: John Gordon	Mr. Jona: Norton

An Order was drawn on Jacob Motte Esqe. by the Ch: Wardens—& Vestry for £275. Current Money payable to the Revd. Wm. Peasely for Six Months Salary due the 25th. March last past—And another was drawn on him for £40 Currt. Money for Parochial Charges for the year 1752. and indors'd over unto William Gough (as Clerk and Sexton) for his Salary for the Year 1752
An Order was likewise given unto the Ch: Wardens, by the Vestry, to pay unto William Gough £56 Currt. Money, being the Interest Money arising from the late Rev'd Lewis Jones's Legacy, for the Incouragement of a School Master in the Town of Beaufort, He teaching such Poor Children as Shou'd be sent by the said Vestry's Recomendation.——
According to a former Agreement, Coll: Barnwell, paid Mr. Richard Rickets £20, in my stead, the Coll: to be reimburs'd by a Subscription among the Gentlemen of the Vestry, at the next meeting
The Church Wardens Acct. was then settled as follows

viz.

74

Dr The Parish of St. Helena To Edward Wigg

1753		
Jan. 26	To Cash paid Alexdr. Grives in full ꝑ Rect.	£.-72,,10,,—
	Do paid Jonathan Norton ꝑ Do. .	15,,12,, 3
	Do. paid William Gough ꝑ Do. . .	10,,13,,—
	Do paid A poor old Man ꝑ Ordr. of Vestry....................	6,,—,,—
April 23d	Do paid Coll: Barnwell for so much due to Mr. Mcfarling. . .	83,,12,, 6
	Cash paid William Gough in full ꝑ Rect.....................	12,, 6,, 3
	Do paid William Waight on acct. Ann Wormsley	6,,10,,—
		207,, 4,,—
	Cash paid Coll Barnwell the balance due to Mr. Mcpharling this Day. from August. 3d	20,, 3,,—
	Balance due this Day from Edwd: Wigg	8,,—,,11
		£ ..235,, 7,,11

The following Gentlemen were again Chose of the Vestry

Revd. Willm. Peasely	Capt John Gordon
Coll: Nathl. Barnwell	Mr. John Barnwell
Coll: Thoms. Wigg	Mr. Charles Purry
Coll: John Mullryne	Mr. Jona: Norton

All of whom were qualified by Samuel Hurst Esq: except Coll: Mullryne who was absent.—

The Inhabitants Ballotted in for Church Wardens for the ensuing Year

Mr. Joshua Morgan
Mr. Benjamin Ladson

———and Then Adjourned———

and John Fripp Church Wardens...........Cr.

1752. Aug: 3d:	By Cash rec'd from Mr. Stuart his Fine for not serving as Church Warden	£ 10,,—,,—
1753 Jan: 26.	Cash rec'd from the Revd. Mr. Willm. Peasely being Sacrament Money	50,,18,,—
	Cash rec'd of Sundry Persons for Poor Tax ℔ Acct. this day render'd	167,,19,,11
	an overcharge of Cash pd. Willm. Waight on acct. of Ann Walmsley	6,,10,,—
		£235,, 7,,11

April 23d
1753

The Parish .... Cr.

By Cash, in the Church Wardens hands........£ 8,,— 11

Cash, being Sacramt. Money.............. 44,,14,,—

£52,,14,,11

Mr. John Hutchinson's Poor Tax pd........ 3,,15,,—

£56,, 9,,11

76

Friday the 18th May 1753 At Vestry
Present
The Rev'd William Peasely
Joshua Morgan }
Benj: Ladson } Ch Wardens

Coll: Nathl. Barnwell	Capt. John Gordon
Coll: Thomas Wigg— —	Mr. John Barnwell
Coll: John Mullryne	Mr. Charles Purry

The above Church Wardens were duely qualified as was also Coll: Mullryne as a Vestry Man.

The Acct. delivered to the said Ch: Wardens

Cash of Mr. Edwd. Wigg	£5,, 5,,11
Mr. Fripp to pay........................	6,,10,,—
	£11,,15,,11
Sacramt. Money	44,,14,,—
Parish Cr.	£56,, 9,,11

For Papers, see the Memorandm. at the end of the Book The Letter mention'd, the 17th. of March past, to be sent to the Representatives for this Parish, having been laid before the Honble: House of Assembly, They were pleas'd to give them to understand, That no more Money would be granted towards the building of the Parsonage House, until proper Vouchers made it appear that their former Grant of £500. was intirely expended, according to the true intent and meaning of the Donation: Upon which the Gentlemen of the Vestry——

Ordered, That the Parsonage House, should be carried on with the utmost expedition, according to the last Resolution, and Coll: Barnwell, Coll: Mullryne and Capt Gordon were Nominated and desired to Oversee the Work——

The Petition of Jno. Lillenton being Read & it appearing he was a proper object of Charity, he was taken on the Parish, and £15. order'd him in Goods for his present Relief——

77

The £20 ℘ ann was agreed to be paid Mr. Richd Ricketts in manner following vizt.

Coll Barnwell	£ 6,,—,,—
Mr. Jno- Barnwell........................	4,,—,,—
Coll: Wigg	2,,10,,—
Capt Gordon	2,,10,,—
Coll: Mullryne	2,,10,,—
Mr. Chas. Purry	2,,10,,—
	£20,,—,,—

Monday July 16. 1753 At Vestry

Present

The Revd. William Peasely

Mr. Joshua Morgan Ch Warden

Coll: Nat Barnwell

Coll: Tho Wigg

Capt: Jno- Gordon

Mr. { Jno- Barnwell
Cha: Purry }

A Letter was Read directed to the Ch: Wardens and Vestry dated 6 May last from James Irving Esq: one of the Representatives for this Parish, in answer to a Letter Sent the 17th. March past, the purport of wch. may be seen on that days entry on the Minutes of Vestry.

An Answer was writ to the above Letter signed by the above Gent. and directed to the above James Irving Esq: both on File.

Mr. Ellicot Story had orders to secure the X beams at the West end of the Church, by proper Pillars as supporters.

78

Monday August 6th. 1753

At Vestry

Present

The Rev'd Willm. Peasely

Mr. { Joshua Morgan
Benj: Ladson } Ch: Wardens

Coll: Nath Barnwell.	Vestry	Capt: John Gordon.
Coll: Thomas Wigg.		Mr. Charles Purry.
Coll: John Mullryne.		Mr. Jona: Norton.

The Vestry agreed with Mr. Joshua Morgan, to make 20,000 good Lime Bricks, and to deliver them, in good Order, on the Glebe Land, near the Spot on which the Parsonage House is to be Built, at £6 ℘ m.

Memorandum———

———October the 9th. The Revd. Mr William Peasely had an Order on the Pub: Treasurer for £275. for Six Months Salary due the 29th. of September last past—

Wednesday Feb: 6th 1754,,——
At a Vestry then held
Present
The Rev'd Willm. Peasely

Joshua Morgan }
Benj: Ladson } Ch: Wardens

Coll: Nath: Barnwell — Mr. Chas. Purry
Coll: Thos. Wigg — Jona Norton
Capt: John Gordon

79

Feb: 6th. 1754——

Ordered, That the Ch: Wardens do assess the Parish This assessmt. was for the Year 1753 in a Poor Tax, at the Rate of two Shillings & six pence for every pound they paid the last year to the Gen: Tax And that the same be paid by the 25th. of March next.

And that such Persons who Subscribed towards the building of the Parsonage House, for this Parish, be desired to make their several payments, unto Capt John Gordon, by the said time, and that proper Advertisements be issued for that purpose.——

Agreed, that the Church Wardens do bind William Sommers, a poor Orphan Child, of this Parish, Apprentice unto Sarah Mathews, of the Town of Beaufort, until he be 13 Years of Age (which will be on the 5th. day of November in the Year 1763) and that they pay unto the said Sarah Mathews Fifteen Pounds, Currency, on the day he is bound, and that they or their Successors—continue the paying the like Sum yearly, on the 5th. day of November in each year, the last payment to be made on the said Day in the year 1757, and from thence to Cease and Determine: and that her Acc[t]. to the amount of £17. be discharged.—Agreed, That Coll: Barnwell & Capt: Gordon do directly purchase Timber & stuff to build a Kitchen, on the Glebe Land, and that Workmen be immediately employed to build the same.

80

Easter Monday 15th April 1754—

——At Vestry——

Present

Rev'd M[r]. Will[m]. Peasely

Coll: Nath: Barnwell	Capt: John Gordon
M[r]. John Barnwell	M[r]. Cha[s]. Purry
Coll John Mullryne	————

An Order was drawn for £275„—on Jacob Motte Esq. Treasurer payable to Rev'd Will[m]. Peasely being for—his 6 Months Salary due the 25th. of March last past.

An Order on the same for £40. Parochial Charges, payable to the Church Wardens, and by them Indorsed to Will[m]. Gough being his Salary as Parish Clerk for the Year 1753 . . . .

Ordered That the Church Wardens pay unto Will[m]. Gough or Order Fifty Six Pounds being the Interest Money due on the Legacy of the late Rev'd Lewis Jones.

M[r]. Daniel Daly was chose one of the Ch: Wardens and M[r]. Will[m]. Hazzard ballotted in as the other ag[st]. M[r]. Andrew Aggnew.——

The same Gentlemen, as acted on the Vestry the last year, were again made choice of & the Six above mentioned were Sworn in.

81

August 5th. 1754.——

This day there was to've been a Vestry but there being present only ————

The Rev[d]. M[r]. Peasely
Coll: Barnwell
M[r]. Jn[o]-: Barnwell &
Coll Tho[s]. Wigg

They broke up to a more convenient Opportunity.

M[r]. Daniel Daly paid his Fine £10. not chusing to stand as Church Warden. ——

August 22^{d}. 1754
At Vestry
Present
———The Rev^{d}. Willm. Peasely———

Coll Nath: Barnwell	Coll: Thos. Wigg
Coll: Mullryne	M^{r}. Jno- Barnwell

M^{r}. William Hazzard & M^{r}. James Steele, were duely sworn in as Church Wardens for this Parish and
M^{r}. Jno- Chapman & M^{r}. Jno- Delegaye were chosen as Gen. of the Vestry, in the Room of Capt John Gordon who resigned, and M^{r}. Chas. Purry, deceased.——
Order'd, That Willm. Trunker be paid by the Ch Wardens at the rate of 12/6 ℘ day for 30 days his Wife nursing & boarding— Tabitha Weatherly in her Lying in————————£18,,15,,—
Order'd That the Widow Mandevill have £15 in Cloaths from the Store and that Mary Wade have £15. in the same manner.

82
Memorandum
October 4. 1754 An Order was drawn on Jacob Motte Esq: for £275 Curr^{cy}. payable to the Rev^{d}. M^{r}. Willm. Peasely or Order for 6 Months Salary due the 29th. September last past———

Nov^{br}. 1st. 1754
At Vestry then held
Present

M^{r}. Jam^{s}. Steele
Ch: Warden

Rev^{d}. William Peasely
Coll: Nathl. Barnwell
M^{r}. Jno- Barnwell
Coll: Thos. Wigg
M^{r}. Jno- Delegaye

M^{r}. Jno- Chapman declining to Act on the Vestry Mr Fra^{s}: Stuart was nominated in his Stead
M^{r}. John Delagaye was qualified as a Vestry Man
Order'd That the Church Wardens do Assess the Parish in a Poor Tax of Three Shillings in the Pound for every Pound they pay in the General Tax, payable the first Day of Jan^{r}. next, and that proper advertisements be put up to give notice thereof.

83

March 31st. 1755
———Easter Monday———
At Vestry
Present
Revd. William Peasely

Col: Nathl. Barnwell — Col: Thomas Wigg
Col: Jno- Mullryne — Mr. John D'lagaye
Mr. James Steele Ch: Warden

An order was drawn on the Pub: Treasurer for £275,,— payable to the Rev'd Willm. Peasely or Order for his— Six Months Salary due the 25th. instant
An Order was likewise drawn on the Pub: Treasurer for £40 Parochial Charges for the Year 1754 and indorsed over to William Gough Clerk &c———
An Order likewise was issued to the Church Wardens to pay unto William Gough, or Order £56 being the Interest Money due on Revd: Mr. Jones's Legacy for the incouragemt. of a School Master in Beaufort &c——
Then the above four Gentlemen of the Vestry, together with Mr. John Barnwell and Mr. Josp: Jenkins were chose as the Vestry—
And Mr. John Chapman and Mr. Saml. Ladson were chose as Church Wardens for the year 1755.
And the Vestry Adjourned to Monday the 13th. of April when they are to meet and be qualifyed for their Offices

84

Dr. St. Helena Parish

		£	s	d
1754 Feb: 6	To Cash pd. Sarah Mathews on acct. of William Somers an Orphan Child	17	,,—	,,—
28 March	To Cash pd Richd. Dale on acct. of Mary Hope a poor lame Woman....	16	—	,,—
15 April	To Cash p'd Mcpherling then due......	30	,,—	,,—
	Cash p'd Linnington	30	,,—	,,—
	Cash p'd Mr. D'lagaye his Acct......	12	1	3
	Cash p'd Col: Flowers for Somer's Fam.	1	14	6
22 Augst.	Cash pd. Wm. Trunker for Tabitha Weatherly	4	3	,,—
	Cash p'd Willm. Gough's Bills, vizt.			
1755 31 March	To Balance Sommers Acct £10,,16–9; Charges & Fees burying the Poor 19,,18,,9; Charges in Ch: and Ch Yard 19,, 1,,3; Writing from 1753 to prest. time 13,,12,,6	63	9	3
	Balance in the hand of W. Gough	4	5	5¾
	£	178	13	5¾

85

	Per Contra	Cr.		
	By Cash from Mr. Ladson...........	5	5	11
	£ { Poor Tax from Mr. Jno. Heyward..	37	„—	3¼
a 2/6 ℔	Do from Willm. Gough......	67	3	7½
	Do. from Mr. Morgan........	33	8	8
	Cash from Mr. Morgan acct. of Sommers	13	15	„—
	Do. from Mr. Daly fine as Ch: Warden	10	„—	„—
	Do from Revd. William Peasely...	12	„—	„—
	£	178	13	5¾

86

Monday April 14th. 1755

According to Adjournment (the 31st. March) the Vestry met, and the Gentlemen before Chose were Qualified as a Vestry, and M^{r}. John Chapman was Qualified as one of the Church Wardens. M^{r}. William Reynolds was chose as the other Ch: Warden in the Room of M^{r}. Samuel Ladson.

And William Harvey Esq: was nominated on the Vestry

The Rev^{d}. William Peasely having declared his desire of leaving the Province, Letters were wrote to D^{r}. Bearcroft Sec^{y}. to the Honble: Society for propagating the Gospel in Foreign parts, to acquaint them thereof, and to desire that another Missionary might be sent over to take charge of the Parish, soon as possible, which said Letter was inclosed with one from the Rev^{d}. W^{m}. Peasely, to the said Honble. Board to notifie the same, and sent by Capt: Coole who set Sail for England the latter end of April 1755——

The Vestry Letter was Signed by,

Coll: Nath: Barnwell — M^{r}. Jno- Barnwell
Coll Thos. Wigg — M^{r} Jno- Delegaye
Coll John Mullryne — M^{r}. Josp: Jenkins
Willm. Harvey Esq:

M^{r}. John Chapman & M^{r}. Willm. Reynolds Ch: Wardens

Copy's of the said Letters are on File See page 104

87

June the 3^{d}. 1755 At Vestry then held

Present

Coll: Nath : Barnwell — M^{r}. John Barnwell
Coll: Thos. Wigg — M^{r}. John D'legaye
Will: Harvey Esq — M^{r}. Josp: Jenkins

M^{r}. John Chapman Ch Warden

Order'd That Susanna Rearden a Poor Woman, having a very bad Eye, shou'd be on the Parish till further Order.

And that the Widow Trunker & Child shou'd be continued on the Parish at 40/„ ℔ Week.

August 4. 1755 At Vestry then held

Present Rev^{d}: William Peasely.

Coll: Nath: Barnwell W^{m}. Harvey Esq:
Coll: Thos. Wigg M^{r}. Jno- Delagaye
Coll: Jno- Mullryne M^{r}. Jno- Jenkins
M^{r}. Jno- Barnwell

M^{r}. John Chapman Ch: Warden

M^{r}. James Steele, late Church Warden, deliver'd in part of his Years Account, and was desired to get in all the Poor Tax, that his Account might be closed the next Vestry Day:
Order'd That all Persons pay in their Poor Tax directly, and Resolved, That all Defaulters shall be served with Executions, after the next Vestry—

88

Friday Nov^{br}. 7th. 1755——

At Vestry then held

Present

Coll: Nath: Barnwell M^{r}. Jno- Barnwell
Coll: Thos. Wigg W^{m}. Harvey Esq
Coll: Jno- Mullryne M^{r}. Jno- Delagaye

M^{r}. John Chapman Ch Wdn

Agreed, That, as William Sommers a poor Orphan Child had lived with M^{rs}. Sarah Mathews for two years past, and the Agreement of Vestry made Feb: 6. 1754 had not been Comply'd with —that she be paid for the said two years care of the said Boy, due the 5th. of Nov^{br}: instant, £30 and that She be paid, from that day, at the Rate of £20 ꝑ Ann during the Term that the Said Orphan Child may remain with her. She finding the said Child Meat, Drink, Washing, Lodging and Apparel.——
Order'd That the Parish be Assessed in a Poor Tax at the Rate of Three Shillings for every Pound paid to last General Tax of this Province, and that the Poor Tax be paid by the first day of January next.
Ordered, That all Defaulters for the Poor Tax in the Years 1753 and 1754, be Advertised to pay the same by the first day of December next, and that the Name of such Defaulters be put to the bottom of the said Advertisement.

The Revd. Mr. Willm. Peasely received an Ordr. on the—Public Treasurer for £275,, Currcy. being his—Salary due the 29th. of Sept last past——

Sign'd by all the above Present

Order'd that William Gough, lend Willm. Harvey Esq: the Parish Book of Laws. but since returned.
And that he write's a Letter to the Revd:.Mr. Clerk of Chas Town concerning some Books sent over by the Honble. Society for this Parish for the Vestry & Ch: Wardens to Sign—— See Folio 107

89

The Parish of St. Helena to Messrs. Steele & Hazzard late Ch: Wardens from Easter 1754 to Easter 1755

	Dr.		
To John Robinson's Child, Sundries for its Funeral £	2	5	,,—
To Anne Wade Sundries ℔ Ord: of Vestry........	15	,,—	,,—
To Tabitha Weatherly's Lying in & Nursing & Midwife	17	12	6
To William Trunker Senr: Sundries for his Funeral & a Coffin	5	15	,,—
To Rees Morgan............Do for his Sickness Funl. & Coffin	10	7	6
To Richd. Dale for Boarding a Sick Man one Week	2	,,—	,,—
To Danl. Reardon's Wife & Child's Board Sickness & Medicines	48	7	,,—
To Mary Hopes Board & Lameness &c............	21	18	9
To Mcpherling and Lenningtons yearly allowance	60	,,—	,,—
To Ch: Yard Hoeing 32/6 a Bar for the Wt. Gate 20/	2	12	6
To Jacob Bona making a New Platform for S: Door of Ch:	10	,,—	,,—
To Julian Moronsy an Acct. for ye Year 1753.....	4	15	,,—
To Lennington Sugar 7/6 a Memorandum Book 2/6	,—	10	,,—
To Wine for Sacrament..........................	1	5	,,—
To a Pub: Advertisement. in the Gazette for P. Tax.	1	,,—	,,—
To Jonathan Norton for Mary Mandevil's Funl....	8	10	,,—
To Mr. Jno. Chapman Ch: Warden Cash at 3 payments	38	5	6
To Mr. Jno. Chapman - - Do. (as ℔ Rect.) Cash as Balance	9	5	11¼
£	259	9	8¼

℔ Contra . . . . Cr.			
By Andrew Bell, Cash being a bal: due to ye Parish	6	„—	„—
By Fines on St. Helena & the Indian Land........	2	15	„—
By Poor Tax for Year 1753......................	33	1	„—
By Sacrament Money	10	„—	„—
By Poor Tax for the year 1754 at sundry times....	207	13	8¼
£	259	9	8¼

90

April 19. 1756 Easter Monday

At Vestry

Coll Nathl. Barnwell — Mr. John Delagaye
Coll: Jno- Mullryne — William Harvey Esq:
Mr. Jno- Barnwell — Mr. Joseph Jenkins
Mr. John Chapman } Ch Wardens
Mr. Wm.. Reynolds }

The Revd. Mr. William Peasely's Ord: on the Pub: Tresur: for £275. was Signed by the Vestry, being his Salary to the 25th. March last past.
Also an Ordr. to the Ch: Wardens on the Pub: Treasr. for £40 Parochial Charges, for the year 1755. and by them Indorsed to William Gough Clark.———
An Order was likewise given to the Ch: Wardens, to pay unto Wm. Gough Fifty 6 Pounds, being the Interest Money due on the Rev'd Mr. Jones Legacy, for the Support of a School Master in the Town of Beaufort.

Officers Chose for Year 1756.

Mr. John Gordon } Ch Wardens.
Mr. John Heyward }

The same Vestry, Rechose

Mr. Jno- Gordon, Qualified accordingly.
N B, At the same time Mr. Peasely had notice that, the Gentlemen of the Vestry & Church Wardens would draw for his Salary no longer then to the 29th of Septembr: next and advised him to make Provision for himself by that Time.

91

Parish of St. Helena to Messrs: Chapman & W: Reynolds late Church Wardens from Esther 1755 to Easter 1756.

	Dr.		
To Mcpherling & Jno- Linningtons yearly allowance £	60	,,—	,,—
To Wm. Sommers an Orphan Child. pd. Sarah Mathews on his Acct.	30	,,—	,,—
To Do. ——— Sundries at his Funl. & a Coffin.......	5	10	,,—
To Mrs. Johnson Sundries..........................	15	15	,,—
To George Hardwick, his Board Funl. Coffin &c....	23	,,—	,,—
To John Wilcox his Board &c.......................	17	7	6
To Jane Jones—Sundries................St. Helena	3	10	,,—
To a Poor Man from Pon Pon 50/ Sullivan a Beggar 30/	4	,,—	,,—
To Danl. Reardon's Wife & Child's Board & Sundries.	74	8	9
To Sundries for the Church.........................	5	12	6
To an Advertisemt. for the Poor Tax in the Gazette	1	,,—	,,—
To Alexander Blane Sundries........................	25	6	,,—
To Dr. Thomson's Acct. for Medicines...............	53	10	,,—
£	318	19	9

ꝑ Contra	Cr.			
By Cash from Dr. Steele	£38,, 3,,—			
By Sundries the Effects of Geo: Hardwick Sold	7,,17,, 6			
By Poor Tax rec'd ꝑ Acct..............	267,, 1,, 6			
By Do. rec'd of Thos. Farr for the year 1754.	4,, 3,, 9			
By Bal: due to Jno- Chapman............	1,,14,,—			
		318	19	9

1756			
Ap: 19 The Parish To William Gough Dr.			
To Tackes for pulpit & Desk Ornamts. pd. Nash ....£	,,—	15	,,—
2 Days Provision for Negro cleaning Ch: yard paths	,,—	7	6
Sacramental Bread for 5 Years past a 10/ ꝑ Ann.	2	10	,,—
Writing Advertisemts. Letters &c and Vestry			

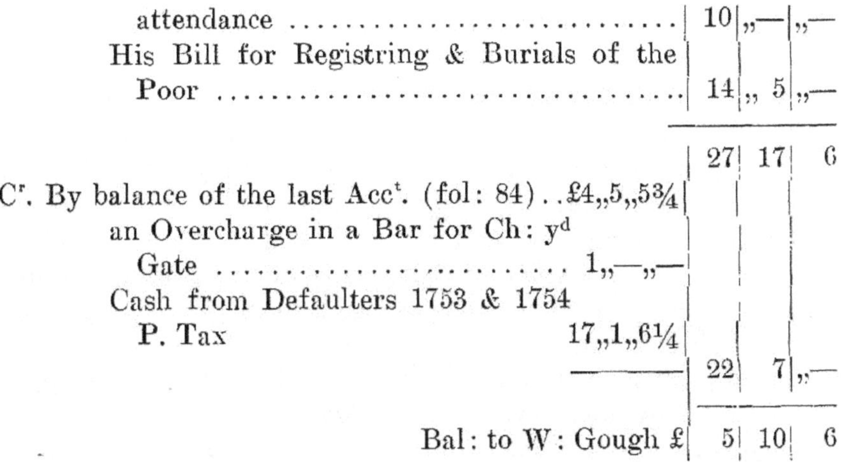

	£	s	d
attendance	10	,,—	,,—
His Bill for Registring & Burials of the Poor	14	,, 5	,,—
	27	17	6
Cr. By balance of the last Acct. (fol: 84) . . £4,,5,,5¾			
an Overcharge in a Bar for Ch: yd Gate .... 1,,—,,—			
Cash from Defaulters 1753 & 1754 P. Tax 17,,1,,6¼			
	22	7	,,—
Bal: to W: Gough £	5	10	6

92.

Copy of a Letter sent ℘

To the Rev'd Mr. William Peasely dated

Revd: Sir

It is now above Twelve months since you acquainted us that your bad Health would not permit your longer stay in this Parish, and we then jointly wrote to the Honourable Society desiring your removal and that we might be supply'd with another Missionary, but as we have not been favoured with any answer its probable our Letters miscarried—and the General discontent of of your parishoners arising from the unhappy Differences which has so long subsisted and still increases to such a Degree as to utterly destroy all Union and Harmony between you and them lays us their Representatives under an Indispensible necessity of endeavouring to Restore and Establish our usual and much desired Tranquillity.

In Compliance therefore of our Duty in this Regard so often and strenuously urged by the Parishioners, We are now Writing to some Friends of the Clergy in Charles Town requesting their advice in the most proper method of application for obtaining the end proposed, by Inviting over from England a Prudent meek and pious Divine whose Precepts may not only Dictate the true Principles of Christianity but his Example forcibly Inculcate them.

But in this affair we shall carefully avoid (unless we are drove to the necessity of it) Entering into any minute—Detail of Grievances or unne'ssary Personal Reflections, as it would be very disagreeable to us, and must be injurious to you and your Family, Whose Sufferings will Affect us in Proportion to our Concern in the Cause, Altho' Self Defence shou'd (which we hope your Conduct will not) make it become necessary to our Justification.

You cannot if you will divest your self of Prejudice Blame our Conduct in this affair Considering the animosities and Feuds which has so long Subsisted in the Parish, and which are now Swelled to such a Degree as to keep the People from the Church and Comunion and if continued must End in a total Degeneracy of Christianity and morals.

This we hope you'll Consider Seriously of and neglect no Opportunity to Provide for your Self in some other Parish by next Michalmas as we are willing to Dispense [93] with your attendance here until that Time and will agreeable to our Promise draw for this Year's Sallary then but no more.

We conclude in heartily wishing you Success and that our Tempers had been better Suited to each other so as to have prevented this Breach. and are

Rev[d]. Sir, &c

Copy of a Letter to the Rev[d]. M[r]. Alex: Garden Sen[r]: in Cha[s]. Town bearing date 24th June 1756.

Rev[d]: Sir

Your long Residence in this Province and your distinguished Zeal and attachment to the Church of England attended with every laudable Endeavor to promote Christianity strongly urges us in behalf of Selves and Brethren of that Communion in this Parish to lay our unhappy Case before you desiring your advice and Opinion in a matter which we doubt not will appear to be of such Importance, as not only to plead our Excuse for this Intrusion but ingage your good offices to Stop the growing Evil.

You have doubtless heard (as its too notorious) of the Differences between M[r]. William Peasely & his Parishioners here and which is now grown to such a height as to prevent his Congregation from attending Divine Worship and Consequently the Communion Table for some time past It being with great Reason urged by many People that they cannot Receive the Sacram[t]. from a man whose Life & Conversation prove him to have little or no Regard for Religion or the Reputation of that sacred Order which he is a member of.

Particulars of this unhappy Mans Conduct wou'd take up your time to read—and give us pain to relate therefore shall only say that we will be always ready to prove our Allegations, if ever it shou'd be thought Necessary, and sincerely wish that his—behavior had render'd this Proof more difficult but its so open and Shameless as to Disgust all Ranks & Degrees of People, and therefore not only renders him incapable of doing the least Good here but his Example may in time be of the most fatal Consequence

We therefore agreed above a year ago to part in mutual Peace. If possible, and in Order thereto did in Conjunction with him write to the Honble. Society He desiring a Removal on Acc^{t}. of his Health and we the favour of another Missionary but have not since received the least answer from them so that we have no Reason to hope for any Relief in that way, and least our present
94
Condition shou'd Estrange People quite from the Church. We most earnestly pray the favour of you to assist us with your kind advice in the best method of Application for getting over A Godly and Pious Divine to Reside among us, and we wou'd Chearfully Contribute towards any moderate Expence for accomodating such a Person from England to this Parish and for that purpose wou'd send Orders to a Gentleman in London. Our Compassion for M^{r}. Peasely's Family has made us very tender of his Character lest he shou'd be deprived of the means to make a Provision for them in some other Parish and this Consideration has been hetherto Privalent enough to keep us from coming to Extremity's nor would we now Willingly hurt him in that Respect If Possible to be avoided—as we pity his Weakness, but our Public and Private Duty calls upon us to guard against that general Depravity of Manners which his long stay threatens us with.

We hope Sir, you'll be kind enough to Excuse this Trouble, and your favouring us with an Answer will greatly oblige.

Rev^{d}. Sir &c

Copy of a Letter from the Rev'd M^{r}. Alex: Garden in Chas Town bearing date the 16 July 1756 in Answ^{r}. to the last
Directed to the Ch: Wardens & Vestry S^{t}. Hellens Par^{r}:

Gent:

Your Letter of the 24 Ultmo: is now before me, and in answer to itt I shall very freely offer you the best advice I can

In the first place it was a very great mistake in you to enter into any Compromise with Mr. Peasely, in Writing to the Society, he for his Remove on acct. of his health, and you for another Missionary to succeed him. This might easily appear a plain artifice on Mr. Peasely's part to put the Evil day as far off as he cou'd, for tho' he might actually Write to the Society to be removed on acct. of his Health yet how easy was it for him to write to them soon after, that he had recovered his Health and desired to be continued where he was. I do not say that this is really the Case, but as you have heard nothing from the Society, it has at least the appearance of it.

In the next place, The Remedy is plainly in your own Hands as Mr. Peasely is not Elected your Minister therefore my sincere advice to you is forthwith to discharge him, from any longer Service of your vacant Cure & immediately draw up your articles of Complaint against him which you're able and willing to [95] Prove (pursuant to the Societies earnest Desire and Request annex'd to the annual account of their proceedings) and transmit the same to them for your Justification.

Tenderness to a Family is indeed very commendable but when it happens in Competition with the Interests of the Church of God & the Souls of the Parishioners it not only ceases to be Commendable but becomes very faulty & blameable.
No Consideration either of Mr. Peasely's or Familys bread ought to be of any weight, when Religion and the Church of God are to be sufferers; and therefore the Society earnestly desire and Request all Persons Concerned that they would acquaint them with the offensive Behavior of their Missionaries, so as they may not only remove them from their present Charges, werewith they Intrust them, but finally dismiss them from their Services and not impose them on any other Parish or People where their behaviour may be equally offensive and hurtful.—
I shall be glad to know your final Resolution in this Affair, if you think proper to commit your Letters to the Society and Bishop of London to my Care, at Least three Copies of each, I will carefully transmit them by the first Opportunities, and at the same time will write my self and use all the little Interest I

have with them to procure you as speedly a Supply of another Missionary as possible. In the meantime I remain

Gent:

Your most abed[t] hum[le]: Serv[t].

Alex: Garden

96

At Vestry Monday August 2[d]: 1756

Present

Coll: Nath[l]. Barnwell	William Harvey Esq:
Coll: Tho[s]. Wigg	M[r]. John Barnwell
Coll: John Mullryne	M[r]. John Delagaye
	M[r]. Joseph Jenkins

Capt John Gordon, Ch: Warden

The Vestry being Qualified. a Letter was Signed by them and the Ch: Warden, and sent to the Rev[d]: M[r]. William Peasely, a Copy of which follows. viz[t]

Rev[d]: Sir

The Gent: of the Vestry that had lately a private Meeting with you, have Comunicated to us the Proposals you made which we reject— We have now before us an answer to the Letter we wrote to Charles Town, requiring the advice and assistance of some of the Clergy there in getting a proper Person to Supply this Cure, and it confirms us in our Resolution to draw for no more than the Currant Six months Salary when it shall become due, and if you do not in the mean time make some other Provision for your self, but persist in Officiating here, to Order the Church Doors then to be shut against you, and farther if we are oblig'd to it, We will transmit to the Society & Bishop of London our Complaints and Accusations against you properly attested.

We are Sir

Your most hum[le]: Serv[ts]

&c &c &c

97

From the Rev[d]: M[r]. W[m]. Peasely to the Vestry

Gentlemen.

As you have been pleased (notwithstanding your repeated verbal promises, and that under your hands in your favour to me of 24th. June that no Complaint or even personal Reflextion should be made) to complain of me to Mr. Garden in very virulent, tho' general Terms, which may cause him to think me guilty of the most culpable actions, and consequently prove of the very worst Consequence to me and my Family: I would be extremely oblig'd to you as I am now bound for Charles Town if you wou'd be so good as to be a little more explicite in a Letter to him by me, and let him know whether by this general Complaint you wou'd have him to understand I had been guilty of actions highly Criminal, or imoral, or indiscretions and imprudencies only; such as—uneasinesses in my Family, my warmth of Temper in resenting injuries and such like. My Reason for requesting that you wou'd be thus particular to Mr. Garden is, lest, from the Scandelous Story raised by Mrs. Cattell's Wench, he should think you intended to prove me Guilty of that base Action.—

I cannot Gentlemen, help thinking it a very great hardship that I am oblig'd to pay House-Rent, as you are not insensible that the Society sent me here on Condition that a House wou'd be provided for me, as is the Custom throughout this Province; and really the Society told me, before I left London, that there was a good parsonage House on the Glebe, and on no other Terms wou'd I have come here. Besides Gentlemen, I believe the whole World will think it—reasonable that the Interest of the money given by the public for building a House on the Glebe, shou'd be applied towards discharging the ministers House-Rent till the parsonage shou'd be ready for his Reception. Was I in Circumstances I wou'd—never mention the House-Rent, but in my present Situation, I really am not able (without greatly distressing my Self and Family) to pay Mr. Weatherly £150.——

If you'll be so good as to take this matter into Consideration and raise this Sum, or even half of it, by Subscription, it will at this Juncture be of great service to my Family and highly oblige

Gent: Your most obedient &c

Copia W Peasely

21st. August 1756

98

Postcript to foregoing Letter—

Believe me Gentlemen, that I would not give you the trouble to raise the Sum, or any part of it, was I not driven to very great straits; as you may plainly see is the Case, by my being oblig'd even to part with my Books. M^{r}. Steell tells me he can raise this half Year's Salary on your Order to the Treasurer, if you'll please to favour me with it: As my stay here will be but for a few days, I beg you'll oblige me with your answer as soon as you conveniently can. As my Family's distress cannot serve you in any shape (nor do I believe you desire it) I make no doubt but you'll be good enough to represent my Case to M^{r}. Garden in as favourable Light as you can.

The Vestry's Answer

Rev^{d}: Sir Beaufort Aug 24th- 1756

We have now before us your Letter of the 21st. Current to which we answer

We refer you to the Vestry Book for a Copy of our Letter to the Rev^{d}. M^{r}. Garden, in which we have not said anything that we are disposed to contradict—We leave you to Judge whither in Justice to our Selves, we cou'd have said less, and what room their is left for us to write ought in favour of you, consequently we hope we shall not be farther urged on that head, As to the Report of you by M^{rs}. Cattels negro Wench, that you seem to hinge on, we wish it was the only bad one laid to your Charge— In regard to the Interest of the money granted by the Public towards building a Parsonage House its being applied towards your present Debt for House Rent, youll please to observe, that the whole of that Interest Money since your arrival here, to this Day, will not exceed £220. and that in lieu thereof the Parish have (in Order to increase the Fund for building the parsonage House) paid more than double that Sum House Rent for you, which is more than has ever been required of us by any Clergy Man. Inclosed we have sent an Order for your Salary for the Current half year, and are Sir

Your very humble Servants

John Gordon C W. Nathl. Barnwell
Thos. Wigg
Copia John Mullryne
John Barnwell
Willm. Harvey

99

£275.,—— St. Helena Parish

Aug: 24. 1756

On the Twenty ninth day of September next pay to the Rev'd William Peasely, or Order Two Hundred and Seventy Five

Pounds Curr^{cy}. for his Salary as Minister of this Parish from the 25th: of March last

	Nath: Barnwell
John Gordon C W.	Thos. Wigg
	John Mullryne
To Jacob Motte Esq:	John Barnwell
Pub: Treas.	Willm. Harvey

The said Rev^{d}: Willm. Peasely left the Parish and went for Charles Town Sept 6th. 1756

Oct. 7. 1756 The Rev'd M^{r}: Peasely returned again from Charles Town and sent the following Letter to the Gentlemen of the Vestry

Gent:

I have been favoured with the Advice of my Friends who to a man, tell me that by quitting the Parish before I hear from the Society, or at least till it might be reasonably expected I could have an answer to my last Letters, I shall be guilty of the highest breach of Trust, and forfeit my Interest in that Venerable Body on whom is my intire dependance: which must be inevitably attended with y^{e}- utter destruction of my Self and Family. In Consideration of the Premises and as I am desirous to part in Peace with the Parish must beg that you will draw for my Salary, and permit me to do the Duties of my Place till Easter next, with which If you'll please to Comply, I hereby Promise to quit the Parish entirely, at that Time, as I may then do it without giving the Society the least offence.

And to this Request you'l the more readily agree if you'l please to consider that your notice on Easter Monday last was too short and that it was scarce possible for me to receive an answer to the Letters, I wrote in Consequence of that Notice by the 29th. of Sept^{br}. which was ingeniously acknowledged by a Gentleman of the Vestry in his own House a few hours after I received the notice: who also was pleased to add, that there wou'd be no difficulty in prevailing on the Vestry to comply with the above Request: A speedy Answer will oblige,

Oct: 7th. 1756. Gent: your most Obed^{t} Servt. W: Peasely.

100

Answer to the foregoing

Beaufort 8th Oct 1756

Sir

The requests you make with the Reasons assign'd for it in your Letter of yesterdays date give us the greatest surprize as you cannot expect our Compliance with it from an Approbation of your late Conduct.

We make no doubt, Sir, but it may be extremely convenient for you to Officiate in this Parish & receive the Salary till Easter next, but the Tranquility of every person in it being at Stake is an Effectual Bar to our Assent, and you are therefore by no means to effect it.

To repeat the Cause of this general dislike is surely needless, and we sincerely wish your Regard for Religion, your Interest in that Venerable Body you mention, and welfare of your Family may be the principal motives of your desire to remain longer among us.

We are Sir
Your most huml Servts.

To
Rev'd Wm. Peasely

Nathl. Barnwell
Thos. Wigg
John Mullryne
John Delagaye
Willm. Harvey

101

Copy of Letter from the Revd. Mr. Richard Clarke Dated in Charles Town Oct: 20th. 1756

Gent:

Application was made by Mr. Peasely to the Clergy who met in Town at the Assizes, desiring that they would hear what he had to say for himself, in vindication of his Conduct with regard to your Parish ——— They thought it unreasonable to condemn a man unheard, and for that Reason complied with his desire. ——— From his state of the Case it appears to them that things are not so bad on his side as they have been generally represented. But as they have heard only one side, it were impossible that they shou'd form a right Judgment upon the whole. Religion has been greatly wounded through this unfortunate Man's Sides: They therefore entreat you, for the sake of our

Common Christianity, as well as for the sake of M^r. Peasely's Character, and his Family's happiness, that you would transmit to them, the first Opportunity, your state of the Case. A Copy of a Letter you wrote to M^r. Garden on this Occasion was produced by M^r. Peasely, which contains only general Assertions without Proof, alledging at the same time that you can, without the least difficulty specifye particular facts, and supported with all reasonable Evidence; there Request therefore to you is, that you would point out those particulars, together with their proofs, that they may be able to Judge for themselves, whether they can Conscientiously give him a Recomendation to any other Cure of Souls in this province.— The Clergy present at this Meeting were M^r. Copp, M^r. Harrison, M^r. Martyn, M^r. Andrews. and my Self who am, Gentlemen

P.S. Your most humble Servant

Direct for me Rich^d: Clarke.
in Charles Town.

102

Copy of the Answer to the Rev^d. M^r. Clerke's Letter

Beaufort Nov: 5th. 1756

Reverend Sir

We rec'd your favor of the 20th past & altho' we had resolved against entering into any further dispute with M^r. Peasely unless he obliged us to it by that strict and expensive account wch. we have been often threatened with by him, Yet the regard we pay to the Request of so many Gentlemen, whose sacred Function we hope ever to Entertain the highest notions of, Prevails not only over that Resolution, but forces us with great Reluctance to point out a few particulars of M^r. Peasely's Conduct, which we apprehend will Sufficiently Justify the steps we have unwillingly taken in the long Contest that subsisted beteen him and his Parishioners.

In this affair it cannot be expected that we should here give full proofs of those particulars or relate many other Facts corresponding with them, as the first might lay us under some future Inconvenience, in Case his Threats should be carried into [1] and the last wou'd be too Prolix for a Letter. We shall therefore omit a Detail of many Feuds and the occasion of them between him and the great part of the Parish, in which the Ves-

[1]A word here has been erased and the place left blank.

try took no part, and begin with his too frequent and ill timed Visits to a Woman who then lived in this Town that gave great umbrage, and occasioned an affidavit much to his disadvantage, about this Time also a Person publickly affirmed before Capt. Fendin that he was witness to some indecent familiarities between them, which the Captain acquainted him with by Letter mentioning the Author, and desired he might clear himself of the Imputation but his not hearing of any Step taken towards it, occasioned a second Letter in which he strenuously urg'd the Author's being called to a strict Account. Upon this Mr. Peasely called a Vestry and made complaint to them of Fendin's ill treatment in giving this Salutary advice, which ended in his Solemn Promise to them never to make her any more visits, but they were notwithstanding repeated that very afternoon, and continued so publickly, that we were oblig'd to remind him of his Promise [103] which only served to whet his passion, or Purpose with assiduity in them to such a degree, that scandelous Advertisements were put up in Public places by Persons unknown, so obviously levelled at those Nocturnal and other meetings, that they seemed to give every Person (but him who was most concerned) the greatest disquiet, this caused such an Example of Tumults and disorder in his own Family & of what shall we call it obstinate indiscretion in himself, to the people, that they totally absented themselves from the Church & Communion.

That this was not the Case before that Example was set them, we shall only appeal to his own Letter of the 25th of January 1754 to the Society, tho anticedent to that Letter, his Conduct in refusing to Visit people at the point of Death, when sent for (of which their was two notorious Instances) and suffering them to leave the World without the benefit of that spiritual Comfort they so earnestly desired was such, as perhaps few Parishes wou'd have overlook'd.

—— To say that Mr. Peasely, and the Woman in Question were seen weeping together a day or two before he left us. —

—— That he stayed with her two days and two nights, about 4 miles from his Wife, after he had parted with her here to go to Charles Town.— That he had late at night on his return home from a Journey gone through a worse Road, and a greater distance to Sleep at her house than it was to his own — That he had beat one Person to the great Effusion of his Blood, and threatened others with the like Manuël Discipline, and that he offer'd to strike on of the Vestry only for differing with him in Opinion, might perhaps sound too much like a Romance, yet all these things (if the Testimony of Credible people have any weight) are certainly true. We will pursue this disagreeable Subject no further but Circumstanc'd as we were, if Mr. Peasely could be of any real Service to this Parish in preaching to bear Walls, and if it was not our indispensible Duty to get him removed and invite over another Minister We Submit to your Judgments and that of every Impartial man,

Jno- Gordon C W We are Revd. Sir &c The Whole Vestry

104.

At Vestry held Nov: 29th. 1756

Present

John Gordon Ch: Warden

Coll: Nath: Barnwell	Mr Jno- Barnwell
Coll: Thos. Wigg	Jno- Delagaye
Coll: John Mullryne	Wm. Harvey Esq.

Order'd, that the Parish be Assess'd in a Poor Tax of three Shillings in the pound (according to the last General Tax) to be paid by the 25th. of March next, and to be Advertis'd accordingly——

Copy of a Letter To Dr. Philip Bearcroft Secy: to the Society for Propagating the Gospel in Foreign parts, dated 21 April 1755

Revd. Sir See Folio 86

We the Vestry & Church Wardens of the Parish of St. Helena Port Royal South Carolina, beg leave to inform the Honle. Society, that Mr. Wm. Peasley our present Minister (for Reasons wch. he will comunicate to the Honle. Board, in his Letter, a Duplicate whereof we send inclosed) chooses to remove out of this Province, which we have agreed to, and wish for his own and Familys Sake, may be to his satisfaction, altho' by that means we shall again be destitute of a minister, and our Parish being one of the outermost Parishes in this Country and is so greatly divided by Bays Creeks & Rivers &c.a from any of the other Districks as renders it very difficult for us to be supplied on any emergency, And as there are great Numbers of Poor Setlers scatter'd up & down throughout this extensive Parish, the ministerial office will be greatly wanted in its Several Branches: We therefore hope that the Hon^{le}. Society in their known pious & Religious intentions to promote the knowledge of the Gospel of our Lord & Saviour Jesus Christ, will take our case into their Serious Consideration, and according to their accustom'd goodness, will supply this our Parish with an able & Religious Divine, as soon as possible, that our people may not live in Ignorance, nor want for Knowledge in the things pertaining to their Eternal Salvation. Your Friendship in securing us such a pious & godly minister will be an additional obligation to us who are

Ch: Wardens   Rev^{d}. Sir &c.   The Vestry

105

Duplicate of a Letter from M^{r}. W^{m}. Peasely, sent inclosed with the former, to D^{r}. Philip Bearcroft of the same date

Rev^{d}. Sir   See Folio 86

I Rec'd your kind favour of October 9th. and beg leave to return the Society my most hearty and sincere thanks for their very seasonable grant of a Library for the Use of the Missionary of this Church, the Books came safe to the hands of M^{r}. Clerk of Chas. Town from whom I hope to receive them by the first Opportunity to this place—The Addition of pious and practical small Tracts which you Sir was pleased to make, claim also my most grateful Acknowledgments, and be assured that when I receive them (for they did not come with the Library) all proper care shall be taken to distribute them where I find they are most wanted. I must now beg leave to acquaint you, that the frequent & severe returns of a Fever & Ague with which it has pleased Almighty God to visit me in this Country, have so far impaired my health, as to render it absolutely necessary for me to Petition the Society for a removal to some northern mission, where (through Divine Mercy) I may enjoy a better state of Health and consequently have it more in my power to contribute towards the promotion of the Society's pious designs. And as my endeavours to serve the Society for almost thirteen years have met with their favourable Opinion I make no doubt, Sir, but through the means of your good offices, they will be pleased to grant this my Request, and remove me to a mission where I may not be so much exposed to the extreams of Cold and

Heat, as I have been for some years past in the very opposite Climates of Newfoundland & Carolina.

I must also beg leave Sir, to join the Vestry of this Church in their application for a minister to succeed me upon my removal, that the invaluable blessing of God's Word & Sacrament may be continued in this place, and to assure the Society, that as there are many sober regular Families in the Parish, it may be in the power of a pious prudent man to do much good among them.

I am Rev^d^. Sir &c

St. Helens parish So. Carolina W Peasely
April 21. 1755

106

Vestry, Easter Monday, April 11th. 1757

Present

Coll: Nath: Barnwell	William Harvey Esq:
Coll: Thos- Wigg	Mr. John Barnwell
Coll: John Mullryne	Mr. John Delagaye
	Mr. Josp: Jenkins

Capt John Gordon }
Mr. John Heyward } Ch: Wardens

An Order was drawn on the Public Treasurer Jacob Motte Esq:

For £60 payable to Recd. Jenkin Lewis for preaching 6 times in this parish since October the 1st.

For £20 payable to Revd. Alex: Baron for Officiating twice

For £40 payable to Ch Wardens for Parochial Charges for the Year 1756, and indorsed to Wm. Gough as his Salary.

An Order drawn on the Church Wardens payable to Wm. Gough for £56— According to Rev'd Mr. Lewis Jones Legacy for the Incouraging a School Master in Beaufort.

A Petition was Signed to the Genl. Assembly for their assistance towards repairing & enlarging the Church. The above Vestry were again chose for the ensuing Year (except Mr. Jno- Delagaye who now residing in Charles Town, Capt John Gordon was chose in his Room) and where qualifyed Accordingly.

and then was chose { Mr. Francis Stuart } Qualifyed
{ Mr. John Cattell } Ch: Wardens

The Vestry Adjourned to Monday ye 18th. at 9 oClock

107

Monday April the 18th. 1757

The Vestry met according to adjournment

Present

Coll: Nath: Barnwell
Coll: Thomas Wigg
Coll: John Mullryne
Capt John Gordon
William Harvey Esq:
Mr. John Barnwell
Capt: Joseph Jenkins

Mr. Francis Stuart Ch: Warden

Order'd That, Mrs. Wade have to the value of £10. in Cloathing
Mrs. Johnson .... 30. in Do.
John Lennington in 2 paymts. 30. in Do.
The Widow Allen be paid .. 20. in Cash

That, Mary Hope be allowed £49, for six months to be to Dr. James Steele & Mr. John Givens and that she be allowed a little Liquor:

That, the Tinkers Wife (Susanna Rearden) be paid what Capt: Jenkins may judge necessary.

Capt: Gordon gave Notice that he had received the Books from the Revd. Mr. Clerk of Charles Town as mentioned Fol: 88—

The list of the Books as follows

2 Volumes	Fol:	Whitby on the N. Testament
1 Vol	.......Do--	Pearson on the Creed
1 Vol	.......Do--	Burnet on the Articles
1 Vol	.....Quarto	Chudens Concordance
12 Vols.	.......8vo.	Tillotson Sermons
4 Vols	.......Do..	Stanhope on Epistles & Gospels
1 Vol	........Do.	Nelson on the Festivals
1 Vol	.......Do--	Wheatby on the Com Prayer
1 Vol	.......Do--	Clerk on the Attributes
2 Vols.	.......Do.	Newcomes Sermons
7 Vols.	.......Do.	Sharpes Sermons
1 Vol.	........Do.	Wake on Ch: Catechism

34 Vols & 15 Marble Cover'd Society Sermons Feb: 15th: 1754

108

Dr. The Estate of Mrs. Jane Jones deceased—

1756. To Cash paid for Wine to Mr. Delagaye £ 3,,10,,—

Do. paid Mr. Norton for the Doctor ...... 3,,10,,—

Do. paid Do. . . for a Coffin .... 5,,—,,—

Do. paid Mary Williams for Nursing &c. . 25,,—,,—

Do. Registring her Death 6/3 Charge of Vendue 1..16. 3

£38,,16,, 3

Cr. By Amount of Vendue £32,,10,,3

due to the Parish 6,, 6,,0

£38,,16,,3

Dr. The Parish of St. Helena

To William Gough

To Balance the Last Acct. Fol: 91 ....£ 5..10..6

Registring & Burying the Poor as ℔ Bill.. 24.. 8..9

Writing and Vestry Attendance to Easter 1757 .... 10,,—,,-

£39,,19,,3

Cr. By Cash of Mrs. Delegall being her Poor Tax for the Year 1753 1754 & 1755 .... £1,,19,,6

Cash at Mrs. Jones Vendue ...... 31,,—,,-

Easter 1757. Cash of Capt Gordon as Cal: 6,,19,,9

£39,,19,,3

109

Dr. St. Helena Parish with Capt. Jno. Gordon Ch Warden

———from Easter 1756 to Easter 1757———

To Cash pd. the Ohio Woman & carrying her off £2,, 1,,3

Do. for Rum Sugar &c at the Burial of Danl. Rearden 3,,11,,3

Do. Bread & Wine for Sacramt 12,,6

Do. 7 yds. Cheque for Alex: Blane 2,,12,,6

Do. a Blanket & Wine for do 3,,12,,6

Do. a Coffin for Mr. Mcpherling.................. 2,,10,,-

Do. a Broom for the Church .... 1,,—,,-

Do. pd. Mrs. Clerk for the Freight of Book Fol: 107 3,,15,,-

Sundrys ℔ Ordr. of Vestry———

To Dorothy Johnston £25,,19,,6

Alex: Blane 46,,11,,3

John Lennington 26,, 6,,9

Susanna Rearden Tinker's Wife... 51,, 8,,1½ 150,,5,,7½

To Cash M[rs]. Dale

Her Acct. against Blane & Ohio Woman 3,,7,,6

To Dr. Jams. Thomson his Bill	£6,, 5,,—	
Julian Moronsy. Do.	4,,—,,—	
Jonathan Norton Do.	5,,—,,—	
Mary Williams- Do.	25,,—,,—	
Coll: Barnwell Do.	20,, 8,, 9	
Mathew Hext-- Do.	8,,12,, 6	69,,6,,3

To Cash pd. Wm. Richards 14 days Blane	1,,10,,—
Do. Wm. Goughs Balance	7,,—,,—
Do: Vestry Order to Wm. Gough	56,,—,,—
Do. pd. the Bal: to Fra: Stuart Ch Warden	157,, 4,,—
	£464,, 8,, 4

℘ Contra Cr

By Sundries Fol: 110 £464,, 8,,4

110

Dr. Capt John Gordon with the Parish

By Cash received of Mr. John Chapman late Ch: Wardens as balance of last Acct- — — —	£10,,15,,—
By Cash of Cato Ash ℘ P. Tax for year 1755 ...	2,,18,, 9
Do. of Edwd- Bellenger for 3 years to 1755	6,,—,,—
Do. of Danl. Blake P. Tax for 1755	3,, 2,,—
Do. for Swearing	7,, 6
Do. of Jas. Williams & Abra: Vauchier no arms in Church	2,,—,,—
Do. of Willm Gough Sacrament Money	19,, 5,, 6
Do. pd. short to Mrs. Rearden at times	7,,18,, 6
Do. of Fras. Stuart 1 yrs. Int: of his Bond	28,,—,,—
Sunday Poor Rate received	384,, 1,, 1
see Fol: 109 —————————	£464,, 8,, 4

111

Monday August 1st. 1757

Present

Coll: Nathl. Barnwell	Willm. Harvey Esq:
Coll: Thos. Wigg	Mr. Jno- Barnwell
Coll: John Mullryne	Capt: Josp Jenkins

Order'd, That the Parish be Assessed at the Rate of two Shillings in the Pound, which they paid into the last General Tax and that Advertisements be published that the same be paid by January the first next (1758)——
That the Westermost X Beam in the Church be imediately secured, it appearing to be very Rotton and Dangerous. ——

An Order was drawn on Jacob Motte Esq: Pub: Treasurer for the payment of £20. Currcy. to the Revd. Mr. Jonathan Copp, for Officiating the 1st & 2d Sundays in May last. and was Signed and Delivered to Coll: Barnwell ——

Order'd That the Vestry Clerk do, in the Name of the Gentlemen of the Vestry, return their Thanks unto Mr. Francis Stuart for his Gift to the Parish of a handsome large Damask Table Cloth, and two Napkins in one for the use of the Comunion Table ——

112

Wednesday Novbr: 16th. 1757 Vestry

Present

Coll: Nathl. Barnwell	Willm. Harvey Esq:
Coll: Jno. Mullryne	Mr. John Barnwell
Capt. Jno. Gordon	Capt Josp: Jenkins

Francis Stuart Ch: Warden

In Consequence of a Former proposal, it was Voted and unanimously agreed by the above That the Rev'd Mr. Alex: Baron of Stono shou'd be Invited to be minister of this Parish: But first, That the Parishioners should have Notice, by Advertisement, to appear at the Parish Church, on Tuesday the 29th. instant, between the Hours of 10 and 12 aClock in the Forenoon, to shew what Objection they or any of them may have Why the said Mr. Baron should not be Invited.

Tuesday Novbr. 29th. 1757
The Vestry and Church Warden met as ꝑ Adjournment

Present

Col: Nathl. Barnwell	Capt Jno. Gordon
Col. Thomas Wigg	Willm. Harvey
Col. John Mullryne	

Francis Stuart Church Warden

Order'd That a long Ladder be made for the use of the Church, and that the Weather Cock be painted Yellow and fixed on the Steeple.
Coll: Wigg being absent the last Vestry day, the Question was put to him, whether he consented to the Resolution of the last Vestry Meeting? to which he answered, in the affirmative: Upon which, as no Parishioner appeared against the said Invitation, a Letter was drawn up & signed to Invite the Rev^{d}. Alex: Baron to be Minister of this Parish a Copy of which follows.

113

Copy of the aforesaid Letter

Rev'd Sir/ S^{t}. Helena Parish Church 29th Nov: 1757-

Having heard that the bad State of health your Self and Family have been afflicted with for sometime past, will oblige you to seek out a more healthy place than that you at present possess; and being anxious to have for our Pastor one whose life and Character we know have been so long acquainted and are so perfectly satisfied with, we are here met to invite you, in the name of the Parish, with one Voice, to supply this vacant Cure. It will be needless to say anything of the advantages of this Situation to you, whom the experience of years hath made it sufficiently known to, All we shall say is that we will do all in our Power to make it still more agreable to you — A speedy Answer that you will accept this Invitation will be particularly pleasing to

To the Rev^{d}. Rev'd Sir

Mr Alex: Baron of Stono Your most Obed^{t} Servants

Memorand:

S^{t}. Philips Charles Town Parish D^{r}.

On Acct^{t}. of Morgan Rees, deceased, To S^{t}. Helena Parish.

1754 To Wine &c } during sickness ....Jno Delagaye £3,,—,,—
Physic } during sickness ....D^{r}. Steel - - - - 5,, 7,, 6
Oct. 18th- - -Coffin 50/ 4 Carriers 40/........ 4,,10 —
Liquor at his Funeral 1,, 7,, 6
Parson's Fees .... 2,,—,,—
Clerk Sexton & Register 3,,16,, 3

£20,, 1,, 3

By Cash p[d]. to D[r]. Steel £5,,7,,6
℔. W Gough Cash rec'd of D[r]. Steel . 11,,6,,3
parsons fees & Liq: at Fun[l]. not allowed .... } 3,,7,,6
Settled as above £20,,1,,3
Dec[br]: 1757.

114

Answer to the Letter Page 113.

S[t]. Paul's parsonage Dec: 12th: 1757

Gentlemen/

Esteem is valued by all mankind; but when it comes from Friends and is reciprocal, its value is much enhanced: this is the Case with me at present. I have received a kind Invitation to be minister for those, who, since my arrival in America, have stood highest in my Esteem, and which (did not a sense of my own inability discourage me) wou'd give me inexpressible pleasure: However I heartily accept your Invitation, and hope to be among you about the beginning of May next, which I think is in Conscience as soon as I can leave my Parish to give them an Opportunity of providing themselves with another Clergyman. If my Service does not answer your expectations, I doubt not you will attribute it to the true cause, my want of Capacity not my want of inclination. In short be assured that I will do the utmost in my power to please you and if I fail, it will be thro' human Weakness from which none is exempted.

I shall endeavor to be with you several times before I come to settle and wou'd in the mean time beg of you to get the Parsonage as forward as possible, tho' this I need not mention, as I make no doubt of having the Common incouragement of a Clergyman in this Province. Your affection for me is sufficiently shewn by the kind concern you express for my Health, and well being, and were I to Sacrifice more than I do, it would not be an adequate return: Gratitude only is in my power, and by Divine assistance I shall be grateful, as long as I have a being. The present Circumstances of my Family (of which D[r]. Thomson will inform you) prevent me the pleasure of waiting upon you, more fully to express the just sense I have of this Last and great testimony of your regard for me: when the causes are removed, which I hope will be soon, I shall make no delay. Meantime you have my sincerest prayers to Almighty God for your prosperity in time, and happiness when time shall be no more. I am with Respect, Gentlemen

To the Vestry & Ch: Wardens — Your Obed^{t}. & hum: Servt.
of S^{t}. Helena Parish — Al: Baron

115

Vestry February 26th. 1758

Present

Col: Nath: Barnwell — Willm Harvey Esq:
Col: Thomas Wigg — M^{r}. John Barnweli
Col: John Mullryne — Capt Josp: Jenkins
Capt John Gordon

M^{r}. Fra^{s}: Stuart Ch: Warden——

Resolved, That the Parsonage House should be finished, and that a Subscription should be made for the same, the first moiety to be paid the first day of April next, and the other moiety to be paid on or before the first day of January following. ———

Order'd That the House belonging to M^{rs}. Elizabeth Wigg be Rented, and put in Repair for the Reception of the Rev^{d}. M^{r}. Baron, until the Parsonage House is fitting.—

[116[1]]

Easter Monday March 27th. 1758

Vestry: Present,

Col: Nath Barnwell — William Harvey Esq:
Col: John Mullryne — M^{r}. John Barnwell

M^{r}. Fra^{s}: Stuart Ch: Warden

M^{r}. Francis Stuart reported to the Vestry, That the Church Wardens of S^{t}. Philips Charles Town had applyed to him for money expended for the Relief of one John Downing (belonging to the Scout Boat stationed at Caliboga) who was for some time Sick in Charles Town; But on M^{r}. Stuarts acquainting them, that the said John Downing was in the Service of the Governm^{t}.

[1]Page 116 is not numbered.

and therefore not a Parishioner, consequently the Vestry could not repay any charge on that Account, the said Church Wardens desisted from their demands, and put the said Charges on the List of Transient Poor provided for by the said parish of S^{t}. Philips Charles Town——

They then proceeded to the Election of officers for the year ensuing when ————

Col: Nathl. Barnwell	Willm Harvey Esq
Col: Thos. Wigg	M^{r}. John Barnwell
Col: John Mullryne	Capt Josp: Jenkins
Capt: John Gordon	

were chose again as the Vestry.

And M^{r}. John Grayson }
M^{r}. Benj: Chaplin } Church Wardens

Adjourned to Tuesday April the 11th. 1758 to settle Acc^{ts}. &c

117

Tuesday April 11th. 1758

The Vestry met pursuant to Adjournment vizt

Col: Nathl. Barnwell	William Harvey Esq:
Col: Wigg	M^{r}. John Barnwell
Capt Gordon	M^{r}. Francis Stuart

The above were qualified as Vestry Men,

Coll: Mullryne being in Charles Town, and M^{r}. Francis Stuart chose in the Room of M^{r}. Josp: Jenkins who refused to Act in the Vestry longer.

Mr. John Grayson Qualified as Ch: Warden

An Order on Jacob Motte Esq: for £20 payable to the Executors of the Rev^{d}- Jenkins Lewis deceased for his Officiating two Sundays since Easter 1757

An Order on D^{o} for £40. payable to the Rev^{d}. Alexander Baron of Stono for his Officiating 4 Sundays vizt July 31st. Jan: 22^{d} & 29th and February the 26th all last past——

An Order on D^{o}. for £40 Parochial Charges for the year 1757 which order was endorsed to William Gough as his Sallery as Clerk—

An Order to the Church Wardens to pay unto William Gough Fortynine Pounds being the Interest Money arising from the late Rev[d]. Lewis Jones's Legacy, to Incourage a School Master in the Town of Beaufort, he teaching such Children as should be recommended by the Vestry & Ch Wardens.

[118[1]]

Vestry, Monday May 29th 1758

Present

The Rev[d]. Alexander Baron
Coll[o]. Nathaniel Barnwell
M[r]. John Barnwell
Coll[o]. John Mullryne
William Harvey Esq[r]
Coll[o] Thomas Wigg
M[r]. Francis Stuart
Cap[t]. John Gordon
M[r]. John Grayson Church Warden

Memorandum, The Reverend M[r]. Alexander Baron in consequence of the Invitation from this Parish arriv'd to his Charge on Friday the 26th Instant and Preach'd here on Sunday the 28th. and this day was chosen one of the Vestry and Qualify'd Accordingly
Order'd That the Church Warden (M[r]. Grayson) do deliver unto the Rev[d]. M[r]. Baron all the Books in his Custody belonging to this Parish and take his receipt in the Vestry Book for them
Agreed That Andrew Aggnew, haveing already acted at the desire of the Vestry as Clerk, Register and Sexton since the death of William Gough, do continue to Act in these offices, And that the Said Aggnew be intitled to the money Left by the Rev[d]. M[r]. Jones for the Education of Poor Children, provided he shall Teach such Children as the Vestry recomend to him for that purpose

119

A List of the Books belonging to S[t] Helena Parish deliver'd to the Rev[rd]. M[r]. Alexander Baron Vizt

1 Vol: Folio, Rich[d]. Hooker, Law Ecclesiastical, Polity
2 do........do... Whitby, on New Testament
2 do........do... Pearson's, on the Creed

[1]Page 118 is not numbered.

1 do........do... Burnet, on the Articles
2 do........do... Comber, on the Com[n]. Prayer
1 do........do... Stillingfleet, on Religion
1 do......Quarto. Crude's Concordance
1 do........do... Moody's, Hugonis Grotu
1 do........do... Edwards, ..Socinanism
12 do........8[vo]... Tillotson's Sermons
4 do........do... Stanhope on Epistle's & Gospel's
1 do........do... Nelson's, Festival's
1 do........do... Wheatly, on the Com[n]. Prayer
1 do........do... Clark's, Attribute's
2 do........do... Newcome's Sermon's
7 do........do... Sharp's, Sermon's
7 do........do... Beveridge's, Sermons, Vol[e]. 1,2,5,6,7,8&10
1 do........do... Wake, Church, Catechism
1 do........do... Burnets, Abrig[mt]. of Reformation
2 do........do... Bragge's, Practical Discourse's
1 do........do... Dernham's Demonstration
2 do........do... Echard's, Ecclesiastical History
1 do........do... The Faith & Doctrine of Religion
1 do........do... Sermon Book.

15 Marble Cov[d]. Society's Sermons
June 5th, 1758 Received the above Books

Al: Baron

[120[1]]

Monday 7th,, August 1758

The Vestry mett According to Law

Present

The Reverend M[r]. Alexander Baron
Nathaniel Barnwell
John Barnwell
John Mullryne
John Gordon
William Harvey Esq[r]
Francis Stuart
} Vestry Men
John Grayson Church Warden

The Vestry agreed that Francis Stuart the old Church Warden should write the Gentlemen Nonresidents in this Parish to pay

[1]Page 120 is not numbered.

up their Poor Taxes— Mr. Grayson the Church Warden was Ordered to Pay Mrs. Gough the Sum of £20—Currency—

Tuesday October 17th,, 1758 121

The Vestry Mett According to appointment

Present

The Revrd,, Mr. Alexander Baron
Nathaniel Barnwell
John Mullryne
John Gordon
William Harvey Esqr.
Francis Stuart } Vestry Men
John Grayson Church Warden

The Church Warden produced a Letter from Mrs.. Gough, beging a further Suply, Upon which the Vestry agreed to allow the said Mrs. Gough the Sum of Thirty Pounds Currency from, this day to Easter Next, to be given out by the Church Warden at the rate of Five Pounds ⅌ Month.

Drawn an Order on Jacob Motte Esquire Public Treasurer in favour of the Revrd. Mr. Alexander Baron, for Four Months Salery, from the 28th. May, to the 29th. September 1758.

The Vestry appointed Messrs. John Mullryne, John Gordon and Francis Stuart, to draw Up a Petition to the Governor and Assembly, Requesting them to Grant the Vestry a Power to Asses the Parish for the Reparation of the Church, and Likewise to grant them, some part of the Money, Granted by Law for the reparation of the Parsonage House & Kitchin.

The Vestry desired the Church Warden to Acquaint the French Accadians, that doe not belong to this Parish, that they Must not remain in it

The late Church warden Francis Stuart was desired to Settle his Accounts and to pay the Ballance in his hands to the Present Church Warden Mr. John Grayson.

[122[1]]

1757 Dr.. The Parish of St Helena

		£	s	d
17th. May	To Cash paid the Vestrys Order to Mary Wade ....£	,,..10,,	......,,	....
25 Augst..	To 50..20d nails for the Church .... ,, 3,,9 1 Spring stock Lock for ditto 1,,16,,3	,,.. 2,,	......,,	....
30.........	To 1 pr. hinges, hook & eye for ditto	,,........,,	15,,	....
7 Septr.	To Cash paid for 34 feet Scantling & 16 ft. 2 In. plank...	,,......2,,	......,,	....
14........	To do. paid Elizabeth Gibbons a poor Woman to help her to C: Town	,,......1,,	11,,	....
19........	To do. paid William Owen....	,,......1,,	......,,	....
21........	To do. do. Mary Dale for 12 weeks & 4 days board of Mrs. Reirden a 40/	,,....25,,	3,,	9
6 Octo.	To paid Linnington ℔ order the Vestry	,,30,,	......,,	....
13........	To Amount Robt. Fairchilds Acct. for worke done to the Church & Church Yard Fence ...	,,......5,,	5,,	....
15........	To paid Thomas Stone hire of a Negroe to Clean the Church Yard............ ...	,,......1,,	10,,	....
21........	To a Broom dd. Willm. Gough for the Church.............	,,........,,	12,,	6
28........	To Cash paid the Church Wardens of Charles Town their Account for Ann Primrose...........	,,....67,,	13,,	4
	paid for a Poor Tax Adverment	,,......1,,	......,,	....
7 Novr.	....paid Dorothy Johnston	,,....30,,	......,,	....

[1]Page 122 is not numbered.

		£	s.	d.
8.........	....paid Thomas Walker his Acc[t]. for Securing the Girder of the Church....	,,......4,,	10,,	....
19.........	....paid William Hutchins a			
21.........	Lame man	,,......1,,	11,,	....
	....paper, Ink powder & 25 Quills (d[d]. W Gough	,,........,,	12,,	6
14 Dec[r].	To paid M[rs]. Shergold for Board of M[rs]. Reirden	,,......5,,	......,,	....
21 Feb[y].	To 1 p[r]. Shoes for (M[rs]. Sacheverill) .... 1,,10,,..			
	... 1 p[r]: Worsted hose (for do.) 1,, 2,,6	,,......2,,	12,,	6
2 March	To Cash paid M[rs]. Givens for Board, Nursing &ca of Mary Hope	,, ..24,,	......,,	....
	To Sundry Necessaries suplyd Mary Hope	,,....19,,	12,,	6
	ditto & Burrying Charges of M[rs]. Reirden	,,....33,,	16,,	....
	Amount of Doct[r]. Thomson's Acco[t]. for do	,,....25,,	......,,	....
	Sundry Necessaries Supplied M[rs]. Shergold & family.....	,,....17,,	13,,	....
	To Sundrys Supplied Parsons the Painter	,,....19,,	3,,	6
	1 Ceader post	,,........,,	7,,	6
	James Steels Acco[t]. for Mary Hope	,,....25,,	......,,	....
	To Sundries for Old Deal, Coffin & Burrying Charges &ca	,,......5,,	12,,	6
1758	To 1 Lock for the Church Yard	,,........,,	18,,	9
13 Ap[l].	To paid the Widow Allan ℔ Order of the Vestry	,,....20,,	......,,	....
	Carried Up——£	384,,	0,,	4

123

To Francis Stuart Church-Warden Cr..

1758	Dr,, Brought Up ....£	384,,	0,,	4
18 Apl.	To...Interest money received ℔ Collo. Wigg & paid Wm. Gough	,,....11,,	13,,	4
	To...Cash paid Wm Gough his Account	,,....12,,	4,,	....
3 May	To...ditto paid Julian Maronsy for a Coffin for a Soldiers Wife ....}....	,,.......5,,	.......,,	....
	£	412,,	17,,	8
	To Ballance paid John Grayson Church Warden 4th. November 1758 ℔ Receipt}..	179,,	12,,	5½
	£	592,,	10,,	1½

Cr..

1757				
4th July	By Sacrament Money received of Gough ....£	,,.....28,,	7..	9
19 Septr.	By...1 Yars Intrest of Thomas Wiggs Bond	,,....28,,	.....,,	....
	5 Months ditto on...ditto..	,,. 11,,	13,,	4
	received of John Gordon Ballce. in his hands ₱ Acct.	137,,	4,,	....
	received of ditto	,,....20,,	.....,,	....
	By Amount of Poor Tax collected to 11th. April 1758....	,,327,,	15,,	6¼
	By Sundry Poor Taxes Collected from 11th. April to the 10th July 1758,,	,, 36,,	17,,	3
	By Sundry Poor Taxes from 10th. July to the 4th. Novemr. 1758	,,......2,,	12,,	3¼
	£	592,,	10,.	1½

Errors Excepted

[124[1]]

Received. 4th. November 1758 of Mr Francis Stuart Late Church Warden, The Sum of One Hundred & Seventy Nine Pounds Twelve Shillings and Five pence half penny, being full Ballance of Money in his hands for the Use of the Parish, Also Received Two Bonds Vizt. Francis Stuarts and Joseph Parmenters Senrs, each for the Sum of Fifty Pounds Stirling, Being the Revrd. Mr Jones Legacy for the Encouragement of a Schoolmaster and Educating of Poor Children in this Parish, for all which I Promise to be Accountable John Grayson

N B. Francis Stuart's Bond was discharged & the money sent Phillip Martinangele }

125

Tuesday 16th,, January 1759,

The Vestry mett according to appointment

Present

The Revrd,, Mr. Alexander Baron. John Mullryne
William Harvey John Gordon
Francis Stuart
John Grayson Church Warden

The following Letter Sent to the Representatives ℘ Capt. John Stuart,

To John Rattray William Roper and John Murray Esqrs. Representatives for the Parish of St. Helena.

Gentlemen

We are Credebly Inform'd that the Inhabitants of the Youhaws have petitioned the General Assembly for a seperate Parish and as Such a Seperation wou'd be productive of Many Ill Consequences to Our Parish at this time too Tedious now to Enumerate, We the Vestry & Church Wardens Desire you will Oppose the Said petition untill we Give Our Reasons for Desiring you to do so, if any Such Reasons Shou'd be thought Necessary

We are

Gentlemen

Your Most Obdt Hue Servts

[1]Page 124 is not numbered.

John Grayson C W

Al Baron
John Mullryne
John Gordon
Francis Stuart
Will[m] Harvey
Tho[s]. Wigg

P S. Coll[o]. Barnwell & his Brother are not in town at Present

S[t] Helena Parish 16th. Jan[ry] 1759

126

Thursday March 29th. 1759

The Vestry Mett According to Appointment

Present

The Rev[rd]. M[r]. Alexander Baron
John Mullryne
John Gordon
John Barnwell
Francis Stuart
William Harvey

Nath[l]. Barnwell Sick

John Grayson Church Warden

Agreed that Nath[l]. Barnwell, John Mullryne and John Gordon, Should agree with Workemen as Soon as Possible, to finish The Parsonage House, and Outhouses and with People to furnish Matierials for that Purpose, And that the sum subscribed for that purpose be Imediately Collected to Defray the Expence of the same

Drawn An Order on Jacob Motte Esq[r]. in favor. of The Rev[rd] M[r]. Alexander Baron for Six Months Salery due the 25th. this Inst[t]. March 1759

127

Easter Monday April 16th., 1759

Vestry Present

The Rev[rd]. M[r]. Alex[r]. Baron
John Mullryne
John Barnwell
William Harvey
John Gordon
Francis Stuart

Coll[o]. Barnwell sick

John Grayson Church Warden

An Order was drawn on Jacob Motte Esq[r]. Forty Pounds Payable to John Grayson Church Warden for Parochial Charges from Easter 1758 to Easter 1759 and endors'd to Andrew Aggnew for his Salery as Clerke

An Order On the Church Warden to pay unto Andrew Aggnew the Intrest Money, According to the Revrd. M^{r}. Lewis Jones's Legacy for the Incouragement of a School Master in Beaufort—

Then proceeded to the Election of Officers for the Ensuing Year, when the Following Gentlemen were Choose as Vestrymen

The Revrd. Alexander Baron	Nathaniel Barnwell
John Gordon	John Barnwell
William Harvey	Francis Stuart
John Chapman	William Reynolds

William Elliott }
James Heyward } Church Wardens

Agreed that John Thomas be intitled to the Intrest Money arising from the Revrd. Mr Lewis Jones's Legacy, for the Educating of Poor Children, Provided he shall Teach such Children as the Vestry shall recommend to him for that Purpose.

Agreed that John William Parsons do Act as Clerke, Register and Sexton of this Parish, in the room of Andrew Aggnew Who declined that Office,——

M^{r}. John Chapman was Choosen Vestryman in the room of Coll^{o}. Wigg Deceased

M^{r}. William Reynolds was Choosen Vestryman in the room of Coll^{o}. Mullryne who declined Acting

128

Recived 2th May 1759 of M^{r}. John Grayson Late Church Warden the Sum of thirty nine pounds five Shillings & aLeven pence halfpeny being the Full Ballance of Money in his hands for the Use of the parish also Recived Two bonds Viz^{t}. Joseph Parmenters Sen^{rs}. & Phileph Martonangels Each For the Sum of fifty pounds Sterling being the Revrd. M^{r}. Jones Legacy For the Encouragement of a School Master & Educating of poor Children in This parish for all which I promise to be Accountable——

W^{m}.. Elliott Junr

The Parish of St Helena Dr—

			£	s	d
1758					
Apr	6	To 2 Spelling Books Deliverd to Mr. Gough @ 8/9	0	17	6
	15	To Sundrys Supplied John Davison	..3	12	6
June	3	To Do.....Do John Wm. Parsons....	..8	14	7½
Aug...	1	To Cash pd for 2 pr of Apprentices Indenrs.	2	0	0
		To 1 Surplice	32	10	0
	7	To Cash Paid Mrs. Gough ₱ order, Vestry	20	0	0
	18	To 100=20D. Nails for ye.. Parsonage House	...0	7	6
		Paid for Nailing up the Doors & windows Do.	..0	10	0
	21	To a Padlock, hasp, & Staples, & putting them on the west Gate	0	10	0
		pd. for Cutting Down the Trees in the Church Yard & Cleaning it	1	10	0
Decemr.	2	To Sundries Supplied Mrs. Robinson for her Child's funeral & Coffin	5	14	0
	11	To Cash Paid to Ambrose Gibbons	4	0	0
1759					
Febry	15	To Do....Do Robt. Fairchild, for a Book Case for the Parish Books	15	0	0
		To Sundries Supplied John Lillenton	30	0	0
		To Do....Do.. Dorothy Johnson....	30	0	0
		To Cash pd Mrs.. Gough at 6 Payments	30	0	0
Apl...	14	To 1 pr of Apprentices Indentures	1	0	0
		To a padlock for the South Gate..	0	10	0
		1 pr. of Apprentices Indentures	1	0	0
May	2	To Ballance pd to Wm. Elliott as ₱ the above Receipt	39	5	11½
			227	2	1

129

John Grayson Churchwarden......Cr..—

			£	s	d
1758		By Cash receiv'd from Francis Stuart, the Late Church warden	179	12	0
Decr.	25	By Sacrament Money	14	2	3
1759					
April	5	By Cash Reced From, Fran: Stuart, Late Ch: W:	8	6	0
		By Poor Tax Reced of Mary Williams	0	19	1½
		By Do....of Geo: Delabere......	1	11	6
		By Do....of John Kennard Delabere	1	8	1½
	15	By Sacrament Money	16	19	0
		By Poor Tax reced of Wm.. Scott	1	18	6
		By Do....of Henry Tabert.......	1	18	3
		By Do....of Thos. Stone	0	7	4
			227	2	1
		Acct. Dr.	187	16	1½
		Ballance	39	5..	11½

Errors Excepted

[130[1]]

Monday April 30,, 1759

Vestry called for this day was adjourned to a more Convenient Opportunity, by reason Some of the Gentlemen Being indisposed or out of Town; the rest not Sufficient to make a Vestry

Monday July 16,, 1759

Vestry Present

The Revd,, Mr. Alex Baron

Nath: Barnwell Fran: Stuart	vestry	John Barnwell John Chapman

Wm.. Elliot Church warden

The above Gentlemen Qualified as Vestry men for this Year

NB.

John Gordon
Wm. Harvey Esq } were not in Town
Wm. Reynolds

Application being made by Mrs Gough for a Further Supply of Maintenance for herself & Family it was agreed to allow her 3 £ Curency ℔ Month until Easter next & to be paid by the Church warden once a Month.

Application was likewise made by Mr. John Barnwell in behalf of the widow Heard & her family It was agreed to allow them the Sum of 22,10,, 0 which money is to be Laid for them in Apparel

Agreed that Mr. Rickets be allow'd the Sum of 20 £ one Moiety of which is to be pay'd Directly & The rest at the End of Six Months

Ordered; that the Inhabitants of this Parish, be Assessed in the Poor Tax one Shilling in the Pound paid to the Last General Tax payable 1 Day of November Ensuing which is Ordered to be printed in the Public Gazette

131

Mr,, Elliot the present Churchwarden is Desired to Acquaint Mr. James Heyward the Other Church Warden Nominated on Eas-

[1]Page 130 is not numbered.

ter Monday; that unless he Qualifies as Such, the fine Stipulated by a Late Act of Assembly will be Levied against him
Ordered That a Subscription be raised, for Defraying the Expence of House Rent. (Occupied by the Rev^{d},, M^{r}. Baron) for the time being—15 M^{os}- being Expired
Proposition made by M^{r}. Francis Stuart, M^{r}. John Barnwell & Col. John Mulry'ne, to build 3 pews on the vacant Ground at the East End of the Church between those already built
Resolved, the Said pews be built uniform to the others in Heigth & Model, the Dimensions of each pew 6 feet in Length & 4½ feet width, to be made of Cedar, by next Easter, Each person to pay 25 £ Cur^{cy}. which money Shall be apply'd to the Use of the Church
Resolved that M^{r}. Elliott do Cause 6 more Benches to be made in the form of the other Two, alredy in the Church which are to be placed on the vacant Ground at the west End of the Church between the Pews & to be pay'd, from the monies arising from the 3 pews which are to be built at the East End
A Letter was produced by M^{r}. Elliott from Magd^{n}- Goiron an Acadian Desiring Relief from the Parish, was Rejected

132

Monday Augst—,, 6,, 1759

The Vestry mett according to Law

Present

The Rev^{d}: Alex Baron	Vestry	John Gordon
Mes^{s}. Nath: Barnwell		John Chapman
John Barnwell		W^{m}. Harvey Esq
Fran: Stuart		

Church wardens { James Heyward
W^{m}. Elliott...........absent

W^{m}. Reynolds, Vestryman not Qualified
James Heyward Qualified as Churchwarden
John Gordon Qualified as Vestryman

Agreed; that the widow Allan be allowed at the Rate of 20 £. untill Easter next

133

Easter Monday Apr 7,, 1760

Vestry Present

Mr. John Chapman } } Wm. Hervey Esqr
Fran: Stuart } } John Barwell
Wm. Elliott } Ch ward

James Steele (Security for a Bond of 50 £ St ℔ with Jos: Parmenter Senr..) being Dead the Vestry have agreed to Accept his Son Joseph Parmenter as his Security in the Room of The Said James Steel Dece'd.
An Order Drawn on the Church wardens in favour of John Thomas for 56 £ Curr being the Interest of the Revd.. Mr. Jones Legacy for the Encouragement of a School master in Beaufort Town, for the Benefit of Certain Poor Children Educated by him & that the Said John Thomas has agreed to Continue the Same another Year & was Orderd to Advertise the Same
An Order was Drawn on Jacob Motte Esq P.. T for forty Pounds Currency Payable to James Heyward & Wm Elliott Church wardens for Parochial Charges from Easter 1759 to Easter 1760 & Endorsed to John Parsons for His Salary as Clerk/
Mr. Wm. Elliott & James Heyward not haveing Collected the Poor Tax the vestry postponed their Settlements of Accts. till Monday the 21 Instant

Elected the new vestry as follows

Nathaniel Barnwell } { John Barnwell
William Harvey..... } { Francis Stuart
John Chapman ...... } { William Waight
William Elliott Junr }

And adjourned to the 21st Inst. appointing

Churchwardens { William Fripp
Nath. Greene

134
Met according to Adjournment on Monday 21st April 1760

Vestry Present

Nathaniel Barnwell } { Frans Stuart
William Harvey }
John Chapman .... } { Wm Waight

Churchwardens { Nath. Greene
Wm. Fripp

Who were qualified according to Law
Mr. John Barnwell & Mr Wm Elliott nominate Vestry Men not qualified being absent.

Agreed to allow the Widow Allan .....£30 p ann.
The Widow Heard .... 30 do...
Prudence Albergottie... 30
Richd. Rickets .... 30 do...
John Lennington ...... 30 do...
Dorothoy Johnson .... 30 do...
} £200.—

Sarah Shergold ... 20d in Goods for the present use of herself & Children

The Revd Mr Cooper at the desire of the Vestry and Churchwardens has wrote to England to the Revd Mr John Gabb of Radnor Shire to come and supply the vacancy of this Parish or in case that he should not be able to come to provide us with a Person properly qualified.

The Vestry and Churchwardens have appointed John Thomas to act as Clerk, Sexton and Register of the said Parish in the room of John Parsons.

135

Receiv'd 3d- of October 1760 of Mr. William Elliott Late Church Warden the Sum of Seventy Eight Pounds, Seventeen Shillings & Nine pence being the full balance of money in his hands for the Use of the Parish also Receiv'd two Bonds Vizt. Joseph Parmenters Senr & Philip Martinangels each for the Sum of Fifty Pounds Sterling Being the Revd: Mr. Jones's Legacy for the Encouragement of a School-Master & Educating of Poor Children in this Parish for all which I promise to be Accountable

Nathl. Greene/. CWd

1759 The—Parish of—St. Helena wth— William Elliott ——— Dr:

	£	s	d		£	s	d
Paid Richd Rickets, at 2 difft paymts	20:	—„	—„	By Cash rec'd of John Grayson late Church Warden	39„	5„	11½
Paid Mrs. Gough at 4 ditto	12„	—„	—„	By Sacrament money rec'd on Whit-sunday	17„	10„	6
Paid Mrs. Frentz for ye care of Caesar	6„	—„	—„	By Axtell and Jno. Hutchinson's Poor Tax for 1757	„	15„	9
To Sundrys supply'd Mrs Johnston by Mr John Grayson......	30„	—„	—„	By Jno- Stanyarns Poor Tax p Do	„	12„	6
To Do-Supply'd Mr Linning by do-	30„	—„	—„	By Sundry Poor Taxe's rec'd by Mr Francis Stuart	188„	15„	6½
To 25 Quils d'd Mr Parsons......	„	7„	6	By Poor Tax collected by J. Grayson	88„	14„	3½
To Sundrys pd Fra Stuart as ℔ Acct	159„	1„	„	By JulienMeronsey's Poor Tax ———	„	3„	7
£	257„	8„	6	By Jos: Parmenters Junr do	„	7„	2½
Balance due the Parish	78„	6„	11½	By Cash recd of Jonathan Norton for Poor Tax	21„	—„	—„
				By do- for Sundry Poor Taxes	10„	—„	—„
£	335„	14„	5½	£	367„	5„	4
To Cash pd- Nathaniel Greene C-W-at Sundry times	110„	17„	9	By Ballance due	78„	6„	11½
£	446:	12„	2½	£	446„	12„	3½

136

Easter Monday March 23rd: 1761.

At a vestry met at the Parish Church of St Helena,

Present

Mr William Fripp, } Ch: Wa:

Nathaniel Barnwell Esqr
Mr Frans Stuart..............
Mr John Chapman............ } Vestry
Mr Wm Harvey................
Mr Wm Wait ....

An Order was drawn on the Public Treasurer for the Payment of £40. Cy, to John Thomas as Clerk, Register and Sexton, another in the said Thomas's favour on the Church Wardens for £56 for the Schooling of the Parish Childn to be paid out of the Interest arising on the Legacy left by the Revd Mr Lewis Jones dec'd for the purpose aforesaid; Mr N Green's absence prevented further Business as to the Parish Accots, The Vestry adjourn'd until the Monday Sevn Night being. the 7th April following— — — — — — electing first a new Vestry as follows ————

Mr Wm- Hazzard } C. Wardens
Mr Wm- OBryen }

Nat Barnwell Esqr
Mr John Barnwell ..
Mr Wm Harvey ....
Mr Frans Stuart ... } Vestry
Mr Wm Elliott Junr.
Mr John Delagay ..
Mr Peter Purry ....

The Parish of St Helena

To Julien Meronsey

1760

To making a Coffin for Owen Mc.Garr ....£5—
To John Thomas Clk &ca.. ℘ his Accot ℘ the Funeral 3,,15,,7½

£8,,15,,7½

137

1760

At a vestry held at St Helena Saturdy Decr 18th Fols

Present

Mr Nathaniel Greene Church Warden. — —

Nath Barnwell Esqr

Mr Fras Stuart ....
Mr John Barnwell ....
Mr John Chapman........
Mr William Harvey.......
} Vestry men.

Agreed by the Board that the Parish aforesaid be Assess'd 2/ in the pound of what they paid to the General Tax, and that an advertisement, for the Parish aforesaid to that purpose be published in the So Carolina Gazette;

An Order at the same time was given to the Revd Mr John Copp, on the Public Treasurer for Preaching here on Sunday the 31st. Augt, 1760. for £10,,—,,— Another on the said P. Treasurer to the Revd Mr. Cooper for Preaching here the 17th Feby. and 9th November last for £20,,——

[138]

At a Vestry met at the Parish Church of St Helena on Tuesday the 14th Day of April 1761. . . . .

Present

Nathaniel... Barnwell Esqr

Mr John Barnwell ....
Mr Francis Stuart ....
Mr John Chapman ....
Mr William Harvey ....
Mr William Elliott Junior..
Mr John Delagay...........
Mr Nathanl Greene late CW-
} Vestry Present

Mr Wm OBryen

Mr Nathaniel Greene having produced and laid before the vestry the Parish accounts, as also rendering an accot of the moneys by him Collected and Mr William Fripp Church Wardens for the Preceeding year 1760, the sd accounts were now settled and deliver'd to the Register to be enter'd Mr Greene also d'd into the

Care and Custody of M^{r} W^{m} O Bryen who now qualified as C Warden, and it is orderd that a Letter be writt to Mr Wm Hazzard, signifying that he is appointed CW for the present year, and that he be and appear at y^{e}-s^{d}, Parish Church, on Tuesday the 12th of May next, in order to qualify for the same then the following Gent^{n} were appointed as the vestry for 1761.

Nathaniel Barnwell Esqr..
Mr John Barnwell ....
Mr Wm Harvey ....
Mr Fran^{s} Stuart ....
Mr Wm Elliott Junr.......
Mr John Delagay ....
Mr Peter Pery .... } Vestry Men for 1761

M^{r} W^{m} O Bryen
Mr Wm Hazzard } C. W

Orderd that an Additional allowance of £10. to be given in Cloathing to Elizabeth Small, and that Letters, wth. relation to our want of a Pastor be here copied

and

139

sent for that purpose, which are as follows

St Helena Parish Ap^{l} 10th. 1761

Revd Sir

Our destitute situation for want of a Pastor, and being almost entirely depriv'd of Divine Service for above 15 months past, will we hope be a sufficient Apology for our Application to you and entreaty, that whenever you can wth conveniency & Propriety leave your own Parish, you woud come and supply our want.

We shall contribute any thing in our power to make your Journey easey to you, and the oftener you visit us youl lay the greater obligation on

Revd Sir

Your most obed^{t} Hum Serv^{ts}

To the Revd Mr Robt Baron

It was first agreed and concluded upon y^{t}. a Letter should be wrote to the Revd Mr Chas Martyn Pastor of St Andrews embracing his kind offer to provide us wth a Clergyman upon his arrival in England wch Letter is Copied in folio: 140.

St Helena Parish 10th April 1761

Revd Sir

When we inform you that we have been destitute of a Pastor and of almost any Divine Service for about 15 mo^{s} past we hope it will Apologize for our applying to you, and entreating that when you can wth conveniency leave your own Parish you may come and Supply our want, nothing in our Power shall be wanting to accomodate you on your Journey & to make it agreeable to you, and the oftener you visit us the greater obligation you will lay on

Revd Sir

Your most Obed^{t} hum Serv^{ts}

To The Revd Mr Tonge

140

It was agreed also that a Letter be wrote to The Revd Mr Chas Martyn Rector of S^{t}: Andrews

Rev^{d}, Sir/

We would long e'er this time have acknowledged the Receipt of yor kind letter, but waited an answer from The Rev^{d}, Mr Coopers Friend, who we hoped woul'd have provided us wth a suitable Pastor to supply our great want. We apprehend the present troublesome situation of this Province might be no small obstacle to The Revd Mr Gabbs endeavours in our behalf

But as it is in your power to represent these Matters in their true & proper light we beg leave to accept of y^{r} very kind offer, and to entreat, you may, on your arrival in England, write Mr Gabb, to desist from his endeavours, and use your best Interest for us in providing us as soon as possible wth a Proper Clergyman.

It would be presumption in us to prescribe to your superior Judgment in the choice of a person proper for us, but we will thus far venture to say; That a Gentleman of a Studious turn, and, regular Uniform, deportment who will maintain the authority of the Church wthout being austere or rigid to the Dissenters (of wch we have a good many in this Parish) would suit much better than one of a contrary Disposition.

We are sorry to say yt ye- conduct of our late Missionary makes an application to the Bishop of London, or the universities seem more agreable to the generality of the Parish, than applying to the Society, but in this we do not chuse absolutely to restrain you, as it is the less matter where our Ministr comes from, provid'd, he is one who teaches ye- Doctrines of Xt, & his Gospel in truth & is of a life & conversation agreeable thereto. If we are happy enough to have such a Person for our Teacher, we promise that nothing on our part shall be wantg to render his situation agreeable & make his life comfortable. Our Parsonage House is not entirely finish'd, & indeed our want of a proper Clergyman, has made yt work go wth less spirit, but we promise that a proper & convenient House shall be provided for our Minr, at our expence, until it is compleated, and a Negro hired for his service, for at least one year after his arrival, as to ye Election of our Minr wch you mentd, to Mr Stuart, we cannot take it upon us, to make any Promis's in behalf of ye- rest of ye- Parish on yt head, but as we have said already, nothing in our Power shall be wantg to make such a Minr, as we like, respectable & easey we are wishing you a prosperous voyage

&

April 1761

P S. When ye- Revd, Mr Cooper was so good as to write in our behalf to Mr Gabb, we then lodged in ye- hands of Mr Richd Shubrick of Londn, £20 Sterlg for his use, or whoever he shou'd pitch upon to come & supply us, and Mr Stuart now incloses you an Order for sd sum (if not already calld by Mr Gabb,) for the use of whatever Minister you may provide for us.

This letter came too late but shoud have——————[1]Mr

141

Mr William Hazzard

Sir

The Church Wardens and Vestry of St Helena Parish having met on Easter Monday the 23rd of March last; Mr Nathaniel Greene and Mr Wm. Fripp having resign'd the Office and Duty of their said Church Wardenship for the

---

[1]Several undecipherable words—destroyed by the cutter when the book was rebound.

Preceeding year 1760, you together wth M^{r} W^{m} OBryen were appointed in their Rooms for the ensuing year, I was orderd by the s^{d} vestry to signify the same to you, and to desire you wou'd be at our Parish Church on Tuesday the 12th of May nex't in order to Qualify for the same; I presume I need not acquaint you that there is a Fine of £10. Proclam^{n} incurred in case of your declining to Act, any Services in the Writing way to assist you therein you may command,

S^{r}

Your very hum Servt

Beaufort 16th April 1760

John Thomas Clk & Reg

142

D[r] :—The Parish of S[t]: Helena wth Nat.. Greene ———— C[r]:

1760	£	s	d		£	s	d
Paid Rich[d] Ricketts.............£	30	.—.	—,,	By Cash of W[m] Elliott at sundry times	110,,	17,,	9
Paid M[rs] Johnston	30	,,—,,	—,,	By Poor Tax recd of Sundry Persons..	54	:	: 4¼
Paid M[rs] Shergold	20	,,—,,	——	By Cash recd by M[r] W[m] Fripp moneys by him collected at S[t] Helena Island	74.	5,,	2,
Paid M[rs] Albergotti	30	,—,	——				
P[d] Linington	30	,—,	——				
P[d] M[rs] Heard	30	.—.	——				
P[d] M[rs] Shergold for Eliz Small	23,,	3,,	6				
P[d] for a Woman & Childs Passage	8,	—,	—,	£2	39,,	3,,	3¼
Provisions found them	3,,	—,,	——				
Liquor supply the People for Burying a Poor Man	1,,	—,,	——	By Ballance due N. Greene..........	19,,	5,,	10¼
Negroes to clear y[e]. Ch: Yard.......	3,,	——	——				
Supplyd M[rs] Small with a Blankett &[ca]..	4,,	10					
Paid for Advertisements	3						
Paid M[r] Thomas	3,,	15,,	7½				
Paid M[r] Meronsey for a Coffin	4,,	—,,	——				
Cash p[d] M[rs] Allen	30,,	—,,	——				
D[o] p[d] M[rs] Small	5,,	—,,	——				
£	258:	9:	1¼	£	258:	9:	1¼

(143

Easter Monday

At a Vestry held at the Parish Church of St: Helena on Monday the 12th. April 1762

Present..

Nathaniel Barnwell Francis Stuart John Delagaye & William OBryen	William Hazard & William OBryen Ch: Ward:

It was agreed and concluded upon, that the present vestry should continue as they were last year, and we accordingly rechosen, as was allso William OBryen Church Warden for the present year, together with David McKees of St Helena Island; They then adjourn'd until Monday the 25 Inst:. as there was not a Sufficient number to do the intended Business of the said Parish

Monday the 25th. April 1762 The Vestry met according to Adjournment

Present

Nathaniel Barnwell John Barnwell William Harvey	Francis Stuart John Delagaye

William OBryen C. Warden

William Harvey resigned as one of the Vestry this present year John Mullryne Esqr: is appointed and chosen in his room; Agreed that the Church Wardens do write seperate Letters to the Non-Residents of the said Parish advising them to pay up their Arrears for two Years Past, as also to acquaint them that they are Taxed this present year at 9d. in the pound and that payment thereof be made in two Months from the day & date of said Advertisement. Nath: Barnwell. John Barnwell. Francis Stuart, John Delagaye, qualified as Vestry Men as did also William OBryen as one of the Church Warden

The following persons (in Compliance with the Act of Assembly were appointed as Overseers of the Poor) Vizt: William Hope for Port Royal Island, Mr. Jonathan Norton for St Helena Island & John Grayson for the Youhaw Indian Land

An Order was drawn on the Public Treasurer payable to M^r^. William Hazzard & Mr William OBryen, and indorsed over by them by them to John Thomas for his Service due as Register &Ca

144)

at the same time another Order was drawn, in his the said Thomas's favour, on the Church Wardens for the sum of Fifty Six Pounds Currency the present Interest Money arising on the Legacy left by the Reverend M^r^. Lewis Jones for y^e^: teaching of Poor Children in the said Parish

The said John Thomas has resigned up the office or Duty on acco^t^. of his removal) of Clerk, Sexton & Register of the said Parish, during his Residence here, in which time another may be procured or offer to do the said Duty

Yearly allowance for the Poor at the meeting of the before going Vestry Vez^t^:

M^rs^. Johnson	.£30. ℔ Ann
Linnington	. 30
Mrs Shergold	. 25
M^rs^. Heard	. 30
M^rs^. Albergotti	. 30
M^rs^. Allen	. 50
M^rs^: Small	. 90

(145

Tuesday 28th: September 1762

The Vestry mett by appointment

Present

Nathaniel Barnwell
John Barnwell
John Mullryne
John Delagaye
William Elliott
Francis Stuart

The Reverend M^r^. John Green mett the Vestry for the first time since his Arrival which was on 20th: of August Last, He was this day unanimously chosen on of the Vestry,

The Vestry ordered that the Church wardens should with all possible Expedition bring the Parsonage Acco[t]: as far as finished to a Conclusion & Colect the Subscriptions due, that they should likewise enter up the Parish Acco[ts]: to last Easter & Collect as soon as possible the Poor Tax & write Letters to several non residents—John William Parsons being represented to the Vestry as an object of Charity & now in distress they they ordered the Church wardens to Supply him with proper necessaries to the amount of £30.. Curr[y]. Andrew Verdure was propos'd as a Schoolmaster in the Town of Beaufort and the Vestry agreed to allow him for a time the Interest money arising from the Rev[d]: M[r]. Jone's Legacy for the Education of Poor Children, he agreeing to Educate a Proper Number

146)

Easter Monday 4th. April 1763

The Vestry & Church wardens met according to Law

Present

The Rev[d]: M[r]. John Green Nath[l]. Barnwell John Mullryne John Delagaye Francis Stuart	Vestry Men
William OBryen David M[c]Gee	C Wardens

An Order was drawn on the Publick Treasurer in favour of the Rev[d]. M[r]. John Green for 8½ Months Sallery, being £538.6.8 Curr[y]. an Order was allso drawn in favour of the Church Wardens for £40. on the Public Treasurer for Parochial Charges £30 Curr[y] for M[r]. Welch & £10 Curr[y] for a Quarter's Salary due John Thomas

There appearing to be a very large sum due the Church Wardens, on Account of the Poor Tax not being Collected The Church Wardens were requested to press the Payment of what is deficient & to press the Non residents, who have not paid for several years

The Parishioners present proceeded to chuse a new Vestry & Church Warens agreeable to Law—When
The Rev^{d}. M^{r}. John Green
Nathl. Barnwell
John Barnwell
John Delagaye
William Elliott
Peter Perry
Francis Stuart.
Where chosen as Vestry men William Hope where chosen Church Wardens

Dr,,——The Parish of St. Helena wth. William Obryen Cr

Dr					Cr			
1761					1762			
To Cash Paid Nathaniel Greene£		19,,	5,,	—	By Cash Received from Sundry's as ℘r. List	£162,,	15,,	8
To Sundrys supplyed Dorothy Johnston		30,,	—,,	—	By Ballance Due W, OBryen.......	168,,	10,,	4
To Ditto...Ditto John Linnington		30,,	—,,	—				
To Ditto...Ditto Mrs. Sheregold		22,,	1,,	6				
To Ditto...Ditto Mrs. Iding		10,,	—	—				
To Ditto...Ditto Mrs. Heard		30,	—					
To Cash pd. Mrs. Albergotti....		30,,	—,,	—				
To Do. Do. Mrs. Small..........	80,,12							
Sundrys Supply'd Hex.......	10,,—	90,,	12,,	—				
To Cash paid Mrs. Allen........	....	50,,	—,,	—				
To Do. Do. Benjamin Burton...	....	2,,	—,,	—				
To Do. Do. John Story pr. Acct..		3,,	—,,	—				
To Do.. Do. Julias Moronsey do..		1,,	10,,	—				
To Do. Do. Edward Tucker.....		3,,	—,,	—				
To Do. Do. John Thomas Do.......		9,,	17,,	6				
£		331,,	6,,	—		£331,,	6,,	—
		sh	d					
To a Ballance Brot. Down ....£	168,,	10,,	4		By Cash recd of Mr. Stuart ....£	24,,	15,,	4
					By Ballance due Wm OBryen	143,,	15,,	—

Do,,———The Parish of St. Helena wth. Wm. OBryen Cr

1763					1763			
To a Ballce. of Acct due last year	......	143,,	15,,	--	By Cash received from people that had no Arms at Chur	9,,	—,,	—
Sundry's Supply'd Linnington	30.—				By Ditto of Francis Stuart	10,,	16..	3
ditto...ditto. D. Jonson	16,,15,,				By Ditto John Delagaye	7,,	10.,,	—
ditto...Ditto. S,, Shergold	25,,				By Ditto of the Revd. Jno-. Greene	12,,	6,,	—
ditto... Mr. Parsons	27,,1,,6				By Do. Poor Tax recd as pr List	101,,	9,,	7
ditto...Mrs. Small	69,,15,,				By Cash of David McGee	36,,	2,,	6
ditto...Mrs. Albergotte	30,,							
Cash pd. Mr. Ston's Acctt......	4,,10							
Cash pd. Mrs. Allen	50,,	253,,	1,,	6	£	177,,	4,,	4
					Deducted for Mrs. Allen	50,,	—,,	—
£		396,,	16,,	6				

148)

Monday 9th. May 1763

The Vestry mett by Appointment

Nathaniel Barnwell John Barnwell William Elliott John Delagaye Francis Stuart	Qualified as Vestry Men

William Hope who was chosen one of the Churchwarden's refused to Qualifie, & pay'd his Fine, being £10.—.— proclamation Money, say £50.—.— Currcy, Richard Stevens was Chosen Church Warden in room of Mr. Hope & Qualified as such

The Vestry agreed to pay Benjamin Green the £50,,— pay'd by Mr. Hope, being for an allowance made Mrs. Allen last year and that money was Deliver'd Mr. Stuart for that Purpose—

The Parish was assess'd according to Law for the Relief of Poor at the rate of 6d. pr. Every Pound Currency paid towards last general tax to be paid the Churchwardens & other proper persons appointed to receive it, by the 1st. day of August next and the Church Wardens were ordered to give nottice of such assessment in both Gazett's & in all publick places in the Parish,

The following Poor were Ordered to be paid paid the sum annex'd to Each of their names

John Linnington	£30.—.—	
Mrs. Johnson	30.—.—	
Mrs. Sheargold	20.—.—	
Mrs. Albergotie	30.—.—	
William Tweedy	30.—	
Mrs. Small at 31/ ℔ week	80..12	£220..12.—

October 1763

The Vestry Drew on the Treasurer for £380.—.—in favour of the Reverend Mr. Green being for 6 Months Sallery——

(149

Easter Monday 23d. April 1764——

The Vestry met according to Law. ——

Present,

The Reverend Mr. Green
Nathaniel Barnwell
John Barnwell
William Elliott
John Delagaye
Francis Stuart
Richard Stevens C, Warden

The Vestry drew on the Treasurer in favour of the Reverend Mr. Green for £380,, for 6 Months Sallery, and in favour of the Church Wardens £40.—.— for Parochal Charges—By an Account rendered the Vestry it Appears that there is due for Work done to the Parsonage House as follows—

To Francis Stuart	£367,,14,, 5	
William OBryan	33,, 7,—	
John Story & Danll.- Stuart . .	183,,19,—	
John Story	87,, 9,, 6	
William Moses	12,,15,—	
Jacob Ruff	15,,10,—	£700,,14,,11

It was agree'd, if Possible to raise the above sum by subscription ——, The Vestry agree'd to pay £28,, to Mr. Verdier for six Months schooling of the Poor Children out of the Interest Arising from Mr. Jones Legacy—

150)

Easter Monday 23th April 1764

The Parishoners Present proceeded to chuse a new Vestry & Church Wardens when the following persons were chosen——

The Reverend Mr. John Green
Nathaniel Barnwell
William Elliott
John Barnwell
John Delagaye
Thomas Middleton
Peter Perry

William Deveaux and Samuel Heyward were chosen Church Wardens——

Friday April 27th, 1764

The Vestry & Church Wardens Met by Appointment

Present The Rev^{d}: Mr John Green	William Deveaux Church Warden
Nathaniel Barnwell	
William Elliott	
John Barnwell	Vestry Men. and was Qualified according to Law by
John Delagaye	
Peter Perry	
Thomas Middleton	William Harvey Esqr.

(151

Friday April 27th. 1764 ———

Agree'd to Allow, John Linnington—	£30,—,--
M^{rs}.. Johnsons	30,—,--
M^{rs}. Albergotie	30,—,—
M^{rs}. Small 40/ p^{r}. Week	104,—,—
John Leach	30,—,—
Alex^{d}. Bland	20,—,–
	£244,, ꝑ^{r} Ann..

Agree'd that a Tax of 18^{d}. for every Slave, and 18^{d}. for every 100 Acres of Land in said Parish be rais'd for to pay the above Sum

That William OBryan and Richard Stevens late Church Wardns do give into the Vestry an Acc^{t}. of all the Defaulters of the former Taxes.

That Thomas Greene do Act as Register, Clerk and Sexton, and to school six Poor Children, to be paid out of the Intirest, Ariseing from the Ligacey left by the Rev^{d}: Lewis Jones Decd. for that Purpose ———

That Jos: Parmenter with Benjamin Green as Security do take on Interest Sixty two Pounds Sterling, being part of the Ligacey left by the Rev^{d}. Lewis Jones Deceased — — — — — — — — There appear'd to be £112,,—,, Curr^{cy}. Interest due on M^{r}. Jone's Legacy to Easter 1764. from which the sum of £28,,—,,— due M^{r}. Verdier for the Schooling of the Poor Children for 6 Months, was deducted and the Ballance £84.—.— was added to the Principal of Joseph Parmenter's Bond for 350 £ and the whole sum £434,, or 62 £ Sterling was by the Consent of the Vestry Lent to Joseph Parmenter & Benjamin Green upon their Joints Bond payable at Easter 1765..

152)

Monday the 6 Day of August 1764

The Vestry and Church Wardens met According to Law

Present

The Revd. Mr. John Green
Collo. Nathaniel Barnwell
Mr. John Barnwell
Collo. Thomas Middleton
Mr. John Deligaye
Mr. William Elliott
Mr. William Deveaux Church Warden

Mr. William Deveaux is Desir'd By the Gent. Men of the Vestry to Demand of Mr. William OBryan and Mr. Richard Stevens, an Account of the Defaulters, a former List of the Poor Raits, and of Mr. William Obryan, a subscription List to Reimburst Mr. Francis Stuart for Money's advanced by him in England, and Moneys Received on said Subscription

By Order of the Vestry
Thomas Greene Clk

(153

Eastr Monday the 8th Day of April 1765—
The Vestry and Church Wordens met according to Law—

Present

Colln Nathaniel Barnwell
Colln Thomas Middleton
Mr- John Barnwell
Mr William Elliott
Mr- John Delagaye
} Vestry

Mr Saml Heyward &
Willm. Deveaux
C Wardens

Order that Mr William Deveaux do pay Mrs. Greene twelve Pounds three shillings & nine pence for Funeral Charges of Poor of the Parish for the year 1764— ———
The Vestry & Church Wardens drew an Order on Jacob Mott Esqr- Public Treasurer for £40 Parochial Charges for the year 1764 in favour of Mrs. Greene—
The Vestry & Church Wardens drew an Order on William Deveaux for Sixty two pounds fourteen Shillings being the Interest

due on The Rev[d] M[r] Jones Legacy for Schooling Poor Children in favour of M[rs]. Greene
154[1])

(155

Easter Monday the 8th April 1765—
The Parishoners Present Proceeded to Chuse a new Vestry and Church Wardens when the following Persons were Chosen—

Vestry	Church Wardens
Coll[n] Nathaniel Barnwell	Co[lln] Dan[l] Heyward
Coll[n] Thomas Middleton	M[r] Lewis Rive
M[r]- John Barnwell	
M[r]- William Elliott	
M[r]- John Delagaye	
M[r] John Fripp—	
M[r] William Deveaux—	

Persons on the Parish ———

John Linnington ℘ a[n]- ————£30
M[rs]. Albergottie 30
M[r]. Alexander Blane 20

Friday the 17th day of May 1765 The Vestry and Church Wardens met—

Present

Vestry	Church Warden
Col[n] Nathaniel Barnwell	Col[n] Dan[l]. Heyward
Col[n] Thomas Middleton	
M[r] John Barnwell —	
M[r] John Delegaye	
M[r] William Deveaux	

and were Quallifyed by William Harvey Esq[r]. according to Law M[r] Lewis Reve Church Warden Elect being called upon to Quallify refused & paid the fine of fifty Pounds M[r] John Story was elected Church Warden & Qualifyed. ——— Agreed that a Tax of one shilling on Every slave and one shilling for every Hundred acres of Land in said Parrish be raised for to defray

[1]Page 154 is blank.

156)
The Poor Tax for the Present year———

Dr The Parish of St. Helena wt, William Deveaux				
1764		£	s	d
April 3d,	To Cash paid for sundries furnishd, Jno-Linnington	30	—	—
	To Cash paid for dito to -Alexander Blane	20	—	—
	To Cash paid Mrs. Albergottie	30	—	—
	To Cash paid Mrs, Richards- for Mentainance of Mrs Small 27 Weeks & three days at 40s/ pr Week	61	5	—
	To Cash paid funeral Charges of Mrs, Small	5	—	—
	To Cash paid for Sundries furnished Mrs Johson	18	2	—
	To. Cash paid funeral Charges of Mrs. Johson	3	10	—
10th Decbr,	To Cash paid a poor man by order of ye. Vestry	2	13	6
	To Cash paid for Sundries Clothes allowd, Mrs, Small	6	—	—
	To Cash paid Julian Maronzey for two Coffins & Negro hire	10	10	—
	To Cash paid for an Advertisement in Wells Gazette	2	—	—
	To Cash paid Mrs, Richards for Mentanance of Mrs. Small From Mr, Richard Stephens,s Last Payment to Easter day last			
	To Cash paid Mrs, Ann Green Parochal Charges of the Poor	12	3	9
	To Cash paid Mrs, Ann Green by Order..	62	14	0
	To Cash paid in the Whole of the Parish Accompt £	268	11	3
	To Balance due from William Deveaux to the Parish	96	12	8
	3	65	3	11

	The Parish — — — p^r. Contra — — — C^r.	£	s	d
1764				
20th Decbr,	By Cash Receivd, of Sundrie persons their poor Tax	246	7	8
	By Cash Receivd of Mr Samuel Heyward poor Tax by him Collected	39	3	9
	By Cash Receivd, of Mr John Barnwell Sacrament money	7	17	6
	By Cash Receivd, of Sundrie persons Since Easter	9	1	0
	By Cash Receivd, of Mr, Jones's Legacy	62	14	—
	By Cash Receivd in the Whole on the Parish Accompt £3	65	3	11

(157

Agreed that the Ballance due by William Deveaux be paid to Mr William Obryan in part of the Ballance due him from the Parrish & that the Fifty Pounds paid by Mr Lewis Reve be Likewise paid to Mr William OBryan on that account — —

Agreed to give an Invitation to the Reverend Mr John Feveryear of Bermuda to accept of this Parrish in the room of the Revd. Mr John Greene Decd. & accordingly the Following Letter was Wrote to him & Signd. by the Vestry & Church Wardens

Beaufort So. Carolina 17th. May 1765

Mr. John Feveryear

Revd. Sir

The Death of our Minister the Revd. Mr. Green, leaves this Parish in want of a Clergyman to Supply his Place; & having been inform'd that you had through Mr. Green, made an offer of yr. Service to the Neighbouring Parish of Prince William, which Parish was Supply'd before Mr. Green's Letter came to hand & having since, by a Letter from Capt. Solomon Joell to one of our Vestry, been assured that you are desirous of quitting the Island of Bermuda; We the Vestry & church wardens of the Parish of St. Hellena, Induced thereto by the Character we have had of you, do make you an offer of this Parish & wish you may think it worth your accepting. We will not Sir attempt to say anything in Recommendation of the Parish, but for our Selves will assure you, that if you think proper to Accept of our offer, we will Receive you with a Sincere & Hearty Wellcome, & with Dispositions & Inclinations to make the Parish as agreeable to you as we possibly can.

We shall Sir, till we receive y[r]. answer, which we wish may be as soon as possible, Receive no offers from, or apply to any other Clergyman, & are

Rev[d]. Sir

y[r]. very humble Serv[ts].

Dan[l]. Heyward } Church
John Story } Wardens

Nat Barnwell
John Barnwell
Thomas Middleton } Vestry
John DeLagaye
Will[m] Deveaux

158)

Friday the 30th May—1765—The Vestry and Church Warden Met—

Present ——————

Col[n]- Nathaniel Barnwell
Col[n]- Thomas Middleton
M[r] William Elliot } Vestry
M[r] John Delagaye
M[r] William Deveaux

M[r]- John Story
Church Warden

M[r] William Elliott was Quallify.d according to Law

That Richard Harrison do act as Register, Clerk, and Sexton, and to School six Poor Children, to be paid out of the Interest, arising from the Legacy, left by the Reverend M[r] Lewis Jones Dec[d]., for that Purpose, & took the oath required of a Register—

Monday the 5th, of August 1765 the Vestry & Church Warden met

Present Vestry

Col[nl]: Nathaniel Barnwell
Col[nl], Thomas Middleton
M[r], William Elliot ———— }
M[r] John Delagaye ————
M[r] William Deveaux

M[r] Daniel Heyward
M[r] John Story
Church Warden

(159

From the Revd. Mr John Feveryear to the Vestry

Dated ye: 24th of June & Receivd here August the 22d 1765 ——— from Bermuda

Gentlemen I received your Letter Last Thursday dated In may 1765 forwarded by Mr Thomas Savage Merchant In Charles Town where in you have shewn me so much Respect as to make me an Offer of your Parish which I accept with Gratitude/ I yesterday acquainted the Governor of this place and my Parishoners here of your Offer and my acceptance of it and of my Purpose of leaving them the first Opportunity (you may depend Gentlemen That I shall Imbrace the first Opportunity of Coming to Beaufort With my family Especially as you have been so long without a Clergy man

My best Compliments are desired to all the Parishoners of St. Helena and do think my self happy to be

Gentlemen your Obedient and Humble Servant
John Feveryear

To the Gentlemen of the Vestry and Church Wardens of the Parish of St Helena in South Carolina

Tuesday the 4th Day of February the Vestry & Church Warden met

Present Vestry

The Revd. John Feveryear
Coln- Nathaniel Barnwell
Coln. Thomas Middleton
Mr. John Delegaye
Mr. John Barnwell
Mr. William Elliott-
Mr. William Deveaux

Mr. John Story
Church Warden

The Reverend Mr. Feveryear produced his Testimonial & was Qualifyed a Vestry man—agreed that five pounds be allowd. John Linnington untill Easter—The Church Warden is desired to put up advertisements to Collect the Poor Tax, agreed that Mr Woodhouse should teach Six poor Children 'till Easter out of Mr. Jones's Bounty, agreed to Repair & Enlarge the Church

160)

According to the plan Given in by Mr. Cornelius Mc.Carty & Coln- Thomas Middleton Mr John Delegay & Mr. William Deveaux are appointed to Inspect the same, & that Mr. John story do repair the Roof of the Church also to ask Mr. Francis Stuart for the Old Subscription for the Church

D^r. Parish of S^t. Helena with Jno. Delagaye — C^r

Dr.	£	s	d	Cr.	£	s	d
To Cash paid Linington	35,,	—,,	—	By Poor tax Collected by Jno. Delagaye for Jno Story	59..	13..	—
ditto paid Alex^r. Bland	20,,	—,,	—	By ditto Collected by Daniel Heyward from Easter 1765 to Easter 1766....	184.	13	
ditto paid M^rs. Albergotè	30	......	....				
ditto paid a poor man	2,,	10,,	—				
ditto p^d William OBryen	18,,	12.	6				
ditto paid Jo^s. Loyd for the parsonage	15	......	—				
ditto paid Messrs. Middleton Liston & Hope	72.	12.	5				
ditto paid into the hands of the now Church Warden H. Stuart	50.	11.	1				
	244,,	6,,			244..	6..	—

Easter Monday 31st. March 1766.—

Many of the Parishioners of St. Helena Parish met at the Parish Church and proceeded to Chuse a new Vestry & Church Wardens when the following persons were Chosen. . Vizt

Vestry	Church Wardens
The Revd. John Feveryear	Gilbert Pepper
Nathaniel Barnwell	Henry Stuart
Thomas Middleton	
John Barnwell	
John Delagaye	
William Elliott	
William Deveaux	
John Fripp	

161

The Vestry agreed that Thomas Smith should act as Clark & Register and allowd him a Salary of Twenty pounds ℔ annm.. & that George Welch should act as Sexton & allowd him a Salary of Twenty pounds pr. Anm..
Agreed that an order be drawn on the publick Treasurer in favr. Mr. Feveryear for 9 months Salary due him this day say for £570.. Cury.. that an Order be drawn in favour of Geo. Welch for £40 for Parochial Charges..
That an Order be drawn in favour of the Revd. Mr. Tongue for Ten pounds for performing Divine Service and preaching in this Church during the absence of of the Late Revd. Mr. Green. and that an Order be drawn in favour of Mrs.. Duncomb. Relict of the late Revd Mr. Duncomb for his performing divine service and preaching in this Church one Sunday during the absence of the Revd. Mr. Green and the said Orders were accordingly drawn & Sign'd by the Vestry & Church Wardens—

Wednesday 16th. April 1766 The Vestry met

Present—	
The Revd. Mr. Feveryear	Henry Stuart C. Warden
Nathaniel Barnwell	
Thomas Middleton	
John Barnwell	
John Delagaye	
William Elliott	
William Deveaux	

Who were qualified according to law by Wm. Harvey Esqr. J. P.

Poor Upon Parish for the Year 1766

John Linnington to be allowed . .	£30. . . . .
Mrs Albergottè	30. . . . .

Examined Jno. Storys Acot. for Sundry repairs on the Church and

162)

& Parsonage House and agreed to allow him in full of Sd. accot. Fourteen pounds Ten shillings. As the Parish has several Times Lent the Sacrament money for the Support of the poor agreed that Messrs. Middleton Liston & Hopes accot. amountg to £72.. 12..3 for sundres for the Parsonage House, Jos. Loyds accot for painting & Glazing the Parsonage House amounting to £15 Cury.. be paid by the last Church Warden out of the money Collected for the poor for last Year and that the ballance be paid to Richard Stevens to pay up moneys he advanced

Monday 18th. August 1766 Vestry met

Present

Nathaniel Barnwell
John Barnwell
Thomas Middleton — Heny. Stuart
John Delagaye — Church Warden
William Deveaux

Agreed that an order be drawn on the publick Treasurer in favour of Mrs. Feveryear for £190 being three months Salary due the reverend Mr. Feveryear deceas'd late Minister of this Parish to the time of his death 30th. June 1766, & an order was drawn & Sign'd accordingly.—

Agreed that a Certificate directed to the public Treasurer be drawn & signd, that six months salary was due to the Reverend Mr: John Green former Minister of this Parish at the time of his death, & the same was drawn & signd accordingly —

(163

Monday 29th. September 1766

The Vestry met. . . Present

Nathl. Barnwell
John Barnwell
Thomas Middleton — Henry Stuart
William Elliott — Church Warden
John Delagaye
William Deveaux

They Agreed that Mr. Middleton should write to his brother to endeavour to get a Clergyman for this Parish, and that Twenty pounds Sterling to be raised by a General Subscription, be paid into Mr. Midletons hands in order to defray sd. Clergymans expenses in coming to this Parish, and in case the money rais'd by general subscription shoud not make up the sum of Twenty pounds Sterg. the deficiency to be made up by the Present vestry & Church warden

That a petition be presented to the Assembly for some assistance for repairing & enlarging the Church.

That a Subscription be set on foot to raise money sufficient to purchas 3 negroes for the use of the parsonage—

164[1])

(165

Easter Monday 20th. April 1767

The Parishioners being assembled at the Parish Church of St. Helena proceeded to Chuse Vestrymen & Church Wardens to serve for the following year when the following Persons were Chose Vizt.

Nathaniel Barnwell
John Barnwell
John Delagayé
William Elliott
William Deveaux
Thomas Rutledge
Henry Stuart } Vestrymen
William Kelsall
John Norton } ..Church Wardens

Monday 3d. August 1767

The Vestry met according to Law & qualified..

present

Nathl. Barnwell
Jno.. Barnwell
Jno. Delagaye
William Elliott
William Deveaux
Thos. Rutledge
Henry Stuart } Vestrymen
William Kellsal..Church Warden

[1]Page 164 is blank.

The poor to be provided for by the Parish for the ensuing year

Prudence Albergoti . . . . . £30 ꝑr. annum
John Leach . . . . 20 / ꝑ week
John Myres for the mantainance of a poor child to be allowed 50/ ꝑ week till the Child can be otherways provided for. Say £10 ꝑ month

166)
The Vestry have assessd the Parish for the ensuing year at the rates following To be paid by the 1st day of November

for every Slave . . . . .2/6 ꝑ head
for every 100 acres of Land 2/6 ꝑ Hundd. acres

Easter Monday 4th. April 1768

The Vestry met at the Parish Church

Present—William Elliott
Wm. Deveaux
Henry Stuart
John Delagayé
Thos. Rutledge——

Parishioners
Proceeded the Elect a New Vestry & Church Wardens to serve for another year and the following members were again Elected—

Nathl. Barnwell
Danl. DeSaussure
John DeLagayé
Wm. Elliott.—
Thos. Rutledge
Henry Stuart,
John Barnwell.

John Norton
Peter Lavein } Church Wardens

May 5th. 1768.

Met at Collo. Barnwells House—according to appointment and the following persons were present & Qualified

Nathl, Barnwell
John Barnwell,
John Delagayé
Thos. Rutledge
D DeSaussure: } Vestry=Men Peter Lavein, Church=Warden

& then we drew an order on Jacob Motte Esqr. in fav^{r}. of Geo. Welch for £40, for Parochial Charges. also drew an order on the present Church Wardens for sixty two p^{ds}. being for Schooling poor Children on M^{r}. Jones Donation also the above Vestry & Church Wardens assess'd the Inhabit^{ts}. & Freeholders to pay two shillings & six pence on every Slave and the Like Sum on every Hundred acres of Land in the Parish—

(167

The poor to be provided for by the Parish for the ensuing year

John Leach . . . .£6 ꝑ Month.

Docto^{r}.. Bartons, Wife, for the Maintainance of a poor Child to be allowed £5 ꝑ moth.

Monday 23^{d} May 1768.

Met at Coll^{o}, Barnwells House, according to Appointment and the follow^{g}.. Persons were present

Nathaniel Barnwell
John Barnwell
Daniel DeSaussure } Vestry Men
Thomas Rutledge
John DelaGaye
Peter Lavien C W:

Then determined, to Accept of the Rev^{d}: M^{r}. Cosgreve's offer, to Officiate in the Parish Church as Minister till the Arrival of one from England, who is already sent for..

Met at Coll^{o}. Barnwells House according to Appointm^{t}.

Present

Nathl. Barnwell
Will Elliotte
Thos.. Rutledge, } Vestry Men.
John DelaGaye
Daniel DeSaussure

Peter Lavien. CW:

Then drew an order in favour of M^{r}: Cosgreve, on the Publick Treasurer, for three Months Salary due the

168)

Saint Helena Parish to Peter Lavien Dr.

Date	Item	Amount
1768		
June 1st,,	To Cash paid Willm: Woodhouse 1 Years Schooling	,,62,,—,,–
1769	To Ditto the balce: of John Delagayes Accot.	,, 1,,18,,9
Augt: 22	To ditto paid Mrs. Barton 8 mo: board of Kellys Child	,,40,,—,,–
	To ditto paid Messrs: John Delagaye & Co.. for Sundries supplied to Revd: Mr Cosgreve .... }	31,, 6,,3
	To Mrs. Murray for Nursing Linton & his Wife	,,20,,——
	To John Grays Accot. for his bill attendg. ye- Leek &c.	,,24,,15,,–
	To Sundries supplied Trattles Funeral a Coffin &c.	,, 9,,12,,2
	To Lewis Accot. for Leaches board ...37,,15– Sundries supplied him & his Funeral Exp's 12,,7,,6	50,, 2,,6
	To Necessaries supply'd Kelly's Child	15,,18,,–
	To ditto.....ditto Linton & his Wife.......	25,, 1,,9
	To ditto Beekford £4,,19/9: To Leach £9,,15/	,,14,,14,,9
	To Mary Trunkard: £34:1/9: To Noulson 104/3	,,39,, 6,,–
	To Powers=35/. To William Barton 95/..	,, 6,,10,,–
	To Sundries supply'd Miss Holland.........	,,—,,17,,6
	To Cash paid Mr: Mc:Carty his Accot: for planns	30,,—
	To ditto: in favour of Allan Mc:Kee	,,40,,—
	To ditto paid Mrs: Butler's passage to London	,,35,,—
	To John Cooke's Accot: for a Coffin for Kellys Child	,, 2,,10—
	To Sundries supply'd by Delagaye & Co. to Mrs. Albergotie	30,,—,,–
	To Cash gave a poor Man 35/=	,,1,,15—
	To hire of 2 Negroes to take down the pulpit & pews 2 dys	,, 2,,—,,–
	To Cash paid Will Woodhouse 1 Years Schoolg	,,62,,—,,–
	To Mr: Welche's Accot: for parish Funerals	,, 8,,—,,–
		£,,553,,7,,8

1768	Cr		
June 1st,,	By Interest Money recd:	62,,—,,—	
1769	By Cash recd: of Jacob Motte..	40,,—,,—	
Ap: 23d..,,	By Interest Money recd.	62,,—,,—	
	,,By Cash recd: of sundry Persons for ye.. poor Rates	354,, 9,,7,,	518,, 9,,7
	Balce: due Peter Lavien CW		£.34,,18,,1

August: 22d: 1769
Errors Excepte'd

Peter Lavien C: Warden.

(169

Easter Monday 27th March 1769

Many of the Parishioners of St Helena Parish met at the Parish Church and Proceeded to chuse a new Vestry & Church Wardens, when the Following persons were Chosen Vizt.

Vestry	Church wardens
Nathaniel Barnwell, Senr.	Peter Lavein
John Barnwell Senr	William Megget
William Elliott	
Thomas Rutledge	
Daniel DeSaussure	
Samuel Grove	
Andrew Aggnew	

Tuesday April 18th 1769, the Vestry met at Collo. Barnwells House According to appointment

Present. Nathaniel Barnwell
William Elliott
Thomas Rutledge
Daniel DeSaussure
Samuel Grove
Andrew Aggnew

who were Qualified according to Law & drew an Order on the Church Wardens in favour of Cornelius McCarty for Thirty Pounds, the same being for drawing Two Plans for Rebuilding the Church

Tuesday May 2d. 1769, the Vestry met at Collo. Barnwells House according to Appointment

Present

Nathaniel Barnwell John Barnwell William Elliott Thomas Rutledge Daniel DeSaussure Samuel Grove Andrew Aggnew	Vestry	William Megget church Warden

when Mr. John Barnwell Qualified as Vestryman, according to Law and also Qualified William Megget Church Warden Asses'd the Inhabitants for the Releif of the poor at 1/3 ℔ head on Negroes & 1/3 ℔ hundred acres of Land, Stock in Trade & Money at Interest @ 5d ℔ Ct to be Advertised immediately & Collected within 3 Months

[170[1]]

Monday August 7th 1769 The Vestry Met according to Law.

Present
Nathaniel Barnwell
John Barnwell
William Elliott
Thomas Rutledge
Andrew Aggnew

Poor upon the Parish

Mary Trunkard .... a £30 ℔ Ann allowed
William Barton .... 30 ℔ do.. do.
Margarett Jones .... 30 ℔ do- - do,

[1]The pages from 170 on are not numbered.

Easter
Monday April 16th. 1770. Met according to Law. when a New Vestry and Church Wardens were Chosen to serve the Ensuing year—

The Reverend Mr. James Pierce,
Nathaniel Barnwell Senr. ——
John Barnwell Senr. ———
Mr. William Elliott ———
Samuel Grove ——— Vestry Men
Andrew Aggnew.
Thos. Rutledge ———
Danl DeSaussure. ———

Church Wardens
William Chaplin—Planter—& Charles Shaw—

This 16th April 1770 drew two Orders on the Treasurer one of two hundred pounds Currencey being the Sum allowed by law for parochial Charges; the Other for two hundred and twenty four pounds: Eleven Shilling & Eight pence Currencey in favr. of the Revd,; Mr. James Pierce being in full of his Salarey to the 13th Instant——

[171]

Monday 16th April 1770; agreed by the Vestry at this meeting to allow .... Margarett Jones .... £30: ℔ Annum
...................Mary Trunkard .... 30.. ℔ Ann—
And also agree to Assess the Freeholders and Inhabitants of said Parish. for the relief of the poor at the rate of 2/6 ℔ head on each Slave. & 2/6 ℔ hundred Acres of Land. Stock in trade and Money at Interest at 5d ℔ Cent. to be Advertised and Collected Immeadiately by the aforesaid Church Wardens for the Year 1770———

The Parish of Saint Helena

To Henry Wright ....dr,

1770

14 March To Amount Robert Porteous & Co. Account
℔ receipt ....£ 24:16:3
Amount James Fraser Account.. ℔ ditto... 29:
paid Peter Lavein.....℔ ditto.......... 2:14:2

Amount John Grays ditto ℘ ditto 7:15:
paid Robert Fairchilds ditto... ℘ ditto .. 10:
paid Mrs. Trunkard 30:
paid William Barton 15:
paid Margarett Jones 30:
Cash paid at different times 1:18:9
Cash paid Henry Stuart ballance of his accot. 25: 1:4

1770
16 April..To Cash paid C:W: for 1770 .... 1: 3:2

£177,,8:8

Cr.

1770
14 april By Amount from tax Collected at different times ℘ Account 123:18:8
By Wm.. Meggett received of him.. 53:10 £177:8:8

Errors Excepted 16th April 1770
Henry Wright C: W

[172]

Thursday May 10th 1770 the Vestry Mett at Colo. Barnwells

Present

Nathaniel Barnwell	John Barnwell	V M
William Elliott	Daniel DeSaussure	
Thomas Rutledge	Samuel Grove	
Andrew Aggnew		

Mrs. Murphey applyd for Assistance, Ordered the Church Warden to allow her ten Pounds till further Orders, also at same time Ordered him to allow Mrs. Jones the Sum of Twenty Pounds for the Support of her Children

at the Same time Qualified Charles Shaw Church Warden

[173]

Monday the 6th August 1770 The Vestry met at Colo. Barnwells

Present

Nathaniel Barnwell...	Revrd Mr. Pierce	V. M
John Barnwell.......	Samuel Grove	
William Elliott.......	Andrew Aggnew	
Daniel DeSaussure....	Thomas Rutledge	

Charles Shaw Church Warden

Agreed to Raise £1000 for Henry Talbird & £500 for Fairchild & McCluer as soon as possible
Agreed to get proper persons to view the Parsonage House and to give in an Estimate of the Repairs that the same may want.

[174]

Saint Helena Parish

To Charles Shaw	Dr
To paid Mrs. Jones	50,——
To paid Mrs- Trunkard	30,,16,,3
To paid Mrs- Moore	13,,10,-
To paid Mrs- Richmond	17,,18,,9
To paid Mrs- Murphey	45,,17,,6
To Amot. D. Desaussure & Co. Accot-	15,, 1,,6
To Amot. R. Fairchild- ditto	15,,—,-
To Amot. R Porteous & Co. ditto	2,,10—
To Amot. John Grays. . ditto	20,, 2,,6
To A Mitchell for Boarding Mose Butler 2 mos.	10,——
To paid Mrs- McKee	4,,16,,3
To paid J. Gray for medicines for ditto	3,,10—
To Mrs- Lewis's Accot. for boarding Lich 12mos	72,,—,-
	£301,, 2,,9

Cr	
By Cash Receiv'd of the former C. Wardens	£ 12,,—,-
By ditto of A. Aggnew Esqr. Clemans's fine for Strikeing Welch	20,,—,-
By Amot. poor tax Collected at dift. times	169,, 6
By Balance due C Shaw	99,,16,,9
	£301,, 2,,9

Monday 1 April 1771 drew two orders on the Publick treasurers one in favour of the Revd Mr. James Pierce for seven hundred & thirty One pound 10/ being in full to the 25th- March last the Other in favour of Mr. Thomas Smith for Forty pound Currency. Likewise an order on the Church Warden in favour of Mr. Wm- Woodhouse

[175]

Monday 1st. April 1771 the Inhabts met at the Church in Beaufort & Proceded to choose a new Vestry & Church Wardens, when the following persons were Chosen viz.

Revd Mr: James Pierce Rector

Nathaniel Barnwell Senr- John Barnwell Senr. William Elliott— Thomas Rutledge Daniel Desaussure Samuel Grove Jacob Deveaux	Vestry Men
Daniel Green Daniel Heyward Junr	Church Wardens

To ball Acco. due Chas. Shaw	£ 99,,16,,9
To Cash paid Thos. Smith for Funs.	8,,10—
To pd. Mrs. Lewis accot. agains Mr. Richmond	1,,13,,9
ball dld D Greene	4,, 4,,7
	£114,, 5,,1
By Cash Recd of Wm. Chaplin being ball Tax recd. by him on St. Helena after paying the Parsa. Charges There	114,, 5,,1-

[176]

Monday 3rd. June 1771 The Vestry Mett at Colo. Barnwells.

Present

N. Barnwell
Jno. Barnwell
James Pierce
Thos. Rutledge
&
Danl. DeSaussure

Danl. Greene Churh Warden

Agreed to Allow Mary Trunkard—— £30
Margt. Jones 30

And also agree to assess the Freeholders & Inhabits of said Parish for the relief of the Poor at the rate of 2/6 ℔ head on each Slave

2/6 ℔ hundred Acres Land Stock in Trade & Money at Interest 5[d] ℔ C[t] to be advertised & Collected by the aforesaid Church Warden for 1771——— ——— ——— ——— ————

Fryday 5th. July 1771. the Vestry met at Coll[o], Barnwells

Present.—

N. Barnwell Sen[r].
Jn[o]. Barnwell. Sen[r].
James Pierce
Tho[s]. Rutledge
W[m]. Elliott—
Jacob. DeVeaux
Dan. DeSaussure.

agreed that the Pew in the N. East Corner of the Church shall be given for the use of the Minister, in Liew of the pew formerly for that purpose—

[177]

Monday 5th. August 1771 The Vestry met at Col[o]. Barnwells

Present

Nath[l] Barnwell Sen[r]
John Barnwell Sen[r].
William Elliott
Dan[l]: DeSaussure ——
Jacob Deveaux ——
&
James Pierce

Agreed to Allow M[rs]. Waide at Col[o]. Heywards £30—
for Cloathing—

Also agreed[1]

Tuesday 11th. Feb[y]. 1772 The Vestry met at Col[o]. Barnwells—

Col[o]. N. Barnwell
M[r]. W[m]. Elliott
Thomas Rutledge
Jacob Deveaux

Drew an order on the Public Treasurers pay[e]. to M[r]. Rob[t]. Smith for £577. 10/ for Nine Months Salary due the Rev[d]. James Pierce—

[1]A blank space shows that what they agreed to do was not recorded.

[178]

Monday 20th: April- 1772 being Easter Monday

The Inhabitants Met at the Parish Church and Proceeded to Chuse Vestry & Church Warden when the following Persons were Chose Vizt-

the Revd Edward Ellington—
Nathl. Barnwell Senr.
John Barnwell Senr.
William Elliott
Danl. DeSaussure
Jacob Deveaux
Thomas Rutledge
Nathl. Barnwell Junr.
} Vestry—

Danl. Heyward Junr
Robert Porteous
} Church Wardens

Then adjourned to the 27 Inst.

Agreed to allow.

Mrs. Trunkard	£30
Mrs. Jones ———	30
Mrs. Wade — — —	30
Polly Uhland. ——	10

[179]

Monday 18 May 1772—The Inhabitants met at the Church agreable to notice given in the Church for 3 several Sundays & there chose John Barnwell Junr. Esqr. a Vestryman & John Bull Esqr. a Church Warden The Pew that was unsold was this day Sold for £505.

The Vestry &a. then adjournd to the house of Colo. Barnwell & were prest. as follows

Revd. Edward Ellington pro Rector
Nathl. Barnwell Esqr.
John Barnwell
William Elliot
Thomas Rutledge
Jacob Deveaux
John Barnwell Junr.
Robt. Porteous CW

Qualified John Barnwell Junr. Esqr. then Agreed to assess the Inhabitants as follows

Slaves ....1/3 ℔ head
Land ....℔ 100 acres ....1/3 ————
Money at Int ℔...............................3^d℔ £100

M^r. Ellington was calld upon to shew his Testimonials which he produced

[180]

D^r. St Helena Parish in Account with

To Sundries Supplyed Polly Uhland	15,, 8,,9		
" Ditto..........Benj^a. Uhland	12,,14,,-		
" Ditto..........Mary Trunkard	33,,12,,5		
" Ditto..........Mary McKee	1,,17,,6		
" Ditto..........Mary King	2,,13,,-		
" Ditto..........James Edwards	20,,11,,9		
" Ditto..........M^rs. Parker & Children	27,,16,,6		
" Ditto..........Jno. McDowall	9. 17,,6		
" Ditto..........Mathew Hardy	9,, 1,,9		
" Ditto..........Francis Fillips	28,,15,,6		
" Ditto..........Mary Wade	20,,15,,-		
" Ditto..........M^rs. Jones	30 — -		213,,3,,8

To Cash paid Doc^t. James Fraser	176 —
" Ditto William Woodhouse	96 —
" Ditto Robt. Fairchild	20 —
" Ditto Doc^r. John Gray	17 —
" Ditto Miss Betsey Williams	2 —
" Ditto Paid Nathl. Greene	8. 10-
" Ditto paid Nixson	6 —
" Ditto Paid 10 Months Board of James Edwards	60—
" D^o. paid Polly & Benjn. Ulands board	65 —
" D^o. paid Washing the Surplus	1 —
" D^o paid for a Bottle Port	1 —
" D^o paid Board of Mathew Hardy...	15.10—
" Cash paid to a Poor Man	2—

"	paid Dudley for a Bell rope & Bury[g], Francis Fillips	2,,10,,11	
"	paid M[rs]. Parker & Childrens Passage	3 ——	475,,10,,11
			£688, 14,,7

[181]

Dan[l]. John Greene .... C[r]-

By Cash Received of Charles Shaw		£ 4,, 4,,7
By Ditto of the Rev[d]. James Pierce		18,,12, 6
By Sundrie Taxes ℘ List	380,,12,,7	
By Tax Received of Cap Joiner	5,, 8,,9	
By Ditto Jn[o]. Drayton Esq[r].	12,, 7,,6	398,,8,,10
By Interest Money Rec[d]. of Henry Talbird	32 ——	
By Ditto of Jn[o]. Barnwell Sen[r].	35. 15—	
By Ditto of Francis Martinangell	28 ——	95,,15 —
By Cash Received of Dan[l]. Heyward Jun[r]	100,, 3,,8.	
By Ditto of Dan[l]. Heyward Sen[r]. for his Tax	71,,10 –	171,,13,,8
		£688,14,,7

April 19th. 1772. ——
Daniel John Greene

[182]

Thursday 15 Oct[r]. 1772 The Vestry met at Col[o]. Barnwell Pres[t].

Col[o]. Barnwell
William Elliot
Jacob DeVeaux
John Barnwell Jun[r].
Rob[t]. Porteous CW

The following Petition Or Letter was read
Gentlemen

We the undermentioned Parishioners of the Parish of S[t]. Helena request the favour of you, that the Church Wardens & vestry may be called forwith to meet at the Parish Church in Beaufort That reasons may be assignd why the Rev[d] M[r] Ellington is continued to Officiate as Pastor his conduct being so very disagreable, & that enquirey may be made whither his Deportment has been agreable to that of a good Clergyman of the Church of England & Whither he has produced any Character from any Congregation that he has before been Pastor of We are

To
The Church Wardens
& other
Gentlemen of the Vestry
for S^{t}. Helina Parish

Gentlemen Your humble Ser^{ts}.

Signd John Joyner
Andrew Aggnew
James Fraser
Henry Stuart

Lewis Reeve
Haz^{d}. Harvey
And. DeVeaux
Ja^{s} Doharty

John Johnson
Robt. Fairchild
Abram Shecutt
Nathl Greene

Willm. Haz^{d} Wigg
James Black
John Grayson
Ch^{s}. Givens

[183]

Subscribers names Con^{d}.

W. B. Kelsall
A Cumine
Ch^{s}. Shaw
Ja^{s}. Vance
Etsell Lawrence
J Linton
J. Lewis

J B Nixon
Benj: Dean
A Emsden
Ja^{s}. Craig
Ja^{s}. Read
E Gardner

In Consequence thereof the Vestry appointed Monday next the 19 Ins^{t}. at 10 oclock & sent their Resolution to M^{r}. Ellington

Monday 19 Octr. 1772 The Vestry met at the Church & were

Rev^{d}. Mr Ellington pro Rect.
John Barnwell Senr.
William Elliot
Thos. Rutledge
John Barnwell Junr
Jacob DeVeaux
Robt. Porteous CW

The Vestry met in consequence of their Resolution of the 15. Ins^{t}. but the Legality of their proceedings being disputed by the Rev^{d}. Mr Ellington who denied their Authority to examine his Conduct the Vestry broke up & appointed to meet on the 22 Ins^{t}.

[184]

The Vestery Men & Church Wardens

Date			£	s	d
1769					
3 Octor	To Cash pd for— 310 feet 2 In, 357 feet 1½ In, 406 feet 1¼ In, 1628 feet In } Cypress boards	97,,1,,11			
1770	pd freight of said Boards from Georgia	30—	£127,,	1,,	11
17 April	To your order in favour Hy Talbird for	......	1000—		
10 May	To your order in favour Mc-Lure & Fairchild		300—		
	To 1017 feet Cypress Inch boards -- a 65/	33,,1—			
	freight of Ditto from Chs Town	5——	38,,1—		
17 Augst	To your order in favr Heny Talbird	1000—			
28th	To your ditto in favr Mc-Lure & Fairchild	500—	1500—		
1771					
25 Jany	To Cash pd Shaw & Stuart for 14m Shingles £	5,,10/—	77—		
2d April	To amount of Accot for Sundrys supplied to 1st January Last		227,,	9,,	9
5 augst	To Cash pd McLure & Fairchild pr accot	1185—			
27	To ditto pd them theire 2d accot	170—	1355—		
1772					
8 Jany	To ditto pd Thos Smith for Carting Shingles		2,,	1,,	10
	To Willm- Smith for Cutting & Glazing 264 Pains Glass 2/	268—			

	James Trench for Painting 600 yds on the Church — a 2/	60—	86,,	8—	
18 March	To Amount of acc[t] for Sundrys we Supplied to the first day of Jan[y] Last		287,,	1,,	7
		£	5000,,	4,,	1

18 March	To above Ballance due us bro[t] down		31,,	12,,	7
29 June	To Am[t]. of Rich[d]. Proctor for his acco[t].	7———			
	To Am[t]. of Robert Fairchild ditto	2.15——	9,,	15	
	Errors Excepted 29th June 1772		£41,,	7,,	7

Then Receiv'd the above sum of forty one pounds 7/7 Currency In full of this Acc[t] by order on Robert Porteous

Daniel DeSaussure & Co

[185]

Acc[t] Currant with Daniel DeSaussure

1769					
1st March	By Jn[o] Delagaye & C[o] Bond for	£	2130—		
1770					
28 April	By Daniel Heyward Subscription	....	100—		
27 June	By 65 feet 2 In Cypress Plank	....	....,,	3,,	9
3 Aug[st]	By Rec[d], of Jos Jenkins Sen[r]- his Subscription	50—			
	Rec[d]. of Coll[o] Barnwell his ditto	100—			
	d[o] of Jn[o] Delagaye ditto.	100			
	D[o] of Daniel Desaussure ditto	30—			

	D^{o} for Rich^{d}. Stevens ....ditto	100.			
	D^{o} of Lewis Reeve. ditto.	50—			
	d^{o} of Stephen Bull Junr- ditto	100—			
	do of Thos Rutledge. ditto	40—			
	d^{o} of John Barnwell Senr- ditto	100	670		
30th	Ball^{ce} of Interest due this day on the Bond		207	. 8..	4
1771 22^{d} April	By so much re^{cd} of Coll^{o} Heyward for his Pew Ground	25—			
	Rec^{d}. of Thos Bowman Senr- his Subscrip^{n}......	25—			
May	Rec^{d} of Samuel Grove his ditto	30—			
8 July	Rec^{d} of Rich^{d}. Guerard his ditto	50—			
9th	Rec^{d} of Jacob Deveaux a pew he bo^{t}	305—			
	d^{o} of James Cuthbert a d^{o}.	394	829	—	
5 Augst	d^{o} of Coll^{o} Barnwell for Coll^{o} Middletons subscription	100			
17,,— — — —	d^{o} of W^{m}- Elliott for a pew he Bot	350—			
1772	d^{o} of John Joyner Senr- for a Ditto	351	801		
18 March	d^{o} of Jno- Delebare for a Ditto	150—			
	Interest on ditto to this day	8,,6,,8			
	d^{o} of Thos Rutledge for a Ballance he owed for one half of a pew	69,,7,,6	227,,	14,,	2
	By ballance due D DeSaussure & Co	——	31—	12	7
			£5000.	4:	1

[186]

Thursday 22 Oct[r]. 1772 The Vestry met at the Church & were as follows

William Elliot
Thomas Rutledge
Nath[l]. Barnwell Jun[r].
John Barnwell Jun[r].
Jacob Deveaux
Rob[r]. Porteous CW

The Vestry met in Consequence of their Resolution of the 19 Ins[t]. & agreed that M[r]. Ellington should no longer Officiate in the Parish Church as his Conduct was extremely Offensive to the generality of the Inhabitants of Beaufort they accordingly drew an order on the Publick Treasurers for three months Salary being in full & gave the Church wardens Directions to shutt the Church & take care of the Parsonage house

29 June 1772 omitted to be

enterd in its proper place
Pres[t]. Nath[l]. Barnwell
John Barnwell
Rev[d]. Edw[d]. Ellington
Jacob Deveaux
Nath[l]. Barnwell Jun[r].
John Barnwell Jun[r].

Sealed with D. DeSaussure & C[o]. & gave them an order on Robert Porteous for the ball[ce]. of their acc[t]. being £41.7.7 at same time it was determind that H[y] Talbird should

[187]

not receive any more payments untill he has Compleatly finishd the Plaistering Steps & Portico
M[r] John Barnwell gave an order on Ja[s]. Doharty for £25—being for the ground on which his Pew stands
Agreed that M[r] Rutledge be wrote to quit the Parsonage house—

5 April 1773

The Vestry met at Col°. Barnwells—
Pres^t- Col°. Barnwell
John Barnwell
Thomas Rutledge
Nathl Barnwell
John Barnwell
Jacob Deveaux
Rob^r. Porteous CW

It was agreed to make out Titles to the purchasers of the Pews —also that D. DeSaussures acc^t. be entird in the books—— R Fairchild deliverd in an acc^t. against the Parish amounting to £

John Bentley Nixon having Officiated as Parish Clerk & Sexton it was agreed he should be paid £20— out of the Parochai money & the overplus to be paid to Rob^r. Fairchild on acc^t. of the above Demand

There having been no Sacrament money accounted for a long time it was agreed that the Revd Mr Ellington late Pro Rector should account with the Church Warden for the same they according sent him notice thereof in Writing—

[188]

Saturday 10 April 1773—

The Vestry met at Col°. Barnwells
Pres^t- Col°. Barnwell
William Elliot
Thomas Rutledge
Nathl. Barnwell Junr.
John Barnwell Junr.
Jacob Deveaux
Rob^r. Porteous CW

The Vestry Signd the Titles for the Pews in the following manner Viz

We whose names are under written Church Wardens & Vestry men for the Parish of S^t. Helena do Certify that . . . . . . hath true & absolute Right & Title to a Pew now standing in the said Parish Church & is distinctly known by N°-   having paid for the same the Sum of . . . . Witness our hands the 10 of April 1773—

Signd by the Church Warden & Vestry men present—

N°. 18—to J Grayson

19........W. Elliot

20........J Joyner

21........H. Stuart A Cumine R Procter & Rob^{r}. Porteous

22........D°- D°- D°- D°-

23........J Black

24........T Rutledge & W. H Wigg

25........N Barnwell

26........J Cuthbert

27........J. Deveaux

29........J Doharty

30........J Delebare

[189]

Sealed with H^{y} Talbird & gave an order on R Porteous for the ballance of his acct, being £1074,,3,,6 they also Drew on him £80 to W. Woodhouse for Schooling the Poor Children — Drew an order on the Treasurers for £40 for Parochal Charges—

Monday 12 April 1773——

Pres^{t}. William Elliot
Thos^{s}. Rutledge
Nathl. Barnwell Junr.
John Barnwell Junr.
Jacob Deveaux
Robt. Porteous } CW
John Bull- }

Being Easter Monday a great number of the Parishioners met at the Church & Ballotted for a new Vestry & Church wardens upon the close of the Poll the following Gentlemen were declared Elected.

William Elliot Thomas Rutledge Nathl. Barnwell Junr. John Barnwell Junr. Col°. Danl. Heyward John Joyner & William Hazz^{d}. Wigg for vestry Danl DeSaussure & Joseph Jenkins for Church Wardens——

Then Qualified William Elliot Thos Rutledge Nathl. Barnwell Junr. John Barnwell Junr. John Joyner & William Hazzard Wigg to act as Vestry ——

[190]

Tuesday 13 April 1773 ——

The Vestry met at the Church

Pres[t]. William Elliot
Thomas Rutledge
Nath[l]. Barnwell Jun[r]
John Barnwell, Jun[r].
John Joyner
William Hazzard Wigg
Rob[t]. Porteous CW

Dan[l]. DeSaussure chosen yesterday Church Warden refused to qualify & agreed to pay the fine according to Law D[r].. James Fraser was chosen in his Room and qualified accordingly———

[191]

May 9th- 1773,, The Vestry met

Pres[t]- W[m],, Elliott
Tho[s],, Rutledge
John Joyner
John Barnwell Jun[r]-
Ja[s]- Fraser—C,, W

And agree'd to offer the Rev[d].. Charles Frederic Moreau, the Rectorship of the Parish; he Received the Letter, and accepted the Cure, the 15th.. Ins[t]. from which his salary Commenc'd—
also agreed to allow,, M[rs].. Trunkard £30—
Mary Uland . . . .
M[rs],, Jones . . . . 30.—.—
M[rs]:

[192]

D[r],, S[t],, Helena Parish in Account with

[193]

—— James Fraser . . . . .C[r] ——

By an Overplus from M[r],, Porteous £22,,7,,6
By Sacrament Cash from M[r],, Moreau. 7,,3,,-

[194]

June 14,, 1773 the Vestry met

Present the Revd,, Chas: Frederick Moreau
William Elliott
Nathl,, Barnwell Junr:
John Barnwell Junr,, V: men
Thomas Rutledge
William Hazzard Wigg
James Fraser CW—

& drew an Order on the Treasurers for five sermons preachd by the Revd. Mr. Smith of Pr,, Wms. Parish to the 12th.. of May exclusive of a Session Sermon preachd. the 30th. April before the Judges & Desird the Church Warden to furnish Mrs. Irvin with necessarys for the children to amount of Ten pounds Currency—

July 27. 1773 the Vestry met at the Parish Church—

Present
William Elliott
John Joyner
Nathl,, Barnwell Junr.
John Barnwell Junr.
Thomas Rutledge

[195]

Monday April 4,, 1774 the Vestry met

Present—

William Elliott John Joyner Nathl: Barnwell Junr. John Barnwell Junr. William Hazd,, Wigg Thomas Rutledge	Vestry men—
James Fraser Joseph Jenkins—	Church Wardens

& agreed to assess the Inhabitants of the Parish at the following Rates

Slaves ....15d ℔ head
Land ....15d ℔ 100 acres
Money at Intst: 3d ℔ £100— — same day the Inhabitants of this Parish met & made choice of the former Vestry & Samuel

Grove & James Garvey Church Wardens except Richard Guerard who was chosen in the Room of Dan[l]. Heyward & Qualified according to Law

Monday April 11. 1774 the Vestry met

Present
William Elliott
John Joyner
Nathaniel Barnwell Jun[r].
John Barnwell Jun[r].
William Hazzard Wigg
Thomas Rutledge
} Vestry men

James Fraser Church Warden

& agreed to allow M[rs]: Trunkard £30—
M[rs] Jones ———— 30—
M[rs] Wade ———— 30—
M[rs] Irvin ———— 35—

& gave John Bentley Nixon an Order on the Treasurers for forty pounds for his Service as Clerk & Sexton—

[196]

Monday Feb[y]. 29th. 1776. the Vestry met at M[r]. Morreaus Lodgings Present
Rev[d]. M[r]. Morreaux
Nath[l] Barnwell
Rich[d]. Guerard
Will[m]. Wigg
Tho[s]. Rutledge,

When M[r] Wigg returned Polly Uland upon the Parish & the Vestry Concluded to Board her with M[r]. Woodhouse till a proper person can be had to have her Bound Apprentice at the same Rate he formerly had her application was made in behalf of M[rs]. Roche & the Vestry Resolved to desire M[rs]. Weston to supply her with such Necessarys as the Case may require——

[197]

Tuesday 29th- of October 1776

The Parishoners met and made Choice of the follow Gentlemen to Represent them in General Assembly . . . . . .
John Barnwell Jun[r]- John Joyner Sen[r]- Dan[l]. DeSaussure

Thomas Rutledge . . . . . Thom[s]- Heyward Jun[r]- & W[m] Reynolds—

The Parishioners met also at the time and made choice of the follow[g]. Gentlemen as their Committee—

John Grayson . . . John Kean— James Fraser. John Frip John Jenkins . . . Benj. Reynolds— Dan[l]- Heyward— Robert Brumston Dan[l] Savage . . . Giden Dupont Sen[r]- James Garvey- Lewis Bona- Phillip Martinangel N[l]. Barnwell- John Chaplin & John Edwards

President Cap[t] Dan[l] DeSaussure.
John Rhodes Church Warden

[199[1]]

Beaufort March 31. 1777

Being Easter Monday the Inhabitants met at the Parish Church and According to Law proceeded to Elect Vestry Men & Church Wardens when the foll[g]. persons were duly Elected——

Nath[l] Barnwell
Jn[o] Barnwell
W[m]. Haz[d]. Wigg
Rich[d] Guerard
James Fraser
Tho[s] Rutledge
} Vestry Men

Dan[l] Jn[o]. Greene & Benj Reynolds C. Wardens

The old Vestry drew an order on the Treasurers in Favour of the rev[d]. M[r]. W[m]. E. Graham for Thirty pounds Curr[y]. for thre Sermons when the New Vestry were Qualified and agreed to make no farther assesment untill the arrears are paid up for which purpose the Church Wardens are hereby Required to give notice that against Evry Defaulter of the Poor Tax after the first day of June next Shall without Distinction have Executions Granted against them & the Rev[d]. Mr. Graham being present they gave him an Invitation to officiate in this Parish duering the present Establishment of the Church of England which he accepted but as the Parso[ge] House is out of repair could not go into it at present nor did he agree to do it at any Future Time

[1]The 198th page is blank.

[201[1]]

Beaufort 3d. August 1778.

The Vestry Met according to Law, at the House of Mr. Mc.Graths

Present

Thos. Rutledge
James Fraser
Wm. H. Wigg
Nathl. Barnwell
Jno Barnwell
Jacob Deveaux. C. Warden

And agreed to allow Mrs. Williams...£30—— for her present subsistence, to be paid by Wm. Norton out of the money in his hands..———

The Church Wardens Informed the Vestry that Mr. Benjn. Guerard, refused to pay his poor Tax Order'd that the Church Wardens do make application to two Magistrates, to Summon the Sd. Benjn. Guerard, to appear before them, to shew Cause, why he will not pay the poor Tax demanded of him——

[202]

Beaufort 23d. Septr. 1778.

The Vestry met at the house of Mr. Natha. Barnwell—

Present

Nathl. Barnwell
Jno. Barnwell
James Fraser
Wm.. H. Wigg
Jacob Deveaux. C. Warden

The Revd. Mr. Graham having quitted the Parish, as Rector of the same, without Informing the Vestry & Church Wardens—Ordered that the Church Warden do wait on the Revd. Mr. Foley, and give him an Invitation, as Rector of this Parish.

In Consequence of the above Invitation; the Revd. Mr. Foley accepted of the Parish; and his Salary commences from this day

[1]The 200dth page is blank.

Beaufort 15th. Novr. 1778.

The Vestry met at the house of Mr. N. Barnwell:

Present

Natha. Barnwell
Jno: Barnwell
Thos. Rutledge
Wm. H. Wigg
Jacob Deveaux C. Warden

As the Vestry & Church Warden, cou'd not Furnish the Revd. Mr. Foley with a House &c., he declined the Rectorship of the Parish— They drew an order on the Publick Treasurers for Two months Salary—being in full—

[203]

The following persons has Subscribed to pay to the Vestry & Church Wardens, the several Sums opposite their names for the Maintanance of a Minister, and that the said sums shall be paid in Annual payments to be Calculated from the time of said Ministers being agreed with to officiate in the Parish Church of Beaufort,, (dated this 12 Apl. 1784}

Nath Barnwell	£7—p^{d}. 105/
Danl J. Greene	7: p^{d}. 105/
And. Aggnew	7:-p^{d}. 105/
Edw. Barnwell	7—p^{d}—178/ being £15,,15/-
John Barnwell	7.-p^{d}.
John Joyner	7—p^{d}. p^{d}::
Jno. B. Barnwell	7—
W^{m}. H. Wigg	7--p^{d}. in full)
Jno. Kean	(10. paid) p^{d}.
Step Bull	10..p^{d}
D^{r}. James Cuthbert	5..p^{d}.
Jno. DeTreville	2 p^{d}
Ab^{m}. Anthony	1..
Jno. Bull	5:-p^{d}.
Jno. Grayson	3—p^{d} in part 43/6
Jno. Rose	3.. 10.
Richd Guerard	2. -p^{d}.
Barnard Elliott[1]	4..-
Mary Barnwell	5: -p^{d}
Arch^{d}: Campbell	2-..p^{d}.
Martha Barnwell	2....p^{d}
Wm Hazzard	3.-
Jno. Heyward Jur.	4 --
	£117:10-

Robt. Barnwell	£5——
R^{d}. Ellis Junr- p^{d}. in full	2:3:6
Ja^{s}. H. Cuthbert	4. —
Rich^{d}. Bolan.. p^{d}. 23/4	2 p^{d} 18/8
Phillip Givens	1——
Richd Adams p^{d}	2——
W^{m}. Joyner	3....
Thos. Grayson	2....
J. M. Verdier, p^{d}:	5.—
James Glaspell	1.—
Ralph Elliott p^{d}.	6.—
Jno. Givens	1.—
Ja^{s}. D. West	5.—
James Yancey..p^{d}.	3..5-
Flelix McClasweitz	1..10-
W^{m}. Boon	1.—
bro^{t}. forward	117.10.
	£162,,5,,
Rob. Porteous	4.—
Winif^{d}. Lewis	1.—
John Johnson. p^{d}.	3,,5,,3
James Stuart p^{d}.—	3 in full
John McKee 2 Ga^{s}.	2..3..6

[204]

The following persons has promised to pay the several Sums opposite their Names, to the Vestry & Church wardens for the purpose of repairing the Church in the Town of Beaufort & inclosing the Church Yard—
12 April 1784

Nath Barnwell	£3..0..0 pd- EB-
Danl. J. Greene	3..—— pd. do-
Andw. Aggnew	3.—..
Edw Barnwell	3.—— pd—
Jno. Joyner	3.—— pd
Wm. Hazd. Wigg	3.—— pd.
Jno. Kean	5.... pd 17/6 to EB-& 4,,2.6 EB
Step Bull	5.—— pd. 15/11
Dr. Jas. Cuthbert	5 ——
Ralph E. Elliott	3.—— pd,,
Jno. B. Barnwell	3,,—— pd- EB
Jno. Detreville	2 ——pd.
Ab. Anthony	0..10:.0 pd. EB-
Rob. Barnwell	3..pd. EB-
Jas. H. Cuthbert	3.–pd. EB-
Jno. Barnwell.. pd.	3.– pd. 3/6
James Yancy	3..5..3
Jno. M Verdier	3,——pd.
Barnard Elliott	4——
Archd. Campbell	2..–pd EB
Jas. Stuart	5—pd. EB-
Martha Barnwell	2—
Wm. Hazzard	2—
	£71,,15..3

Amt. brt forward	£71,,15:3
Rd. Ellis Junr. pd.—	1,,1,,9
Rd. Bolan	2.pd EB
Jno. Leacraft	3.pd EB
Jno. Johnson pd.	3......
Phillip Givens pd.	2: 10—
Wm. Joyner	2.——
Richd Adams	1—— pd..
Thos. Grayson pd.	2——
Jno. Cross	1——
Ro Givens ...pd	1——
Thos. Talbird...pd:	3 ——
Jas. D. West	1.. 10 pd. EB
Jno. Bull pd.	3——
Jno. Grayson pd.	3——
Felix McClasweitz	1——
Jno. Rose	2..10——
Rd. Guerard	2..—℔ EB
Jas. Glaspell	5——
Wm. Boon	1—pd. EB
	£105,,10,,3

[205]

State of S^o. Carolina

At a Meeting of the Parishioners on Monday the 17th May 1784 to Elect Seven persons to Serve as Vestry Men The 7 following $Gent^n$. was duly Elected—— ———

$Natha^l$ Barnwell John Barnwell $Will^m$. Hazzard Wigg John Joyner Andrew Aggnew John Kean Danl. John Greene	Vestry Men

W^m. Joyner & John Mark Verdier C. Wardens and on the 7th- July Qualified as Vestrymen & Churchwardens.—

Resolved That the Church Wardens do write to M^r. Jacob Deveaux demanding of him the Bonds that was in his Care & the Monies arising from the Poor Tax, which he collected While Church Warden of this Parish & to Inform him that on Examination of the Vestry Book there appears to be a Leaf cut out of it while under his Care & also to know the Reason for the same

Resolved That the following Letter be

[206]

Wrote to M^r. John Kean requesting him to procure a Clergyman of the Episcopalian Church

Beaufort 7th- July 1784

Sir,

You are hereby requested and Empower'd to procure a Clergyman of the Episcopalian Church for the Town of Beaufort South Carolina on the following Terms.

An Annual Salary of One hundred & fifty Pounds Sterling—

We are with Respect

Sir Your most $Obed^t$. hb^{le} $Serv^{ts}$-

John M. Verdier Wm Joyner	Church Wardens—	John Joyner Andrew Aggnew $Nath^l$. Barnwell Danl. John Greene $Will^m$ Hazzard Wigg John Barnwell John Kean	Vestry

The Vestry adjourn'd to the First Tuesday in August

[207]

The foll^g^. letter was wrote Jacob Deveaux.
Beaufort 14 July 1784.
Sir At a Meet^g^. of the Vestry on the 7 Ins^t^. they came to a resolution which we herein Inclose you, by which you will see they wish to have an Explanation and an account of your transactions whilst Chu Warden, including an acco^t^ of all Monies rec^d^. for Poor Tax & the Bonds belong to the Parish &^c^. And to know the reason of the Said Leaf being cut out of the Vestry Book which acco^t^ Bonds &c. we wish you to furnish us by the first safe Conveyance

We are Sir

Y^r^. Mo. O^b^.

W. Joyner } C. Wardens
J. M. Verdier }

To
M^r^. Jacob Deveaux.

At a meeting of the Vestry the 7th- September 1784. Agreed to give orders to either of the Stores in Beaufort to Supply the Church wardens with Locks bolts &^ce^- for securing the Church Doors & Windows to prevent Horses. Cattle &^ce^- going into the Church & Damaging the Pews &^ce^- and that an Estimate be obtained as soon as possible of the Total Cost of the repairs of the Church such as the Workmans bil Lumber Nails Locks &^ce^—

present
N Barnwell } Vestry Men-
Jno Barnwell }
Jno- Joyner }
Danl- John Greene }
W^m^- Hazzard Wigg }

John Mark Verdier Church Warden

[208]

Beaufort- Novr. 22^d^ 1784

At a meet^g^. of the Vestry
At the report of M^r^. John Kean of his succeeding in obtaining a Minister—„ who being now arrived in Charleston, they came to a resolution of sending for him—so soon as a Boat & hands coud be obtained—„ and in the meantime a place must be pro-

vided for him to Lodge at the ministers name—The Rev[d]: Step. C. Lewes—

		Present.	
		John Barnwell	Vestry Men
		W[m] Haz[d]. Wigg	
		John Kean	
W[m] Joyner	Church Wardens-	Nath[l] Barnwell	
John M Verdier	———	And[w]. Aggnew	

At the above meet[g]. the Vestry came to a resolution that the Church Wardens do send Advertisements to Ch[s].ton, and through the Country for to engage w[h]. a workman to put the Church in order—and that they do write to the Rev[d] M[r] Lewes by the above boat which is to be sent for him———

Beaufort 30th. Nov: 84

At a Meeting of the Vestry the following Gentlemen were present

Gen: Jn[o]. Barnwell	Vestry Men
Nath[l]. Barnwell	
John Joyner	
W[m].. Hazzard Wigg	
John Kean	
Andrew Aggnew	
Dan[l]. Jn[o]. Greene	

W[m]. Joyner
Church Warden

[209]

Resolv'd. that M[r]. Nath[l]. Barnwell & Maj. Wigg
do agree for the
repairs of the inside of the Church—
And that the Church Wardens do endeavour
to procure the Lumber as Soon as possible
Likewise that the Church Wardens do immedeatly
have the Church Glazed . . . . ———

NB the Surplice was receiv'd from M[rs].. John Barnwell & Deliver'd to M[r]. Thomas W[m]- Wood Clerk of the Church—

& the following Books viz[t]-		
	1 Bible	Letter'd
	1 Common Prayer	
	1 Old D[o]-	
	1 D[o]- Administration of Sacrament —	were receiv'd

by the said Clerk from Doc[r]. James Cuthbert

1 Bible bound in Calf Skin	receiv'd from M[rs]. Mary Barnwell
1 Book Common Prayer — —	

receiv'd 21st.. December 1784,, from M^{r}. Richard Russell Ash the 5 first & the 10th.. Volume of Tillotson's Sermons the Book of Homilies 2nd. Volume Sharp's Sermon's & Lelands View of Deistical Writers—

the Rev^{d}.. Stephen C. Lewis arriv'd here the 28th.. Nov^{r}- & preached the Sunday follow^{g}———
M^{r}- Thomas W^{m}- Wood- Declined acting as Clerk of the Church 17th- December & Deliver'd up the Books accordingly
Receiv'd of M^{rs}.. Elliott a Cup & 2 Silver Stands belong^{g}. to the Communion with Capt- John Bull's Name Engraved thereon.

[210]

At a Meeting of Vestry Beaufort 11 January 1785 when the following Gentlemen were present

	John Kean	Vestry Men
	John Joyner	
William Joyner C- W-	Daniel John Greene	
John M- Verdier CW	Andrew Aggnew	

the Rev^{d}. M^{r}. S C. Lewis—
they came to the Resolutions follow^{g}— Viz^{t}—

That the Church Wardens be directed to enquire for & get if Possible a Person to act as Sexton of the Church & to have the Bell toll'd (during the Winter Season) at Nine OClock Ten O.Clock & a Quarter before Eleven & ring till the Minister goes into Church in the Morn^{g}- & to ring the Bell at 2 oClock & a Quarter before 3 ^{o}Clock & continue ringing untile the Minister arrives in the Afternoon Untile further orders—
And that the Church Wardens do immediately collect three fourths of the Subscriptions for the maintaining the Minister & the whole of the Subscription for Repairing the Church—
And to agree with some person to saw the Lumber &^{ce}- for the Repairs of the Church & fencing in the Same.
And that the Wardens be Directed to settle the Rev^{d}. M^{r}. S. C Lewis's Expences from the time he left Boston till his arrival here

[211]

The following letter rec^d from Jacob Deveaux.

Charleston 17th July 1784

Gent^n.

yours of 14th Instant inclosing a resolve of the Vestry I receiv^d. and in answer thereto have to inform you that about the time I left Beaufort I Carefully put the Church plate, Surplice, Book, List of poor Tax, with defaulters and remaining Ball^ce.. into my Desk under the particular care & Charge of Doct^r John Gray with directions to deliver them when call,d for to any persons properly Qualified for that purpose with respect to the Bonds I do not at present recollect ever to have had any of them in my hands nor do I know of any leaf being Cut or taken out of the Book alluded to or that the said Book or any other matter ever receiv^d. any injury while under my care having ever paid that decent respect & Duty to the Church becoming the Christian & man of Honor, this Gent^n. to the best of my knowledge is a true representation of the facts and if necessary will make oath when calld on, permit me Gent^n. to assure you it is with regret I learn these things, and you may rest satisfied that shoud any thing hereafter occur to me I shall immediately inform you therewith and think my self happy in giving you & the Gent^n of the Vestry every Satisfaction in my Power—

I am with respect

Gent^n

(Signd) Your most Obedient

Jacob Deveaux

The Desk was open'd by
Doct^r.. Gray & the plate & Surplis delivered to Mr Barnwell as by a letter from him soon after it happend British officers & others opend it at—J..D—
other times—

Messrs.
Wm Joyner
&
John M.. Verdier
} Church wardings Beaufort

[212]

17/6	Recd. of Mr Kean ten Guineas	10..17.. 6	
Jany. 29.	Recd of Wm H. Wigg for his Subscription	£7—	
	Recd. of Mrs. Martha Barnwell	2.. 0.. 0	
31st—	Recd. of Dr. Archd. Campbell..	2. ..—	
Feby 1—	Recd. of Mr. Nath Barnwell	7.. 0 —	
	Recd. of Mr. Aggnew	5.. 5 —	
	Recd. of Mr. Danl Jno Greene..	5.. 5 —	39:7:6
17—	Recd. of Step Bull	2..12..10	
Mar 22d.	Recd. of Richd. Ellis Junr.	2.. 3.. 6	
21/9	Recd. of ditto for his Subscription the Church	1.. 1.. 9	
3/6 29..	Recd. of Mr. Richd. Guerard in part 2 Guins	2.. 3.. 6	
60/,,	Genl. Barnwell two sums	£10..——	
	Capt- John Joyner for Minister	7.. 0.. 0	—25:1: 7
	Do- for Repairing the Church	3,,—,,—	
On May 9.	recd. of Genl. Bull 2½ Guineas..	2..14..4	
	Recd. of Jno. M. Verdier his Subscription	5.——	
	— of Jno. Bull his... do.	5.——	
	— of Rd. Adams his...do........	2.——	
	— of John Johnson his ...do...	3.. 5.. 3	
July 26.	of Jno. Grayson 2 Guins	2..3.. 6	
30	—recd. of Genl. Bull 5 Guins..	5.. 8.. 9	
	recd. of James Glaspell	1..———	
5/.	recd. ditto for the Church..	5 —	
160/.	recd. of Maj. Wigg for the do	3.——	
Augt 3d	—recd. of Rd. Bolan in part..	1.. 3.. 4	
	recd. of Mr James Johnston for Mr Lewis	2.. 3.. 6	
		36:3:8	
	£12. 3.8 belonging to the Church	25.1..7	
	88.9.1 to Mr Lewes	39.7.6	
	£100:12:9 Totall	£100:12:9	

[213]

Rec^{d}. Feb^{y}.. 4th.. 1705 of the Church Wardens Thirty Guineas being for my Expences to this place, allowd by the Vestry—

S C Lewés

N. B......Mr Lewes's Salary Commenced 1st. Octr. 1784

Paid the Rev^{d}. M^{r}: Lewis 7 Pounds 12/3 which was Cap^{n} Joyner's Subscription

£20:0:0 May 26th. 85—
15:0:0. June 11th- . 85— } receipt below

Rec^{d}. May 26. and June 11^{h}: 1785. The Sum of Thirty five punds.

£35— S C Lewés

Jul 30 paid Mr Lewis 5 Guin^{s}.

1786 April 27 Genl. Bulls Subscription up to 1 Jan^{y}.

1786	£2:14.4½
M^{rs}. John Barnwell	2. 0.0—
Octr. 6th. Doctor Stuart paid one years subscription up to the 1st. October. 1785	3—0.0—

[214]

Easter Monday being Mar. 28. 1785. an Election took place at the Parish Church for Vestry Men & Church Wardens for the ensueing year.

Genl. Barnwell
Nath Barnwell
Edward Barnwell
And^{w}- Aggnew
Willm. Haz^{d} Wigg
John Joyner
Danl Jno Greene } Vestry Men

Willm.. Joyner & Jno. M. Verdier } agreed to Serve as Church Wardens for the present Year——

At a meet[g]. of the Vestry & Church Wardens at the Parish Church this 25th April 1785—they where qualified to serve for the present year——

Present—Nath[l] Barnwell
Jn[o]. Barnwell
Andrew Aggnew
Will. Haz[d]. Wigg
Dan[l] Jn[o] Greene
John Joyner
Edward Barnwell

Will[m]. Joyner & Jn[o]. M. Verdier } Church Wardens

At the above Meeting they came to the following Resolution that Co[l].. Edward Barnwell do go to Charleston to meet the Vestry of the Parishes of S[t]. Philip & S[t].. Michael on the 10th- May next agreeable to a Letter receiv'd from that Parish.

[215]

July 25th. 1785.. J. M. Verdier paid Jos. Lloyd in part 8 Guin[s].

At a Meeting of the Vestry and Church Wardens at the Parish Church this 17th.. November 1785.

Present.

Andrew Aggnew
Nath[l]. Barnwell
John Barnwell
Edward Barnwell
Dan[l]. John Greene
William Hazzard Wigg } Vestry Men.

William Joyner Church Warden.

When they came to the following Resolutions

That the Inhabitants be assessed at the following Rates

Negroes at 2[d] ℔ head—
Land at 2[d]- ℔ 100 Acres } for the relief of the Poor said Parish—

& that the Rev[d]. M[r]. S. C Lewis be allowed to officiate every third Sunday on the Island of S[t]. Helena

That Mrs.. Barlow & Child be allowed the Sum of Ten Pounds Sterling ℘ annum—

That the Church Wardens have a Surplice made before Christmas Day——

[216]

at a meetg. of the Inhabitants at the Church in Beaufort Easter Monday the 17th. April 1786. Proceeded to an Election for a Vestry & Church Wardens for the Ensuing Year—When the followg. Gentlemen Were duly Elected.

Genl John Barnwell Genl Step Bull Colo- Edw. Barnwell Capt. John Joyner Maj W. H. Wigg Andw. Aggnew } Esqs. Nath Barnwell }	Vestry
Danl John Greene & James Stuart	Church Wardens.

Carried forward

[218[1]]

Dr. Revd. Mr. Steph. C. Lewes his Accot:

1785							
Feby 4.	To Cash paid you 30 Guineas	....	..	..	£32..	12..	6
	To ditto paid you........	...7..	12..	3			
1 May	To ditto paid you........	..20.	—	—			
11 June	To ditto ... do.........	—15	—	—			
1 July	To ditto ... do. 5 Guineas	.. 5..	8..	9	„48	..1–	
Jany. 2d	To Cash paid you.......	...	...	...	...9	..8..	2
	To 2 Cords of Wood... of R. B.............		18..	8	£90	„1,	.8
	To cash of Mr. Ralph Elliott fine	 10	—	—			
	To cash pd. you recd of Capt Treville	.. 2	—	—			

[1]The 217th page is blank.

	To cash of Mr Yancy.....	.. 3.	5..	3			
	To so much of Dr. Cuthbert	... 8.	.10.	.			
	" of Genl Bull - - -	2	..14.	.4			
	Mr. Greene Subscription	.. 3.	.10	—			
	Mr Porteous- do - -	.. 4	—	—			
Sepr. 20	of J. Verdier - - - -	- 10	—	"			
	Doct Stuart — —	— 3	..	.			
	of Mrs Jno. Barnwell—	- - 2	—	..			
	of Mr R. Elliott — —	- - 3	—	.			
	of Mrs: Mary Barnwell - - - - - - -	- 5	—	-..			
	of R. Elliott - - - -	- 1.	2	—			
	of Jno. Kean — — —	—12.	.10	—	71	,,10	:3
					£161	:11:	11

wth. John M Verdier & Wm. Joyner, C. Wardens. Crs.. [219]

1785					
Jany. 29.	By Cash recd. of John Kean	£..10	..—	—	in full
	By ditto of Willm. H. Wigg	7	....	....	in full
	By do. of Mrs. Martha Barnwell ...	2	—	—	in full
	" of Dr. Archd. Campbell	2	....	.....	in full
	" of Nathl. Barnwell	7	.. ..	—	.do.
	" of Andrew Aggnew	5	.. 5	—	in part
	.. ..Danl Jn: Greene	.... 5..	5..	—	in part
	.. ..Step. Bull....	 10	.—	—	in full
	" of Richd Ellis Junr	... 2..	3..	6	in full
	" " Richd. Guerard	...2.	—	—	in full
	...of John Barnwell	...7	...	..	in full
	...of John Joyner	...7	...	..	in full

	....Jno. M Verdier	5	...	..	in full		
	....Jno. Bull	...5	...	..	in full		
	....Rich^{d}. Adams .	...2	...	...	in full		
	....John Johnson.	...3..	5..	3.	in full		
	....John Grayson.	...2..	3..	6.	in part		
	....James Glaspell	...1..	...	..	in full		
	..—Rich^{d}. Bolan..	...1..	3..	4	in part		
	- —James Johnston	...2..	3..	6	in full		
		£88	„9„	1:			
178	By Rich^{d}. Bolan. for 2 Cord wood	.....	..18.	.8.:			
May 8.	Paid Mr Lewis a ten pound bill had of R Elliott	.. 10	——	..—			
1786 Sepr. 26	By So much rec^{d}. of M^{rs}: Barnwell	 5	..	..	in full		
	" " rec^{d}. of Jno.. Detreville..	2	...	.	in full		
		£106	:7	9			
	D^{r}. Cuthbert,.. 8.10 Yancey.. 3..5..3 R Porteous 4—— othe side 36.12						
	52:7:3 Add	52..	7.	3 is	158	:15.	
	The Parson rec^{d} M^{r}. Greene	Subscrip^{n}	..	..	– 3..	10	
					£162	: 5	

[220] D[r]. The Church

		£	s	d
1785				
July 25.	To Cash paid Jos. Lloyd in part 8 Guineas	£.. 8..	14	. —
	" ditto paid Jos. Lloyd at.......	.....	18	. 8
May. 20.	Paid Jos. Loyd in full..........			
	by J. V..—	.. 10.	7.	4
	allowed for fencing the Yard	£ 20	—	
	to My acco[t]. ..for materials......	.. 5..	5..	10
	to pay Col[o]. Barnwell ......7..18.6			
	then I owe 9.4	8	. 7.	:10.
		£ 33:	13	. 8

This finelly Sett[d]. the Acco.
after I pay 9/4-the 9 April 1787.

There appears on subscript: for repairs of Church £105:10:3—Col[o]. Barnwell's Acco[t]. for the Lumber &[c]. is Seventy pounds & the above £33:13:8. am[t]. to nearly the Subscription Saveing one or two bad debts on the Subscription.

Wth. John M Verdier & Wm. Joyner. C. Wardens Crs. [221]

1785 from this time till	Recd. of Jno. Kean in part	....	17..	6	.....	in	full
	Recd. of Richd. Ellis Junr. in full....	.... 1.	.1.	.9..	.		
	....of Richd. Guerard	......	.3.	6	in	part	
	....of John Barnwell	...3.	...	...	in	full	
	....of John Joyner.	...3.	...	..	in	full	
	....of James Glaspell	....	5	—	in	full	
	....of Wm. H. Wigg	..3.	..	...	in	full	
1786	....of Stepn. Bull in part	.....	15	11	in	part	due 84/
		£12	:3	:8			
Feby. ..8 J. V	– By Rd. Adams....	— 1	—	—	in	full	
	" assumed to pay Jos Lloyd the Ballce for repairs ———of £20—						

Jno. Detreville	£2.	these I have asmd to receive as I have assumed to pay Loyd the Ballce. due him £17.10
Jno. Johnson	3..	
Jno. M. Verdier.........	3.	
Phil Givens	0..10	
Jno Givens	1–	
Tho Talbd	3..	
Jno. Bull	3.	
Jno. & Tho Grayson £3: & 2=	3	
	£20.10	20..10 £33 :13 :8

£33. 13.. 8

[227][1]

At a meet.g of the Parishoners on Monday the 17th. April 1786. they Proceeded to Elect a Vestry & Church Wardens for the Ensueing year; when the following Gent. where duely Elected——

Genl John Barnwell——	qualifd.	Vestry
Genl Step Bull	×	
Colo. Edw. Barnwell	.. do	
Majr. Will. H. Wigg—	. do	
Captn. John Joyner	.. do	
Nathl Barnwell	×	
Andw. Aggnew	. do.	
Danl,, John Greene & James Stuart	Ch. Wardens	

That the former Church Wardens do Collect the Poor [tax[2]] in the Course of three Mos..— . and advertize for the same Immediately— .. a return of the Deaufters then be made to the Majestrate in order to recove the same:—[3]

The Church Wardens are directed to write immediately to all defaulters who have not pd. up their Subscription to the clergiman—and desire their answer thereto—

---

[1]Pages 222, 223, 224, 225 and 226 are blank.

[2]The word tax has been cut out in the course of removing a seal or other wax attachment. Written in pencil on the back of the page is: "The Plat that was here is given to Dr Stoney after being sold & the money paid"

[3]On a separate (loose) sheet is the following:

Poor Tax Charged for 1786 by D. J Greene—

Vizt

Martha Barnwell 6/2 Nathl Barnwell 15/ Wm Joyner 3/6 Jno Joyner 8/9. John Johnson 4/3 Rachl Black 6/1 Jno Rose 9/6 R Ellis Jun 2/2 Jno Leacraft 2/4 Jno Kean 14/4 Rid ash 13/3 Charles Givens 1/6 Robt Porteous 8/2 James Ellis 1/ Eliza. Ellis 1/ Mary Barnwell 5/2 James Stuart 23/8, Jno Barnwell Senr- 10/6 Richd Fairchild 8d- ————

£6:17:6

I did not recolect when in Beaufort that the Parish owed me Money which I ought to deduct from my Tax. You will see by the Parish Book what it is — — — — — — — — — — — — — — —D J Greene

The above was addressed to: Mr. Jno. Rhodes

The "Senr" to John Barnwell had been written "Genl" and the "Senr" was written thereover.

[228] Dr. The Rev. Stephn. C. Lewes his
1787

Jany.	To Cash pd you by Mrs Lewes	£2..5—
	To Cash pd you by Docr. Stuart	4 ——
	ball due to acco for D Greene — — —	50..2—1
		£56:7:1
	To setd. wt. Mr. Lewies in accot.	£4..—..—
May 14.	To Cash pd Dr Lewis by J. Stuart £6–, & 5£...	11..—..—
	To Cash pd. Dr. Lewis by Wm. Hazzd. Wigg in full for his Subscription to 1st. Jany. last	8.. 15..——

[229]

Acco. with Danl Greene & James Stuart Cr.
1786

June	By assumpn. for F. M Laswitz	£1..10—
	By ½ year Subscribn for D Greene	3.10
Decr 31st.	By one year Subscribtion Do	7 ——
	By my assumn for Mr N. Barnwell	8,,15—
	By Cash recd of Mr Jno. Johnson	3,,5:3
	By my Assumpn. for Jno Joyner	8.15.—
	By Do for Wm. Joyner[1]–this to be Setd wth Mr Lewis	..6.15–
	By Do for Richd Ellis Jun.	2:14:4
	By Do for Jno Rose.. his Subn	7.17.6
	By Cash recd of Mr Lewis	2.5.—
	By Cash recd. of Docr Stuart	4.——
		£56:7:1
	By ball due brot. down	£50,,2:1
	By assd. for Genl Barnwell	8:15—
	By Doc Campbell assumed by me	2.10—
		61:7:1
	April 9th. 1787 deduct to Settl. w. Mr Lewes	6.15.—
		£54:12.1

[1]This has been marked out; as also has amount 6.15

Dan[l] Jn[o] Greene

By Rob[t]. Porteous..............................£4

By Rob[t]: Barnwell pd	....	5—
By Rich[d] Adams p[d]	Set[d]	2–10 in full
By James Cuthbert p[d]	wth. M[r]..........	2 — — —
By Jn[o] M. Verdier p[d]	Verdier	5.8.9–

1787

May 14th By Rob[t]. Barnwell p[d]. James Stuart..........5.– —

By James H. Cuthbert p[d]. ditto.............6..–..—

[230]

D[r]. The Parish S[t] Helena in acco.

1787

Jan[y] 1st. To Sundries Supp[d]. M[rs]. Barlow Coleman &c ———— ℘ acco	2„ 18„ 2
T[o] Cash p[d] M[rs] Robinson for Board & Nursing Coleman	4„ 7„—
	£7„ 5: 2

To ball due me ————————————————7/8—

paid for 2 bottles wine..........................6/

paid for 6 ditto by Doc Stuart —

p[d]. Bell Man ———

[231]

with D Greene & James Stuart C. Wardens C[r]

By Poor Tax assumed by me for Sundry Persons...........	........£6„ 17„ 6
By ball due me..	7.8
	£7„ 5„ 2

By my own Poor Tax for 36 Negroes 6/. 858 acres Land 1/5 is 7„ 5

April 9th. 1787

Dan[l]. Jn[o] Greene

[232]

At a Meeting of The Parish^rs^. on Monday 9th: April 1787 they Proceeded to Elect a Vestry & Church Wardens for the Ensueing year when the following Gentlemen where duly Elected—

Col^o^.. Edward Barnwell Capt Jno Joyner— Genl Jno Barnwell Maj. W^m^. Haz^d^. Wigg Nathl Barnwell And^w^. Aggnew Jno Jenkins —	} Vestry
Jno. Rose — Bigoe Henzie	} Church Wardens—

[233]

At a Meeting of the Vestry held at the Parish Church of S^t^. Helena — on Tuesday 1st. May 1787—

Present

Rev^d^. M^r^. Stephen C: Lewes Rector	Maj^r^. W^m^. H: Wigg
Col: Edward Barnwell	Andrew Aggnew
Capt. John Joyner	
Genl. John Barnwell	

The five latter Qualified according to Law.
also John Rose qualified as Church Warden

James Philips and Family are receiv'd on the Parish and to be allowed £10- -- ℔ ann:

Orderd that the Church Wardens do enquire for a proper person to bind Henry Healy to, as an apprentice

Resolved that so much of the monies arising from the Sale of the Lotts (adjoining the Town of Beaufort) as will discharge the Rev^d^. M^r^. Lewes's House Rent from the time of his arrival here, be appropriated to that purpose—

Orderd that the Church Wardens, do write to M^rs^. Martinangele, requiring her to send the Bond formerly given by her husband Philip Martinangele for Money belonging to the Parish, being part of the Rev^d^. M^r^. Lewis Jones's Legacy, which Bond it is said she has taken up of Doctor James Fraser formerly Church warden—that if it should appear to be the case recourse may be had to said [234] Fraser, for recovery of the same; and

that shou'd she not comply with such request, she will be sued for the same—
Orderd that the former church wardens do furnish an account of Subscriptions, for the maintinance of a minister up to the first day of January last, which Subscriptions the present church wardens are required to insist on immediate payment—
Orderd that the Church Wardens do draw up a Subscription for the maintenance of a Minister, to commence from the first day of January last which shall continue so long as the Subscriber shall reside in the Parish—to be payable to the Vestry & Church Wardens for the time being & their Successors—

[235]

At an adjourn[d] meeting of the Vestry held at the Parish Church of S[t]. Helena on Monday 14th. of May 1787——

Present.

Rev[d]. M[r]. Stephen C. Lewes Rector,
Col[l]. Edward Barnwell — Major W[m].. H.. Wigg
Cap[n] John Joyner — Andrew Aggnew
Gen[l]. John Barnwell
Bigoe Henzey Qualified as Church Warden

The Vestry came to the following resolution—of assessing each Pew in the Church, Three pounds St[g] annually to be paid on The first day of January—the first payment to commence the first January 1788
Order[d]. That the Church Wardens do advertise a Meeting of the Parishoners upon particular Business, at the Parish Church on Tuesday the third of July next in The forenoon——

[236]

The Inhabitants met the 24th April 1788.— And chose the following Vestry=men & Church wardens

Gen[l]. John Barnwell
James Stuart
Andrew Aggnew
Maj[r]. W[m] H: Wigg
Col: Edw[d]. Barnwell
Cap[t] John Joyner
John Mark Verdier
} Vestry=men

John Rose
William Elliott
} Church=wardens, who qualified

At a meeting of the Vestry on Tuesday 1st May 1788 at the Church

Present

Wm.. Hazzd. Wigg
Edwd: Barnwell
John Joyner
Andrew Aggnew
John M. Verdier
James Stuart
} Vestry men, who qualified

John Rose. C: Warden—

Ordered that the Church wardens do have the North west window of the Church Sash'd & Glazed the Expence to be paid out of the Subscription for repairing the Church—

[237]

Allowed Mrs: Wood £5:—. for amo. of Accot. for Carting the Stuff for the Church yard to be paid out of the Subscription for repairing the Church.

Orderd that the orders made out at a meetg of the late Vestry on the 1st May last, that are not complied with be attended to by the Church Wardens

---

At a meeting of the Vestry & Church Wardens held the 5th. day of May 1788 at the Parish Church

Present

Genl John Barnwell
Majr. Willm. H: Wigg
Capt- John Joyner
John Mark Verdier
Andrew Aggnew
} Vestry men.

Willm. Elliott
John Rose
} C: Wardens.

A Letter from the Revd. Mr Lewes was presented the Vestry & Church wardens, which was read–

a Copy of which is as follows

Gentlemen/

As my health is very much impaired & since the warm weather hath set in, seems to be on the decline, I have been advised by

Doctor Turnbull the physician who attended me in Charleston to take a voyage to Europe as the most likely means of restoring it. I have therefore to solicit leave of absence from the parish for that [238] purpose: Your concurrence herein will be a favour ever gratefully asknowledged by

Gentlemen

Your most devoted and
Obliged humble Servant
S: C:: Lewes.

Beaufort 5h. May 1788.

To the Gentlemen Vestry & Church Wardens of the Parish of St: Helena—

To which an Answer was wrote by the Church Wardens at the request of the Vestry: a Copy of which follows.—

Revd. Sir/

Yours of this date was handed to the Vestry who have desired us to inform you that you have permission to be absent from the parish for the space of six months from the date hereof—

We wish you an agreeable passage & safe return among us: And hope the Voyage you propose taking to Europe may have the desired Effect of restoring you to health—

We remain Revd. Sir
for ourselves & Vestry
Your most Obt. Servts.

Willm. Elliott
John Rose } C: W

Beaufort May 5th. 1788

The Revd: Mr: S: C: Lewes—

[239]

At a meeting of the Vestry & Church Wardens on the 16th. Februy 1789 at the Parish Church

Present

The Revd. Mr. Lewes Rector
Genl. John. Barnwell
Capt. John Joyner
James Stuart
John M: Verdier
Andrew Aggnew } Vestry Men
William Elliott
John Rose— } Church Wardens

Orderd that those persons who have not paid up their Subscriptions and Pew assessments be applied to by the Church wardens for immediate payment—

Orderd that the Inhabitants of Portroyal Parris Island, & Ladies Island be Taxed 3d. ꝑ head for Negroes & 3d. ꝑ 100 acres of Land for the support of the Poor of the sd. Islands—

The Vestry adjourn'd to Tuesday Fortnight—

[240]

At an adjourn'd meeting of the Vestry on Tuesday 3d. March 1789—

Present

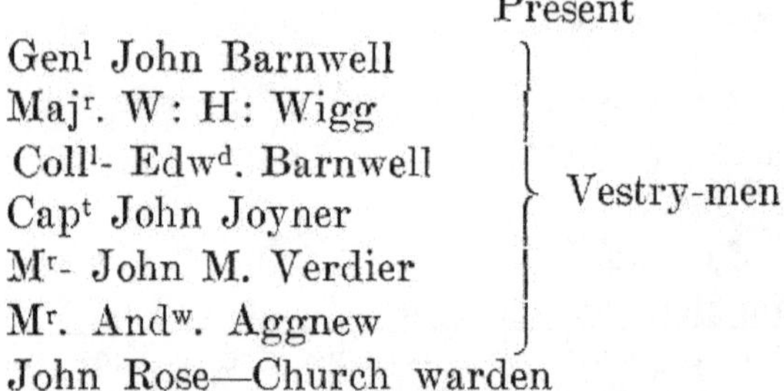

Genl John Barnwell
Majr. W: H: Wigg
Colll- Edwd. Barnwell
Capt John Joyner
Mr- John M. Verdier
Mr. Andw. Aggnew
} Vestry-men
John Rose—Church warden

Resolved that the Subscription for the maintenance of a minister commencing 1st Januy 1787 be no longer in force than the 1st day of January last, that when all the subscriptions due to that time are paid up that the subscription paper be destroy'd—

[241]
Easter Monday
13th: April 1789

The Vestry met

Present

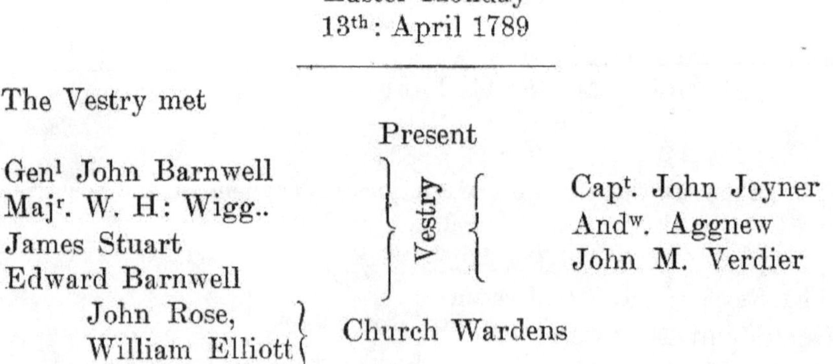

Genl John Barnwell
Majr. W. H: Wigg..
James Stuart
Edward Barnwell
} Vestry {
Capt. John Joyner
Andw. Aggnew
John M. Verdier

John Rose,
William Elliott
} Church Wardens

agree that the same Vestry be continued and Robert Barnwell & Michael OBrien were elected Church Wardens for the ensuing Year—

At a meeting of the Vestry on Tuesday 13th. October 1789—

Present

The Revd. Stephen C. Lewes Rector Edward Barnwell Andrew Aggnew John Joyner James Stuart John M. Verdier	Qualified as Vestry Men—

Col: Edward Barnwell was elected Church warden instead of Michl. OBrien and qualified accordingly—and was taken out of the Vestry and William Elliott was elected Vestryman in his stead

Robert Barnwell also Qualified as Church Warden—

[242]

D^{r}– The Parish of S^{t}. Helena-repairs of Church–Acc^{t}.
Jany. 1790. To Cash p^{d}. for 100 Nails-repai^{g}.
Church Yard.. £0,, 1,,3—
d^{o}- for the Hire of 2 negroes. for d^{o}–.. 3,,—
for a large Pad Lock.................
4 Lightwood Posts........2/6........

[243]

with— Edward Barnwell—Church Warden—Cr—

Jany. 1790. By Cash recd. of John Rhodes–in full.......£0–1„3—

[244]

D^{r}. The Parish of S^{t}. Helena–Acc^{t}-with

Jany. 1790. To Cash p^{d}- D^{r}- Lewis................£7,———
Balance Carried Fõrward......33——

£40—

[245]

Edward Barnwell Church Warden—C^r^—

Jan^y^
1790 L. By Cash rec^d^. of Edward Barnwell in full.£7,———
L. By d^o^- of Captn. John Joyner in full........3,,——
L. By d^o^- of John Barnwell in full..........10———-
L. By d^o^. of James D. West....in full.......11..10—
By d^o^. of J. Rhodes for T. Talbird in part..3,,— —
By d^o^- of Dr. Campbell for R Guerard in full..2,,10—
L- By d^o^- of Dr James Stuart in full..........3,,——

£40

[246]

Dr- The Parish of St Helena–Poor Tax–Acct–

1790–To Cash pd. John Flinn for a Coffin for Mrs. Barlow ———————	£1,, ——
Balance Carried forward..........——.....	33–15–3
	34–15–3

[247]

with — Ed Barnwell—Church Warden—C^r—

1790. Cash Re^d- of $Capt^n$. John Joyner-in full	Poor Tax	......£1,,14,—
d^o. Re^d. of John Rhodes-in full.........		...... 1,,3—
Balance Brought forward................		.33—
		£ 34..15..3

Balance due the Church tro dues & Carried to his $acco^t$- in 1807 — — ———————— £33-15-3

[248]

Easter Monday—

5st April 1790–

The Vestry met—

Present—

John Joyner John Barnwill Wm Hazz Wigg	Vestry	James Stuart Andrew Aggnew

when they proceeded to an election of a Vestry when the same persons were re-chosen and Coll Edwd Barnwell and John Rhodes were elected Curch wardens for the insuing Year

At a Meeting of the Vestry on the 4th. May 1790—

Present

John Joyner John Barnwell Wm. Hd. Wigg Andrew Aggnew. James Stuart–	Qualifyed Vestry Men

Edward Barnwell & John Rhodes Qualfd. as Church Wardens

[249]

Mrs Culverson & family are received on the Parish & to be allowed £10 Stg-₰ Annum-

At a Meeting of the Vestry on the 7th. Sept. 1790

Present–

John Barnwell— John Joyner
Andrew Aggnew— James Stuart—
John Mk. Verdier–Qualified–
Ed Barnwell & John Rhodes—C– W–

The Vestry Unanimously agreed that the Revd- Dr Lewis's Bond for the purchase of a Square in the New Town should be given up to him, in consideration of the Losses he has sustained, by his SalAry not being paid up Regularly–
They also agreed that the Church Steeple should be repaired-Which repairs to be left to the C. Wardens—
Agreed.that Mr. Isaac Hird. as Sexton should be allowed 75/Stg. ₰ ann for ringing the Bell cleansing the Church &c &c—

[250]

7th.. Sept- 1790-

Ordered, that the Church wardens, do apply to Mr Richard Russell ash to know, if he has any property in his hands belonging to Docr. Fraser—

At a meeting of the Vestry held Wednesday Novr. 3rd. 1790

Present

John Barnwell Andrew Aggnew	Vestry	James Stuart Willm Elliott Jno M. Verdier	Vestry

John Rhodes church warden

It is unanimously agreed by this meeting that the church Wardens do without delay collect the Pew tax & arrears due to the Revd Mr. Lewis- as also the Interest money due on the Several Bonds herein annexed—and where the money is not paid that Notes of hand, be taken from all persons without distinction—and shoud any person or persons refuse to Comply with so Just a requisition.their names be reported to the Vestry.at a future meeting—

It is further agreed by this meeting that as monies is due to Mr. Lewis from this Parish that We give him a Certifycate from under our hands to pay to him or to his order one hundred pounds Sterling by the 31st. Jany 1791..in part of what is due him—in order to enable him to pursue his intended Voyage to England for the recovery of his health,,=accordingly a certificate was given //

The Church wardens have in Consequence of the above order, Coll'd in Mr- Ash, who Says. he has no property in his hands belonging to Docr. James Fraser—

[251[1]]
[252]

Dr John Rhodes for Poor Taxes Rec[d] from the Following

Date	Name	Amount	Name	Amount		£	s	d
1790-								
August 12.	Thomas Witter	..3..6	Stephen Bull	1..7.9	.........1.		11	3
13	John Johnson	1..6	Phebe Waight.	—.2-	1		8.	0
	Hannah Dider	..2..	Winefred Lewis	..11..	....		13.	
	M. OBrien	..1..	Mary Barnwell-	..6..	....		7.	
16.	James Cuthbert Sen[r].	3..2–	Ralph Elliott..	1..17..6	.........4.		19..	6.
30..	Est Dan[l] Heyward	2.16–	Jam[s] Cuthbert Jun[r]-	3..2..6	.........5.		18..	6
Sep[r]. 7.	Elizabeth Ellis	9	W[m] Joyner	18..6	1		7..	6
	Rich[d] Ash	2.16.3	S Odingsell	1..16–	4		12..	3
	James Bowman	3..2..	G. Roupell	3.5.6	.........6.		7..	6
	M Perriclair	1.2..8	Est McCarty & Shep[d].	2— .	.........3.		2	8
	Francis Salters.	..5..	Isaac Hird	..1..	....		6	
21	John Cross	..3..	Nath[l] Barnwell	2..7.–	.........2.		10–	
	Dan[l] Jn[o] Greene -	1.12.6	....		1–		12.	6
Dec[r]. 3	James Ferris	..1..	Ric'[d] Adams	1..8.6.	1.		9.	6
Jan[y]. 15.	Est wm Elliott	..8..	W[m] Elliott	..18..	1-		6-	
Feb[y]. 24	Rich[d] Ellis Sen[r]	3..1..	Est Jn[o] Grayson	11..10-	3		12	10[d]
April-	Rec[d] Jn[o] Joyner	1-11.10	....		1–		11–	10
July-91.12[th].	Rec[d] from M[rs] Blake	1—	....		1–			
					£43–		15..	10

[1]Page 251 is blank.

[253]

Persons ——— for the years 1787.1788.1789. & 1790– . Cr—

1791					
march 10th- 22	By Cash paid Isaac Hird..per Acco & rect		5..	1-	
	paid Thomas Grayson for a pew in the Church late belongg- to Danl John Greene ——————— —	———	2.	12	1-
april 27.	By Mrs Cuthbertson.. paid her one years Allowance-	—	10-	-	
august 4th.	By Mrs. Cuthbertson paid her ¼ years allowance. -	—	2	10-	
octr. 5	By Mrs. Cunninghams quarter allowance due this day	—	2-	10-	
Novr.. 4	By Mrs. Cuthbertson paid her ¼ years allowance	...——.	2.	10-	
92 Jany 5	By Mrs. Cunningham..—do- - - -	--------	2-	10-	
Feb 8-	By Cash paid Philip Givens for 40 Posts @ 2/............	—	4		
4	By Mrs- Cuthbertson paid her a quarter allowance ———	——	2.	10	—
april. 5	By Mrs. Cunningham paid her...	—	2.	10	
	Paid Isaac Hird 1 years salary due 24th last decr.......	—	3.	15-	
	Paid Mrs. Yake ¼ years salary		1..	5-	
	By John Rhodes's Acco Current for Balce His Acco..........	——	2.	2.	9
		£	43..	15..	10

Mrs Culbertson Es. £2.10

Errors Excepted 9th- April 1792

John Rhodes Church warden—

[254]

Dr Revd.. Stephn.. C.. Lewis

Date	Particulars	£	s	d	£	s	d
1790							
Sept. 24	To Cash paid you Mr Nathl Barnwells pew tax –	3	-				
	To. do. . . . . . Mrs. Pheebe Weights– do-.	3-					
May 20.	To. do. Stephen Bull . .	6-					
	To.. do.. - John Grayson.	4.	11.	6			
	Philip Givens. —	2.	5-				
	Wm Joyner . . .	6..	15				
	John Givens.. .	2.	5-				
	Winifred Lewes . . . — — . . .	3					
	Francis Salters . . —	12-					
	Est John Grayson –	6					
	Est Richd Fairchild-	9-			,,57,,	16,,	6
					,,57,,	16,,	6
	To so much overcharged by Mr Lewis on Interest Money	. .	.	. .	.19..	13..	9
	To an order on Danl Stevens for 4 years Interest on his bond	43	8				
	To your order on Majr. Talbird in favr- Mr Phillips for	1-		4			
	To an order on Danl DeSaussure for Blacks pew tax—	9			,,53	:8	:4
1791							
July 5–	To yr. Security for Ballce. due on D J. Greene Bond to the Beaufort Society.	......	.	...	30..	16..	3

	To yr. order on the Vestry in fav. Beaufort Society for yr Bonds due them–bearing Interest from 3d Novr 1790	..	..	..	.88..	8..	8
	To 1 yr. House rent due to Maj Wigg	....	...	...	50	—	..
				£	300.	3..	6
	ballce. due Revd Mr. Lewis			—	388.	11	..1
				£	688	.14	.7
1790 6 April	To James. H Cuthberts note paid into the hands. J Rhodes	10-	1–	4			
do-	To Ralph E Elliotts– do	22	2-	4			
1793	——— do —— do—	22	2-	4			
17 Augt-	To Jno. Joyner Bond £67. Interest to this day £5.17.6	72.	. 1.	.6			
88 . 8 . 8 30.16 . 3	To Danl Stevens Bond £155. Int. to this day £14:9:4	169..	9..	4	273	,,14,,	6
	£	273.	14.	6			
119:4. 11	to be pd. to the Society for wch: they will take Bonds.						
	To his order in favor of Ths. Stone March.88—				56,,	13,,	4

in a/C with Parish St Helena Cr–

1790 April 5	By Balance your acct to this day.... 602.2.4.				602	2	4

1790 Octr. 1.	By half years Salary.—@ £150 ₱ Ann. £75.....				75	—	
	"The Sum of five pounds to Mr Lewes c^r. wch Maj^r. Wigg agreed to take from his acco^t - - - - - - - £5="	C^r.			£677.	2.	4
5 Oct^r.	1790 Interest on £332.2.4 being ball^ce. of £602.2.4				11.	12.	3
1791				£	688.	14	7
July 5	By Balance brought down from Contra ———	....	...	...	388..	11..	1–

[256]

Beaufort 4th January 1791–

At a meeting of the Vestry this day the following Gentlemen were present–

Andrew Aggnew	William H Wigg	Vestrymen
John Joyner	James Stuart	
John Barnwell		

John Rhodes Church warden–

Ordered, that the Church wardens, do call on Mr Isaac Hird, and desire him to have the Church Swept, and otherwise kept clean and decent, and that the same be done before he receives his Sallary——

Mr Danl DeSaussure gave notice, that from this day, he woud not pay the assessment of the Pew belonging to the Est James Black—

The vestry agree. and desire the Church wardens, to waite on the Rev^d- M^r. Gardiner. and gave him an Invitation to officiate in this Parish

6th. In Consequence of the above desire. the Church wardens waited on the Rev^d. Mr Gardiner who accepted of the Invitation as above.—

[257]

Easter Monday - April.25.1791-

The Vestry attended —

Present-

John Joyner Wm- Hd Wigg,— James Stuart Andrew Aggnew- John Barnwell	Vestry-

Rvd- John Gardiner— —

John Rhodes— Ed Barnwell	Church Wardens—

Resolved- that the Pew late the property of Danl. John Greene sold under Execution & bought in by the Church wardens, be reserved as a Public Pew—

Proceeded to an Election when the following gentlemen were

Elected, John Barnwell John Joyner Wm. Wigg—	Vestry	Wm. Joyner James Stuart- John Mk. Verdier John Rose—

Ed Barnwell John Rhodes	Church Wardens—

[258]

Dr ——————————————————William

Date	Day	Particulars	£	s	d	£	s	d
1789								
July	4	To 1 years Interest due on your Bond this day.	13-	0-	4	13-	0-	4
90. July	4	To 1 years Interest due on your bond this day	13..	0-	4			
		To your assessment of your pew	- 3-					
		To Cash you Rec[d] from Capt Joyner	9..	7..	6	25.	7..	10
Oct[r] - -		To Richard Ellis's note & Interest to this day.- -	5-	14-	4			
		To your assumption in fav[r] Doc[r] Cuthbert	6.			11-	14.	4
1791 July	4	To your assumption 5 years Interest on J Floyd's bond	9-	8-	9			
"	–	To one years Interest due on your Bond this day	13..	0.	4	22-	9.	1
Nov[r].	24	To so much for bal[ce]: Jn[o] Genovleys acco[t] - – ..	1-	19.	2	1	19-	2
92.. 9th april		To 1 years pew assessment for 1791– ————	3			3	—	
		To Interest on £13-0.4 to 12th. march 1792— ...	2-	8-	10			
		To Interest on– 25-7..10.. to ....d[o]	3-					
		To Interest on—11-14-4-to .... d[o].........	1..	3..	6			
		To Interest- on–22–9..2-to .... d[o].........	1..	1..	8			
		To d[o]....–on– 1 - 19/2— to........ d[o]........	.....		9	7..	14-	9-
		To Cash paid our order in fav[r]. Rhodes Bold & Co.	—	—	—	28-	14.	6
						£114	—	—

[259]

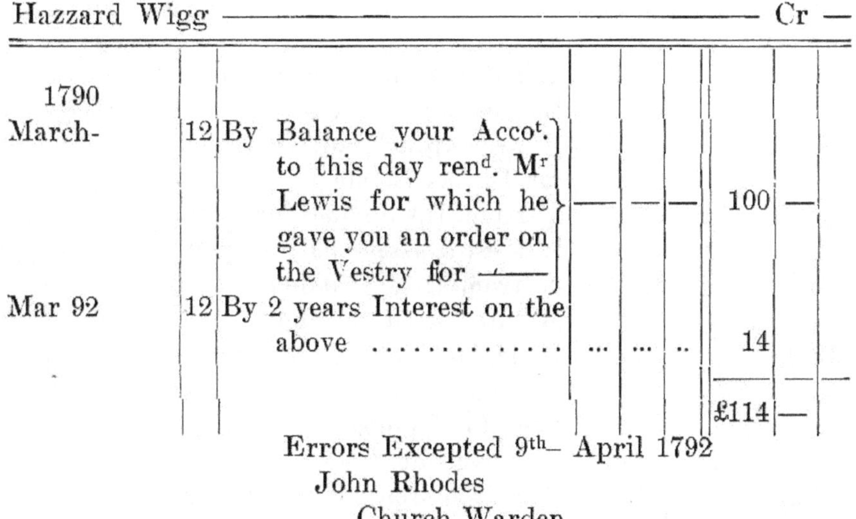

Hazzard Wigg ——————————————————— Cr —

1790							
March-	12	By Balance your Acco^{t}. to this day ren^{d}. Mr Lewis for which he gave you an order on the Vestry for ——	—	—	—	100	—
Mar 92	12	By 2 years Interest on the above	...	...	..	14	
						£114	—

Errors Excepted 9th– April 1792
John Rhodes
Church Warden

[260]

At a meeting of the Vestry Monday July 5. 1791

Vestry

Genl Jno. Barnwell	James Stuart
Maj. W. H. Wigg	John Rose
Jno Joyner	Jno M. Verdier
Wm Joyner	

Edwd. Barnwell }
Jno Rhodes — } church wardens.

It was resolv'd this day that the Church wardens do pay M^{rs}. Lewes as Executrix of Revd Mr Lewes—the Ball^{ce}. due him as ℘^{r}. acco^{t}.. in the Notes of hand of the Several persons who owes Interest money on their Bonds due to the Vestry—and that the same be enterd in this Book particularly——

See this mentioned in a following Leaf

Dr=		John Rhodes for Interest			
1791					
April.		By Cash Rec^d from Danl Stevens for Interest on his Bond..........	43-	8	
		To d° Rec^d from Danl DeSaussure for Blacks Estate	9		
..	25	To d° from Jn° Joyner for 1 years Interest & assessment for pew—	7..	13-	9
May - -	14.	To- d° from Richd Adams for part of Interest on his Bond ——	17-	14..	8
July . . .	6	To d° Thom^s Bell for his note & Interest	12		
		Rec^d for Thomas Talbirds pew assessment . ——	3	—	
92 april-	9	Rec^d from John Joyner for one years Interest due on his Bond the 4th July next.....	4-	13-	9-
		To Balance of Poor Taxes brought this Acco^t- ——	2-	2-	9-
			99..	12..	11

[261]

money & Pew assessments............ Cr

1791					
april-		By Cash paid Mrs Lewis..........	52-	8–	
Aug^st^.		By Cash paid for 6000 Singles from Town	0.	0	0
92 april	9	By Maj^r^. Wigg Paid him this day..	28–	14..	6
1792					
Octo^r^...	8	By Cash rece^d^. of M^r^. John Rhodes in full of poor Tax	2	2	9
	.....	......Balance in the hands of John Rhodes	16..	7..	8
			99	12.	11

Error Excepted John Rhodes Church warden–

[262]

At a Meeting of the Vestry. Beaufort April 25th. 91–

Present–

John Barnwell, John Joyner, James Stuart } Vestry Qualifyed { Wm. Wigg, Wm. Joyner, John Gardiner–

John Rhodes, Ed Barnwell } Church Wardens—Qualified—

At a Meeting of the Vestry Monday July 5. 1791

Genl Jno Barnwell
Maj W. H. Wigg
Cap Jno Joyner
James Stuart
John Rose—
Wm Joyner—
Jno M. Verdie

Edw Barnwell, Jno Rhodes. } church wardens

It was agreed this day that the church wardens do pay into the hands of Mrs. Lewis Executrix of Revd Mr. Lewes. notes of hand of the several persons who are in arrears for Interest Money due on their Bonds, and that a discharge be taken for the said Ballce. due to him of £388..11..1—

That the Church wardens do as Soon as possible have the Church Yard repair'd– & that they get the plan of a Steeple wanted by the Next Meeting. & the Cost thereof———

It is also agreed this day that M^rs^. Cunningham be allowed annually the Sum of Ten pounds for the support of her & Child & that the Church wardens do pay the Same in quarterly payments if possible——

[263]

At a Meeting held Oct[r]. 4. 1791

Present

John Barnwell	John Joyner
W[m] H Wigg	James Stuart
W[m] Joyner	Jn[o] M. Verdier

E. Barnwell C. Warden

Orderd: that an order drew on the Vestry & church wardens by the Rev[d]. M[r]. Lewes some time ago. in fav[r]. Tho[s]. Stone & w[ch]. was accept[d]– That the said order be paid by the wardens agreeable to the Instalm[t]. act——& that the same be deduct[d]. out of the Ball[ce]. which is due The said M[r]. Lewes—

—That the Sum of five pounds be paid ℘ yr for the Support of M[rs]. Ann Yake & that the Same be paid in quarterly payments,,——

It is further orderd that the Church Wardens do without delay. obtain personal Security (if possible). or mortgage on the Lots for the Several purchasers in order to secure the respective debts.———

[264]

Beaufort Easter monday 9th- April 1792

This day the Vestry met:

Present—

Will[m] H. Wigg.	William Joyner	Vestry
John Joyner–	Jn[o]. M Verdier	
	Col[o]. Edw[d] Barnwell	Church wardens
	Jn[o] Rhodes – ———	

There not being a sufficient number to make a Vestry the Church wardens proceeded to Elect a new vestry; when on casting up the votes the following Gentlemen were duly Elected to serve for the insuing year—Viz—

J Barnwell

Wm. H. Wigg-

A Aggnew-

Wm. Joyne

John Joyner – – there being equal Votes between Jacob Deveaux– A Campbell & Js- Stuart, the other two could not be determined, so that the Church Wardens advertised for an Election on Monday Next- being the sixteenth Instant—

Recd from Mr John Rhodes, the late Church warden the following Books Viz– one Book of Homilies. Two Common prayer books, one Bible, 5 Vols- of Tilliston Sermons. say 3rd. 4th, 5th. 10th & 11th Vols- 1 of Sharps Vole. 2nd, one Vole— of Lelands View of deistical writers, also the following Bonds & notes viz—

John Joyners Bond for £67
Danl. Stevens- do- – for .... – – —155
Charles Capers- do—do .... — – —100—
Richard Ellis Senr—do .... — 69—10-
Ralph Elliotts- ——do - - - - - - - - - - - - - - - - 79—
Thomas Bells - ———do ....— 40—
Joseph Lloy'd - – –do .... 27—
Willm. Hazzard Wiggs...do ....186—
Barnard Elliotts.......do - - - - - - - - - - - - - - - - 96—
Thomas Pringles - - —do - - - - - - - - - - - - - - - - 30,,5-
Richard Adams - - - - - -do - - - - - - - - - - - - - - - - 99—
James Hazzard Cuthberts - - - - - - - - - - - - - - - - 36 - —
James Stuarts - - - - - - do - - - - - - - - - - - - - - - - 71—
Nathl. Barnwells.. – do. - - - - - - - - - - - - - - - - -116—
John Barnwells.... - do - - - - - - - - - - - - - - - - -131- -
John Bernis Barnwells Note - - – - - - - - - — — — 19. .15—

at same time Recd Thomas Edens and John Guys Bonds for the maintenance of two Bastard Children. and a Bill Sale for a pew in Beaufort Church No- 29- .

Ed Barnwell. C. Warden

[266]

Agreable to the advertisement on Easter Monday the Inhabitants of Port Royal met here on this day being the sixteenth of April, & upon casting up the Votes the two following gentlemen were unanimously Elected- Viz- John Mark Verdier & Dr- James Stuart,— also Dr- Archibald Campbell was Elected Church Warden—

J Barnwell } Qualifyed——
Wm Hd. Wigg— }
James Stuart } qualified 1st May.
John M. Verdier }
Edward Barnwell also as church warden–

Agreed, that from Jany. 1st– 1792, the Pews shall be assessd at the rate of 2 Guineas ℘ Annum- also agreed that the Revd. Mr Tate should be invited to officiate in the Parish Church
A Aggnew & Wm- Joyner having declined serving as Vestry men James Hd- Cuthbert & Dr- James West were Elected in their room— on the 14th. May 1792—

[267]

At a Meeting of the Vestry– June.5.1792-
Present.
J. Barnwell–
Wm. Hd. Wigg
J. M. Verdier—
Js Stuart
J D. West } Qualfd. 5 June
J. H Cuthbert } 92 —
E Barnwell. Church Warden—

According to invitation Rd. Mr. Tate attended- & produced his ordination. & several other recommendatory papers–
Agreed That Rd. Mr. Tate should officiate in this Parish at the rate of £140 ℘ Annum & that it should commence from 1st Jany. last—

At a meeting of the Vestry– September.4th. 1792
Present
J Barnwell– Wm- Hd Wigg- J. Mk. Verdier–
Js. Stuart- J. D. West- J. Hd. Cuthbert
E Barnwell. C- Warden

Dr. Campbell refusing to serve as Church Warden & also refusing to pay his fine the Church Warden is ordered to commence an Action against him for the recovery- Mr- Ralph Elliott was Elected in his room—
Resolved. That the Revd. Mr. Tate be requested to meet the Ecclesiastical Convention in Charleston, 18 Ocr– 92

[268]

Easter Monday- Beaufort April 1.1793

The following gentlemen were Elected for the present year—vizt-

John Barnwell James Stuart— James. D. West- James. H. Cuthbert John Mk. Verdier Robt. Porteous Wm. H. Wigg-	Vestry-
Ed Barnwell Ralph Elliott-	Church Wardens—

At a Meeting of the Vestry this Day, (May 7th- 93- the following gentlemen were present—

John Barnwell Wm- Hd- Wigg- James Stuart Rt. Porteous- James D. West J. Mk. Verdier James H. Cuthbert	Vestry Men & Qualifyed—

Ed Barnwell. C. Warden, Quald-

[269]

Mr. Rhodes as Attorney to the Revd. Mr. Gardner having laid a Demand of 5 months Salary before the Vestry they were of Opinion that as Mr. Gardner had not complyed with the Agreement made by him with the Vestry of taking Priests orders & Returning to the Parish- they were not at liberty to comply with the same, & the said Account was unanimously rejected—

At a Meeting of the Vestry the 9th. Augt. 1793.

Present.

Robert Porteous	James Stuart
Jas. D. West	John M. Verdier
Jas. H. Cuthbert.	

M^{r} Jno. Grayson presented a power of attorney from M^{rs}. Mary Wall Executrix to the last Will & Testament of her late husband Rev^{d}. Step. C. Lewes. demanding payment of the Vestry for the dett due to her late Husband.—M^{r}. Grayson proposed Receiv^{g}. Bonds in payment— on Consideration the Vestry agreed to pass to him Danl Stevens's Bond of £155. and £14.9.4 In^{t}..
is £169.9.4
also John Joyners Bond Bond of £67. and £5.1.6 In^{t}. is.72.1.6

£241.10.10

which Bonds are delv^{d}. to him in part of said debt so oweing. the Ball^{ce}. In said Est^{e}. to remain a further time till a full and final adjustment of acco^{ts}. can take place—

Then Rec^{d}. this 9th. Augt. 1793 from the Vestry & Church Wardens Danl Stevens Bond of One hundred and Sixty nine pounds 9/4 and Jno. Joyners Bond of Seventy two pounds 1/6. as also Ja^{s}. H. Cuthberts note of Ten pounds 1/4. and Ralph E. Elliott note of Twenty two pounds 2/4. in part of Mrs. Mary Wall demand on behalf of her late Husband Rev^{d}. Stephen C. Lewis——

Jno Grayson
Att^{y} for Mrs Wall

[270]

Drs. Revd Mathew Tate

1793

May 7th..paid in Cash by Genl Jno. Barnwell for Pew in full to. 1st January last wh.............. 5..3..6

June 1st..To Cash pd. Mr Tate..(recd. of D. Stevens 1 yr Int. on his Bond).......................... 10:10–

Augt. 7. To do. pd. do.. (recd. of Mrs. Lewis for 3 yrs. pew Tax) .... 8,,3..6

21. To do. pd. Mr. Tate (recd. of Jas. Stuart on a/c Pew Tax) .... 9..0..0

5th. To So much paid you by Major Wigg in part Int. due the Church on his Bond......... .14..2..6

To Jno. Barnwell Esqr. order on Messrs. Geo. & Thos. Tunno .... 30.......

21st April To Cash pd. you. recd. of James Stuart pd- by-
1794 E. Barnwell.. 3—

Augt 6. To Cash Recd. this day of Jas. H Cuthbert being on accot Interest on his Bond 10......

Octr,,17th: To so much Genl Jno. Barnwell pd. in you in part Interest due on his Bond.... 36..8=

126,,7,,6

95

March To Cash pd- by J. B. Barnwell being in full Interest Note E B– 6,,17,.11

do- by T. Bell being 4 years, April 94 - - E B. ,,11,,4,,—

Order on Thomas Talbird for 4 ys Pew Tax. 95. 9,,10,,6

do- Mrs- Winifred Lewis for. 2 ys. do. Jany. 1.95. 4,,7,,—

do. J. Barnwell for balance Ints- & do– do– .. 9,,2,,2–

10th Mar...To Cash pd. Mr Tate being Recd. of Richd Ellis for his Bond & Int. 78..8.:6

carried other side £119,,10,,1

1798

1 Jany To So much recd. of Rd. Adams, by J. M Verdier for Int. money due on his Bond to this day £61..19..1

20 May. To So much recd. by do. of Chs. Capers Interst money on bond. 50..0.0

To So much pd. by J. M Verdier.....19..3..4,,–,,=131..2..5

1 July 1801 To Ballce. due revd Mathw. Tate..267..18..4

transfd. to J. M. Verdier accot.. £518,.10..10

[271]

1793 Contra Crs.

1st Jany. By 1 yrs. Salary due you this day.......... £140
By Interest on £63–3–6–2 years–£8-16-10- 8,,16,,10
94- By 1 Ys- Salary due this day— 140,,——
By Interest on £90,,12- - 1 Year - 6,,6,—
95 By 1 ys. Salary due this day- - - 140

435,,2:10
Dr brought over- 126,,7–6

308,,15,,4

Oct. 7th. 95-
By 9 ms. Salary due this day - - - - - - 102,,12,,—

Crs., £411,,7,,4

By Intermediate Int. to 1 Jany. 1798...61..2..0
1798 By Ditto.....to 1 July 1801.... .46..1..6
1 Jany —— 107..3..6

£518..10..10

[272]

At a Meeting of the Vestry, Sept. 3. 1793

—Present–

J. Barnwell – Wm. Hd. Wigg— J. Stuart—
J. Mk. Verdier- J. H. Cuthbert– R. Porteous—
E Barnwell. C. Warden–

Resolved That the Rvd. Mr. Tate be requested to meet the Ecclesiastical Convention to be helt on the 17h- October 1793-in Charles-ton-

Easter Monday, April- 21st- 1794

The following Gentlemen were Elected to serve as Vestry Men & Church Wardens—

John Barnwell - } - Qualified
Wm- Hd- Wigg - - - - } - do.
J. H. Cuthbert } Vestry Men
J. Stuart - }
R. Porteous } Qualified March 3- 95-
J. M. Verdier - - - } - Quald.
J. D. West — — } — — — do

E Barnwell } do
Thos. Fuller — } Church Wardens— do.

[273]

At a Meeting of the Vestry held on Monday the 6th. Augs. 1794
Present.

J Barnwell - W. Hd Wigg- J Mk. Verdier
J Stuart - Js. D. West-

E Barnwell } C- W-
T Fuller- }

Resolved. that the Church Wardens to write to the different bond Debtors & request of them an immediate payment of their Interest, which if not complied with that the principal as well as the Interest shall be recovered-

At a Meeting of the Vestry held on Tuesday March- 3rd- 1795
Present

J. Barnwell- Wm. Hd. Wigg— J. Mk. Verdier
J. Cuthbert— Robert Porteous. Quald-

Ed Barnwell } Church Wardens
T Fuller — }

Resolved that the Church Wardens do employ an Attorney at Law to recover a certain sum of Money Dr James Fraser received as Church Warden of Mrs- Martinangel

[274]

that they also get a Copy of James Daly Will

that they allow the family of Mr. William Faris the sum of ten pounds—

Easter Monday April- 6th- 1795-

The following gentlemen were Elected to serve as Vestry men & Church Wardens—

John Barnwell	Qd
John Mk- Verdier	- qualifdd.,, the 19th Octr: 1795
	Vestry
Wm. Wigg—	Qu..
James Stuart—	do..
James Cuthbert—	do
	Men
Robert Porteous—	quald..
James- D. West—	do..—
	do
Ed Barnwell	Church Wardens—
Alexr. Porteous-	do-

[275]

At a Meeting of the Vestry Octr. 19. 1795

Present

Wm H Wigg	James Stuart
James D West	John Barnwell
Robt,, Porteous	Jno. M. Verdier.

on Tuesday Evening the 7th. Octr. 1795 The Revd. Mr. Tate our Clergyman departed this Life-,,-,,—,,— and this day the Vestry met in order to procure a Minister in his Stead.—

The Revd. Mr. Mc.Cully being proposed, Resolved that the Inhabitents have notice to meet at the Church on monday next,,—,,

At a Meeting of the Vestry- Oct[tr]. 26, 1795

Present-

J Barnwell- | Wm. Hd- Wigg-
J. West- | James Stuart
R Porteous | J M. Verdier
J: Cuthbert—

E Barnwell
A Porteous- } Church Wardens—

The Inhabitants agreeable to the notification met this day, & were against an Election-

[276]

Easter Monday March- 28th. 1796

The following Gentlemen were elected to serve as Vestry Men & Church Wardens—

John Barnwell quald.,,
Wm. Hd. Wigg- quald.,,
Robert Barnwell qualifyd.
James Stuart- ..do,,.,,
Dr. James West-
James- Hd-. Cuthbert-,,
Wm- Elliott. -quald,, } Vestry Men-

E Barnwell
Qualify'd J. Mk. Verdier } Church Wardens—

[277]

Easter Monday April 17th: 1797

The following Gentlemen were Elected to Serve as Vestry Men & Church Wardens for the Ensueing yr.

qualfd John Barnwell
do: Wm. H. Wigg=
(sick) Robert Barnwell
do- Jas. Stuart
do. Jas. Cuthbert
do Wm. Elliott
do Thos. Fuller } Vestry

qualifd Edwd. Barnwell
do,, Jno M Verdier } C. W

At a Meeting of the Vestry on Tuesday Sep[r]. 5. 1797,,–

Jn[o]. Barnwell
W[m]. H. Wigg
Ja[s] Stuart
Ja[s]. H Cuthbert
W[m] Elliott
Tho[s] Fuller } Vestry. Edw[d]. Barnwell } ch- w-
Jn[o] M Verdier }

Resolved that the Church Wardens do write M[r] Elias Saltus that unless he Incloses the church and finish the Steeple or enters into a written agreem[t] for that purpose—that they Commence an action ag[t] him for Damages—

[278]

At a Meeting of the Vestry September– 4th– 1798

Present–

John Barnwell—— W[m]. Elliott–
J[s]- Stuart— Th[s]. Fuller
J[s]. H. Cuthbert— Rob[t]. Barnwell. V. M-
E Barnwell & J. M[k]. Verdier- C– W–

M[r]. W[m]. Joyner was duly Elected as Vestry man, in the room of Major W[m]. H[d]. Wigg—deceased—

Resolved– that the Church Wardens do write to the Rev[d]- M[r]. Graham– inviting him to accept the Beaufort Church which has been without a Minister some time– which was accordingly done & M[r]. Graham return'd his answer that he would officiate gratis, untill a Minister could be procured–

At a Meeting of the Vestry on the 10th- Nov[r]- 1798

Present—

John Barnwell— W[m]. Elliott—
Rob[t]. Barnwell— Th[s]. Fuller
J[s]- Stuart– W[m]. Joyner- Quald[y]–
J[s]- H[d]- Cuthbert— — — — — — — — — — — —V– M—
J. M Verdier— C- W–

The Rev[d]. M[r]. Graham repeated to the Vestry that he would accept of the Church as their minister and [279] that he would expect a Salary from Jan[y]- 1st- 1799– it was then agreed that the sum of one hundred pounds be the Salary for the Year 1799– which M[r]. Graham assented to–

At a Meeting of the Vestry on Tuesday August. 6th- 1799

Present–

John Barnwell — — — Ths. Fuller–
Robt Barnwell — —— Wm. Joiner—
Js. Stuart—— V. M—
Ed Barnwell- - J. Mk. Verdier– C- W–

Resolved– That the Church Wardens– do make out an exact list of the sum that can be yearly collected on Acct of the Poor Tax as two more applications are made for Relief. (by Mrs. Jones & Mrs. King-) that if the present rates are not sufficient, the Tax to be raised–

At a meeting of the Vestry– Feby– 4th- 1800–

Present-

John Barnwell— Robt– Barnwell–
Js- Stuart - — Js. H. Cuthbert–
Wm. Joiner– V. M-
Ed Barnwell– C– W–

Resolved– That the 1 years Salary given by the Revd- Mr. Graham for the use of the Church, shall in the first [280] instance go towards glazing & repairing the same– & the Church Wardens- are desired to have it done as soon as Possible—
—That the Church Wardens– do apply to Colo- Talbird to know if he is prepared to build the tabby wall round the Church yard on the former conditions spoken of between the Vestry & himself–
— That the Church Wardens be directed, in case Colo.– Talbird declines his former proposals, to endeavor to have the work compleated by some other person—
—That the assessment on the pews shall be four pounds each annually commencing the 1st. Jany- 1800- & that the poor Tax shall be four pence ℘ head for negroes & four pence for every hundred Acres of land to be paid by the Inhabitants on Port Royal, Paris's & Ladies Island–
—That all the Lotts now belonging to the Vestry, in the town of Beaufort shall be sold to the best advantage on a Credit of five Years—the Interest to be paid annually, provided they shall not be sold under forty pounds a Lott the purchaser to give bond and mortgage of the property & paying for the Titles—

[281]

—That Mr. William Joyner & Colo. Robert Barnwell be authorised to sign the Titles—Mr. Joyner in behalf of the Vestry & Colo. Robert Barnwell as surviving Commissioner

At a meeting of the Parishoners held at the church in Beaufort on Easter monday the 14th. April 1800. the following Gentlemen were Elected as Vestry men & Church wardens for the yr following.

Genl Jno Barnwell	James Stuart Qualfd
Robert Barnwell	Jas. Hazd Cuthbert do
Wm Joyner Quald	Willm. Elliott do
	Thos Fuller– do-

Edwd Barnwell } church wardens—
Jno M Verdier }

At a Meeting of the Vestry held at the church on 28th April 1800

Present

Ths. Fuller-	Js Stuart
J. H. Cuthbert-	Wm- Joyner
	J. M. Verdier C. W-

Resolved unanimously– That Wm. Joyner be fully empower'd. to make sale & sign Titles– in behalf of this Vestry, of such Lotts of Land thereunto belonging– orderd to be sold at a former meeting & to take bond & mortgage of the property as security for payment–

[282]

Dr. John M Verdier

So much pd. Isaac Hird for his Services Some time past	3..15-
Paid Bristol ringing Bell up to the death of Mr Tate	4..4..6–
So much pd Mr Tate, being over the Subscript. raised 1st. yr—	5.—
paid John Johnsons accot. reparg church Yard	5.—10
pd Tho. Stone in part his demd. agt Vestry on accot. Revd Mr Lewes	29.—
Ballce. pd. to Revd. Mathw. Tate by J. M. V..–	19..3..4
	£66..3..8

1798 for Repairs &c.

Mar 17. Paid for 22 m Shingles @ 15/2 pr. m...... 16..13..8
1 m feet fether Edge Boards £6:10 500. feet Norwd. 67/........................9.17.
freight boards 30/. frt. Shingles £5.10 7. 16..17—

4 m Shingles bot. afterwards @ 20/2. 1st parcell not Enough .... 4..0..8
Cash pd. Elijah Swift his Bill for the Steeple, shingling the church & painting the Steeple .... } 101.———
Paid Step Lawrence his Bill for Lightning Rod & other work 18... —
„ Paid Gibbony for Turning the top the Steeple .... 3..17—
„ 5 Galls. oil 45/.4 Large Kegs whi Lead £6 .... 8..5–
„ 76 lb 10 & 20d nails 96/. 49t rope 49/10 .... 7..5..10
.. 2 m brads 16/8 6½tt Verdigrease 30/4 160 Turpnt 3/6 2..10..6
..184tt. Shingling Nails @ 1/2 .1. Augar 3/ - - - - - - - - - - - 10..17= „28„18„4

„ Paid Tho. Talbird for white washg church. Patching &..— .... 16 ———

£205..6..8

1798

1 July J. M. V recd. for Rent Heywards Pew yr 1799 .... 2..3..6
To Jas. Stuart Pew Tax.99. 43/6. 1800. 80/ 6:3:6
Int. on new Bond to 30 apl. 1801.. 11:4.0
Int. on old Bond to 4 July 1801...25,.18.

£43:5:6

deduct Lepd for Mr Grahams Tomb stone 16.18.8 26..6..10

To Rich[d]. Ellis. 2 y[s] In[t]. on his Bond
to 6 March 1802................ 22..8.0
½ Pew tax y[s] 99 & 1899.
between him & Givens 3..1..9.—25=9..9

To Ralph Elliott 2 y[s] pew Tax 99.43/6.
1800. 80/ .... 6..3..6

To Ann Joyner Pew Tax 1800. 80/. W[m]
Joyners 99. 43/6 .... 6..3..6

To J M Verdiers Pew tax y[s]. 99 43/6. 80/.2
y[s] In[t]. on Bond to 30th. ap[l] 1802
£29.8/. (.4.) .... 40..11..6

To Tho Bell Bond & Interest £59:12/. D[r].
Campbell pew tax 99 43/6. 1800. 80/..... 65..15..6

To W[m]. Smith 1 y In[t]. on his Bond to 30
ap[l] 1801 .... 11..4..0

To John Barnwell Bond and Interest to
april 1802 .... 195......

To Ja[s]. Aggnew pew tax 99.43/6. 1800. 80/. 6..3..6

To D. Screven 1 y[s] In[t]. on his Bond £14.
to 30 ap[l]. 1801 .... 14..0..0

To Sarah Waight 1 y[s]. In[t]. on her Bond to
ditto .... 15..19..2

Will[m]. Elliott 1 y[s] In[t]. on his Bond to ditto. 33..12–

. M[rs]. Joyner pew tax 99 34/6. Mich Perry-
clear pew tax 99 43/6. 1800. 80/. ..... 8..7..0

. Phebe Waight pew tax 99 43/6. 1800.80/.
Ph. Givens half pew tax 99. 1800. 61/9... 9/5..3

. P. Givens 1 y. In[t]. on Bond due 30 ap[l].
1801. is .... 11..4..0

£477..9...

[283]

1796 Credit—

Jan[y]. 1st. By J. M. Verdier Pew tax 89.90.91.92.93.
94.95. .... 17..14.

J. Johnson's D[o]. 89.90.91 .... 9——

Winf Lewis D[o]..y[r]. 95 .... 2..3..6

Ph. Waight D[o]..up to Jan[y]. 1.96. 13..1–

rec[d] of R[d]. Ellis In[t]. on his Bond....... 24..5..2

£66..3..8

1798

March., So much rec^{d} for Capt Jno. Joyner dec^{d} Legacy .... £50. —

„ for Doct. West Subscrip^{t} .... 3. - —

Ths. Fuller Subscrip^{t}. 60/. Ths Talbird D^{o}. 60/ .... 6—

Jno Barnwell Subscrip^{t}. 5–
and in p^{t}. In^{t}. money due on his Bond to Church ....16..5. 21..5—

Rec^{d} of Rob. Barnwell for his order on ch^{s}.ton .... 15—

Ja^{s} Stuart Subscrip^{t}. 68/9 Wm Elliotts £5... 8..8..9

Tho. Bell Subscrip^{t}. £2- Jno M Verdier's £5. 7—

Tho Graysons £2- Ralp Elliotts £5. Jno Guerards 60/. J. B. Barnwells 40/ 12= -

M^{rs}. P. Waights £2. Winf^{d} Lewis 60/. Math^{w}. Tates 60/ .... 8.—

Ph Givens's 40/. Tho. Witters 20/. Jon^{a}. Witters 30/. .... 4-.10—

James Scanlans 10/. M^{rs}. Talbird £6. Mrs Grayson £5 .... 11..10—

So much rec^{d} of M^{rs}. Mary Barnwell on Ladies Subscrip^{t}.. 25—

Ball^{ce}. due to J. M Verdier—33..12..11

£205..6..8

„ By Ball^{ce}. bro^{t}. down due J. M Verdier....33..12..11

1 July 1801. By Ball^{ce}. due Rev^{d}. Math^{w}. Tate......267..18..4

By Ball^{ce}. due Thos. Stone he assumes 1 July 1801 .... 78..18.—

By So much church owed Revd And^{w}. Mc-Culley he assumes .... 30—

£410..9..3

By So much J. V. p^{d}. Mulhen & Flin on acco- work to Church...£65

By ditto he p^{d}. Jno. Goddard Surveyor ....1..17..4 66..17..4

£477..6.7

By over cast D^r^. Side mark'd ×......... . 5.

£482..6..7

acco^t^. carr^d^. forw^d^–

[284]

At a meeting of the Vestry held at the Church on the 7th. Octr. 1800—

Present

Tho. Fuller	James Stuart
J. H. Cuthbert.	Willm. Joyner
	W^m^. Elliott.

Edw. Barnwell C W.

on the 4th. of this month The Rev^d^ M^r^. W^m^. E. Graham minister of this church departed this Life— The Vestry in Consideration of his disinterested Services and in testimony of their respect & Esteem for him, Resolve that the church, wardens do with all convenient dispatch procure a plain marble Tombstone with a Suitable inscription to be placed over his Grave–

Col^o^. Tho. Talbird was elected a Vestry man in the room of Genl Barnwell dec^d^.–

At a Meeting of the Vestry on the 3^d^ Mar 1801

Present

Tho. Fuller	Rob. Barnwell
Ja^s^ Stuart	Wm Elliott
Wm Joyner	Tho Talbird Qlf
	J. H. Cuthbert.
	Edw Barnwell } C. W.
	J M Verdier }

Resolved that the church wardens do immediately write an Invitation to The Revd Mr Moore of Lexington Kentucky inviting him to this Parish and offer^g^. him a Salary of one thousand Dollars ℔ ann and a House for his family to reside in—

[285]

At a Meeting of the Parishoners held at the Church in Beaufort on Easter monday 6 April 1801 the follow^{g}. Gentlemen were duly Elected to Serve as Vestry men & Church wardens for the ensueing year—

Robt Barnwell. Wm Elliott– James Stuart- Willm Joyner- Tho Talbird John M Verdier and James H Cuthbert, as Vestry, and Edward Barnwell and Tho. Fuller as church wardens— at Same time Elected Robert Barnwell– Ralph Elliott & Thos Talbird Comm^{rs}. The Streets.——

At a meeting of the Vestry on the 7th. July 1801–

Present–

Robt Barnwell Q^{ed}-	W^{m}. Elliott. Q^{ed}-
J. H. Cuthbert– d^{o}	Th^{s}. Talbird- d^{o}
J. M. Verdier- d^{o}–	W^{m}. Joiner– d^{o}

E^{d} Barnwell Q^{ed}
Th^{s}– Fuller..d^{o}- } Church Wardens—

Resolved that the proposals of Col^{o} Talbird for Build^{g} a Parsonage House be agreed to– paym^{ts}. to be made in the foll^{g} manner Three Hundred pounds at Commencem^{t} the Build^{g}.– three hundred p^{d}. when the build^{g} is raised, Three Hundred pounds when the build^{g}. is Compleated, Three Hundred pounds twelve months after– that the Two Lotts of Land N°. 418 and 419 be given for that purpose that the Square Consisting of Lotts n°. 65.66–91-92 be reserved for public use— The follow^{g}. Letter was rec^{d} from the Presd^{t}. of the Beaufort College... Gen^{tn}— "I am instructed to request from you to have layd of whatever part of the Glebe Land you may think proper for the use of the College as the trustees are called upon to fix a place for the College building. the Trustees request that you woud be as liberal as possible and that you will also take into Consideration the appropriation of two Valuable Lotts in the town of Beaufort made by the Trustees for Building a Parsonage House upon

I am Gen^{n}. Y^{r}. Ob. Serv.

(Signed) R Barnwell
Presid- Board
Trustees

Beaufort 14 July 1801

[286]

At a meeting of the Vestry held at the Church, July- 14th. 1801

Present-

Robt Barnwell- Wm. Elliott
Wm. Joiner- Ths. Talbird
J. H. Cuthbert- J. M. Verdier- V. Men-
E. Barnwell- C. W—

At a Meeting of the Vestry held at the Church Tuesday 4th. augt. 1801

Present

Robt. Barnwell Wm Elliott
Wm Joyner Js. Stuart
J. H. Cuthbert Jno M Verdier. V. M.
Edwd Barnwell }
Tho. Fuller- } C. W.

Resolved that the church wardens be directed to have the within Part of the church repaired in a Neat & workman like manner on the best terms—

Agreeable to said Resolve the church wardens agreed with Mess: Mulhern & Flyn to do the Same & by articles Signd they are to Complete the Same on the 1st Novr. next for the Sum of £95–

In Consequence of a Letter recd. from the President of the Board of Trustees of the Beaufort College dated 14th. July 1801. It was Resolved that the Vestry do hereby grant to the Trustees of the Beaufort College and their Sucessors in office in Fee Simple. Twenty acres of the Glebe Land, next adjoining and bounded by the West Line of the town of Beaufort, to be included in a Line to be run paralel to Hamar Street at the distance of 525 feet from the Said Street, beginning at the Bluff on the River, and resolved that the Church Wardens do immediately engage Mr. Goddard to Survey & Lay off the Same & make a return of the Plat thereof to the Vestry at their next meeting for their approbation—

[287]

At a Meeting of the Vestry held on the 2d. feb. 1802

Present

Rob Barnwell Jas Stuart
Jas. H. Cuthbert Wm. Joyner
Wm Elliott Thos Talbird
Jno M Verdier V. M—
Ed Barnwell. C. W.

Resolved that the church wardens write to Rev[d] M[r] Bowen at Providence Rhode Island. Inviting him to the Rectorship of this Church– agree[a]. to said resolution M[r]. Bowen was written to—

At a Meeting of the Vestry at the Church in Beaufort April 5. 1802

Present

Rob. Barnwell	Jn[o] M Verdier
J[s]. H Cuthbert	Will[m]. Joyner
Tho Talbird	J[s]. Stuart
W[m] Elliott	

E. Barnwell C. W.

Resolved that the Church Wardens do pay to Col[o] Talbird the Sum of Three Hundred pounds as 1st paym[t]. toward the Parsonage House so soon as the first Box of tabbey is made

---

At a meeting held at the church in Beaufort on Easter Monday April 19th– 1802. the following gentlemen were duly Elected to serve as Vestry men & Church Warden– for the ensuing year– Robert Barnwell– William Elliott, James Stuart– John M. Verdier- Thomas Talbird, William Joiner James. Cuthbert– V. M. E Barnwell & T[s]. Fuller C. W–

---

at the same time Elected Robert Barnwell— Ralph Elliott & Thomas Talbird Comms[s]– Streets—

[288]

At a meeting of the Vestry at the Church in Beaufort May 14th 1802—

Present—

Robert Barnwell- qul[d]–	James Stuart q[lg]–
James H. Cuthbert- d[o].—	Thomas Talbird d[o]–
William Joiner—d[o]—	

E Barnwell- C. W- qu[ld]–

The church Wardens having received an answer from M[r] Bowen declining the offer made him agreably to the resolve of the 3. Fe[by]—.

Resolved- that the church wardens write to A Garden Eq- who is on his way to Europe to endeavor to procure a minister for the church on the same terms as offered M^{r}- Bowen- say one thousand dollars & fu^{rn}– with a comfortable dwelling house free of rent–

Resolved- that the church Wardens– do-advertise the remaining Lots belonging to the church for sale on the 22nd. June next on a credit of five years with Interest from the date payable annually with mortgage of the premises–

[289]

At a Meeting held at the Church in Beaufort on Easter Monday April 11th- 1803– the following gentlemen were duly Elected to serve as Vestry men & Church Wardens for the ensuing year—

V men

Robert Barnwell— William Elliott. J^{s}. Stuart– J. M^{k}. Verdier–– Thomas Talbird, W^{m}. Joiner. J. Cuthbert

C. Wardens

E^{d} Barnwell—& R. E. Elliott—

at the same time Elected R- Barnwell. T. Talbird & Stephen Lawrence comms^{s}– Streets – —

At a meeting of the Vestry held 1st June 1803.

Present

Robt Barnwell	James Stuart
Ja^{s} H Cuthbert	Thos Talbird
Willm Joyner	John M Verdier
	E Barnwell C. W.

Resolved that the Church Wardens do Invite the Rev^{d}. M^{r}. Connor to officiate in the church for the space of three months with a Salary of two hundred & fifty Dollars for that time„.

At a meeting of the Vestry held 1 January 1804—

Present

Robt. Barnwell	Jno M Verdier
James Stuart	J^{s}. H. Cuthbert
W^{m}. Elliott	

E. Barnwell C. W.
R. E. Elliott C. W

Resolved that an Invitation be sent to the Rev^{d}. M^{r}. Hicks. with an offer of the Church together with a Salary of Fifteen hundred Dollars ꝑ ann, & the Parsonage House to reside in— which Said offer M^{r}. Hicks accepted.—

[290]

D^{r}.	John M. Verdier Acco^{t}.	
	To am^{o}. Debits bro: forward....	£477..9..0
	To so much rec^{d}. of Tho. Fuller pew tax 1799	2..3..6
the am: rec^{d}. of E. B. ꝑ his order on S. & Yates	To Step Lawrence 1 y^{r} In^{t}. on Bond £11.4/ ½ pew tax 99. & 1800. 61/9........14.5..9 ..J. B. Barnwell 1 y^{r}. d^{o}. 11.13.4.. Jos. B. Cook D^{o}. 1 y^{r}. 70/ ....15..3..4 Rob. Houston 1 y^{r}. £5.12/. Wm Joyners pew tax 1800. 80/ ....9.12.0 F. Saltus pew tax 99.43/6. 1800. 80/. E Barnwells d^{o}. £6.3.6 ....12.7.0	,,51..8..1
	for Jno Johnson's pew tax 99.43/6. & 1800. 80/........	6..3..6
	To Ja^{s}. H. Cuthbert Bond £36. 8 y^{r}. In^{t}. £20.2.8........	56..2..8
		£593..6..9

Dr- Edward Barnwell Acct—

Date	Item	£	s	d
Sept. 1802	To Cash recd. from J. M. Verdier–	£ 104,,	16,,	8–
	Mary Barnwell– Pew Tax - - - - -	6,,	3,,	6–
	Nathaniel Barnwell–part Interest–	30,,	—	—
	William Heyward, bond in full & Interest-	175,,	18	—
	Joseph B. Cooke. Interest - - - - -	3,,	10,,	—
	James Hogg- Senr. 2 ys Interest - -	22,,	8,	—
	Robert Houston - - Interest - - - - -	5,,	12,	—
	Elizabeth Gough. Intr 2 ys - - - - - -	25,,	4,	—
	James Scanlan. Int. 1 yr - - - - - - -	5,,	12	,,–
	Est. John Screven. P. T. . .1800 - -	4,,	—	
	Richard Screven. Int - - - - - - - - - -	14,,	—	
	Stephen Lawrence- do - - - - - - - -	11,.	4	—
	James Stuart - - - old bond in full	70,,	—	
	William Elliott - - - - - Int. - - - - -	33,,	12,,	- -
	William Hutson Wigg- P. Tax- in full	6,,	3,,	6
Oc 5. 1802	do do part Interest - - -	128,,	17,,	10
Nov. 6.	Ralph E. Elliott in full Int. £70.1.2. prin £14.0.5 - - - - - - - - - - - - -	84,,	1,,	7–
	Barnwell Deveaux- part Interest - -	10,	3,,	
Jay- 1803	Estate N Barnwell . . . do - - - -	75,,		
		£816,,	6	,,1

[291]

Credits—

By Credits bro^{t}. forw^{d}. .... £482..6..7
p^{d}. John Johnson on his acco............... 6..3..6
Ball^{ce}- paid the 17th. Sep^{t}. 1802 to Col^{o}. E. Barnwell C. W. 104..16..8

£593..6..9

Credit–

1802				
Sep^{r}.	By Cash p^{d}. W. Joyner in behalf Rv^{d}. S. Lewis-	£23,,	6..	8
	d^{o}- Trustees B. College in behalf. R^{d}. N Graham	30,,	—	—
	d^{o}- d^{o}– d^{o}- —— Beaufort Society	7,,	—	—
	d^{o}- p^{d}. Thomas Talbird - - - - - - -	539,,	4,,	—
Nov. 6.	d^{o}- p^{d}- Robert Brown in full. Est M^{r}. Graham	78,,	6,,	8
Dec 16.	d^{o}. Samuel Firth for lightning rod..	7,,	9,,	4..
	T. Talbird. assumption for B. Deveaux - -	3,,	3,,	—
	Cash ℔. Trustees. B. College. B. Society –.	75,,	—	
	d^{o} - - . – d^{o}— d^{o} –d^{o}– – ..	55,.		,,—
	d^{o}- p^{d}- D^{r}. Smith, prince-ton....—.	4,,	13,,	4
		£823	,,3	,,
	D^{o}. brought over.–.	816,,	6,,	1
	due E. B. . C. W.	£ 6	16	,,11

[292]

Dr– Edward Barnwell- C. W acct

		£	s	d
Jany 1803	Estate N Barnwell in full Interest, P. T„	£ 4„	16„	8
April-	Frederick Fraser. in full Interest- —	16„	16„	—
May. 27	Richard Ellis- do– do - - - - - -	11„	4„	—
	Barnwell Deveaux in pt. do - - - - - -	6„	9„	4–
April 1802	James Stuart. do. - - - - - - - - - - - -	11„	4„	—
1803	– do- do- . do - - - - - - - - - - - - -	11„	4	—
	do- - - - do note in full — — — —	2„	13„	2–
June - - -	J. B. Barnwell in part note - - - - -	23„	6„	8–
	Stephen Laurence Int. - - - - - - - - -	11„	4„	—
	Richard Adams bond & Intr- - - - -	136„	10„	7
	William Elliott – – Int - - - - - -	33„	12„	—
	Robert Houston - - – do- - - - - - - - -	5„	12	„—
	William Smith—Int– 2 years - - -	22„	8„	—
	John Loyd balance in full - - - - -	16„	13„	4
	T. Talbird. bond & Int- in full	292„	19..	6–
1804	- - - - - - - Pew Tax - - 2 years - - - - -	6„	3„	6–
Jany-	P Givens – – Interest - - - - - - - - - -	29„	8	—
	E. Gough— do- - - - - - - - - - - - -	12„	12„	—
	Joseph B. Cooke - - - - - - - - - - - - - -	7„		—
	J. M. Verdier so much red. W Joiner	39„		—
	J. M- Verdier Interest - - - - - - - - -	14„	14	—
	J. H. Cuthbert— do- - - - - - - - - - -	45„	13.	9
	– – – do- - - - - - - - -	6„	3„	6–
	W. Hutson Wigg - - - bond - - - - -	186„		—
	- do - - - Interest in full	48,	16	„11
1805	J. M. Verdier. Interest - - - - - - - - -	14„	14„	—
		£1016	18	11

[293]

Credit— Cr,

		£	s	d
1803	By balance brought over - - - - - -	£ 6,,	16,,	11-
June	By Cash pd- T. Talbird - - - - - - - - -	200,,		,- -
	By R Adams - - bond & Int- to T. Talbird	136,,	10,,	7
	By- John Loyd open acct & int- - - do- - - - - - - - - - - - - -	16,,	13,	4-
	By Thomas Talbird- bond & Int- do—	292,,	19,,	6-
	- - - do- - - - - - - - Pew Tax - - - -	6,,	3,,	6-
Decr–	By Cash pd- Wm. Joiner- as ℔ Acct			
1804	Curt- £677..18..3	25,,	11,,	4
	By Cash pd Revd Mr Connor - - - - -	58,,	6,,	8
Jany	By do- pd. Brister ringing bells–	1,,	3,,	4
	By Cash pd- T Talbird in full. P, house	5,,	6,,	1-
	By do- pd. Firth for Repairing lighg rod–	2,,	16–	
	By do- - 10 M bricks - - - - - - - - -	28,,		,–
	By do- freight do- - - - - - - S 5 ℔ M.	11,,	13–	4
	By do- McCallister- Church yard- -	140,,		,, –
	By do- Caps &c &c- pillars - do- - - -	45 :	9.	
	By do. McCallister ———— do- Ellis-	11,	13.	4
	By do. Mulheron & Flynn. Parsonage.	35,,	—	—
Sepr.	By do- pd. Brister ringing bells - - -	1..	11–	6–
	By do- Burnett- painting. Parsonage	11–	13–	4
		£1037,,	7,,	9
1805	By do. Monroe in full-do- - do- - .	9,.	19	.2
Jany.	By do- pd Brister ringing bells - - - -		17..	6–
	B do- pd- N Wench for taking care Pars. house		14,,	—
	By do- McCallister - - - - - - - - - -	18,.	16,.	8
		£1067,,	15,,	1

[294]

Dr. Edwd. Barnwell C. W. accot–

		£	s	d
1804 May.	amount brought over £	1016,,	18..	1..
	James Stuart- Interest- 2 bonds- in full.	£ 28,,	5,,	6
	Joseph Johnson do- upto 1803 - - -	5..	14..	4
	James Bowman- do- in full - - - - -	22,.	8–	
	Richard Ellis - - do- - - - do- - - - - -	11,–	4–	
	Charles Stewart- - do- - - . 2 ys. Interest—	—22,,		
Octr 9	Joseph Loyds bond &- Interest - - -	52,,	0,,	2.
	Philip Givens - - - - - - - do- - - - -	14,,	,,	4
	Stephen Laurence- do- 2 years. do- -	22,	8,,	
	Alexander Brown. do- do- - - - - -	16,,	2,,	–
1805	James Scanlan- do- do- - - - - - -	11,,	4,,	–
Augs. 5	William Elliott - - - - 1 ys. do- - - -	33..	,,	..
	Robert Barnwell - Pew Assesment. 2 ys 10	18,,		,,
	Edward Barnwell- do – do £10	18,,		,,
	John A Cuthbert - - - - - - - - - - -	10,,	3,,	6–
	Archibald Campbell- - - - - - 1 ys- - -	5,,		,,–
1806	Estate W Lewis - - - - - - - - - do- -	5,,		,,—
Jany	Charles Stewart - - - 1 ys Interest - -	11,,	1,,	2
Feby- 28	Moses Forster- - - 4 do- - - do- - - -	36,,	11,,	4
	John Flynn- - - - - - - 3-do- - do- - -	14,,	1,,	3–
	John Mulheron— 3. do— do	21,,	8,,	3–
	do- - do. 2 ys. assessment Pew - - -	10,,	,,	—
	John M. Verdier- 1 do. up to April 1805	14,,	14,,	—
	do do. 2 ys. assessment Pew	10		
Apl. 1805	Thomas Bowman 1 ys. Interest- - -	5,,	12,,	—
	Thomas Fuller- Int up to Jany. 1806 - - - - - - - - - - - - - - - -	79,,	6,,	8
	do do assessment Pew for 1800-1801	6,,	3,,	6
	£	1504,,	6,,	11

[295]

Credit—

		£	s	d
1805	Amount brought over - - -	.£1067,,	15,,	1,,
July.	By Cash p^d Brister - - - - - - - - -	1,,	12,,	8.
	By d^o- Forster Burnet painter in full.	5,,	0,.	2
	By d^o- McCallister - - Church yard -	30,,	,,	—
Decr. 3	By d^o p^d Brister - - - - - - - - - - - -	1,,	5,,	8—
April 22	By d^o. p^d. Finlay. freight of bricks £37..17..10	35,,	,,	—
Ag^s– 5	By d^o- p^d- C. Graves- d^o- - - - -	33,,		,,—
1806 Jan^y.	By d^o- p^d S Firth, Church gate hinges. &c. . –	11,,	6,,	4—
Fe^by. 28	By d^o. p^d. Treasurer of the College -	36,,	11,,	4
	By d^o- p^d. Rev^d M^r- Hicks. - - - - - -	100,,	,,	—
	By d^o Mulheron & Flynn Parsonage Yard full	67,,	1,,	8
	By — d^o —— d^o- gates &c Church yard-	79,.	19,.	8
	By d^o Rev^d M Hicks T Fullers note	85,,	10,,	2-
	By d^o. M^rs McKee for schooling Farris..	7,,	3,,	9.
	£	1563,,	5,,	6

[296]

At a Meeting of the Inhabitants of Beaufort on Easter Monday the 2d apl. 1804 the follg Gentlemen was Electd to serve for the ensuing yr

Rob. Barnwell quald.
Js. H Cuthbert– do
Jho M Verdier. do.
James Stuart
Wm Elliott
Tho Grayson–qualifd
Jho G. Barnwell. do–
} Vestry men

qualifd. Edwd. Barnwell
Do– R. E. Elliott.
} Church Wardens

At a Meeting of the Vestry on Friday the 20th. July 1804

Present

Rob. Barnwell
Js. H Cuthbert
Thos. Grayson
Jno M Verdier
Jno G Barnwell
} Vestry

Edwd Barnwell
R. E: Elliott
} C. W.

The Revd- Mr Hicks having stated his health to be in such a precarious situation as to demand a journey to the Northward & in consequence thereof requested leave of absence untill November–

Resolved– that leave of absence be given the Revd– Mr– Hicks during the time requested in his application

Resolved— that the Pews be assess'd at the rate of five pounds commencing from April 1st– 1804 & to Jany– 1805

Mr. Charles Stewart by his petition, informing us that three fourths of a Lot (No 70) bought of us in June 1802 [297] was in the ponds commonly call'd the sisters–

Resolved– that fifty pounds shall be taken off the purchase money–

At a meeting held at M[r] Verdier s Feb[y]- 11th- 1805

Present–

Rev[r]. M[r] Hicks–

Rob Barnwell		
Th[s]. Grayson	V	
J[s]. H. Cuthbert	E Barnwell	C W–
J. M. Verdier–	R E. Elliott	

M[r]. Jacob Guerard was Elected a Vestry man in the room of James Stuart—who declines serving—
Resolved– That R E. Elliott. C. W. & M[r] John Rhodes be appointed deputies to meet the convention to be held in Charleston on the 18th. Instant–

[298]

At a meeting held at the Episcopal Church on Easter Monday the 15th. April 1805 the foll[g]. Gen[t]. were Elected to Serve as Vestry men & Church Wardens for the Ensueing y[r].
Vestry men Rob Barnwell. Jacob Guerard. John M Verdier Tho[s] Grayson. James H Cuthbert.. John G Barnwell & D[r]. Arch. Campbell Church Wardens Ed. Barnwell & Ralph E. Elliott.—[1]

At a meeting of the Vestry on Monday Feb[y]- 10th- 1806

Present–

Robert Barnwell–	J. G Barnwell,	J M. Verdier
J H. Cuthbert	A Campbell Sen[r]–	Ves Men–
		E Barnwell C. W.

The Vestry having received the following resolution Viz–
Resolved that the Vestry of this Church do, in the name of its members, forthwith write circular letters to the Vestries of the several Episcopal Churches throughout this State, recommending to them to convene their respective Congregations to determine on the mode of Electing delegates to represent them in the convention of the Protestant Episcopal Churches to be held in S[t] Michaels Church Charleston on the 17th– day of Feb[y] next—
Therefore. Resolved that the Church Wardens do summon the

[1]Interlined above Robert Barnwell is Q[ly]; above Guerard is Qu[ly]; above Verdier is Qu[ly]; above Grayson is Qua[ly]; above Cuthbert is Q[ly]; above John G. Barnwell is Q[ld]; above Campbell is Q[ly] and above Edward Barnwell is Qu[ly].

members of the Episcopal Church to meet at the Church in Beaufort between the hours of 11 & 1 to morrow A. M– to chuse delegates for the above purpose—

[299]

At a Meeting of the Members of the Episcopal Church in Beaufort on Feb[y] 11th– 1806 for the purpose of Electing delegates to meet a convention in Charles-ton on the 17th. Instant-

Edward Barnwell was appointed Chairman The Chairman having read the following letter——

Charles-ton Dec[r]- 3. 1805.

Gentlemen

At a meeting of the members of S[t] Philips=Church, in this City, in August last, the enclosed by-law was adopted, accompanied with a resolve, we have also the honor of enclosing you.

It must have long been manifest to those who are attached to the Protestant Episcopal Church within the United states, that to maintain an uniformity in its doctrines, discipline & worship, it had become necessary for its professers to confederate, & frequently confer together. A National Ecclesiastical Convention was accordingly held in the City of Philadelphia. Provincial, or Diocesan Conventions have also been held in this state, since the year 1786: but the latter have never yet debated or confirmed the Canons agreed to by the former, or have they even established such articles of local regulation, as are essential to our mutual agreement. We will not confidently undertake to assign the causes which may have led to this indecision; but are nevertheless induced to believe they have arisen from an undue representation in our State Conven=[300]=tions, which have hitherto been either composed of the entire body of the vestries of certain of the Churches, of a delegation from others; or of a deputation by Vestries, of persons not members of their body. Whereas we know of no instance amongst us wherein the Vestry of any Episcopal Church are empowered by Law, or have been otherwise authorized, to adopt a constitutional system of government, without the intervention of their constituents. In recurring to the journals of the state convention, in Oc-1797- we found it was on the 19th. of the last mentioned period– "Resolved that as four churches only are represented at this "meeting, it be recommended to the Episcopal Churches of this "state, to convene their respective congregations, & elect three "Deputies from each Church, to meet the State Convention of "Episcopal Churches, on the thursday after the third wednes-"day in October, to form a constitution, for the government of "the aforesaid churches

Our own minutes also testify that this recommendation was fully approved of by the vestry on the 15th. July 1798. they how-ever afford no information why it has hitherto been unattended to, but so thoroughly convinced were the members of our Church that no efficient system of general polity would ensue, untill a Convention was constituted, conformable to the recommendation of such of the Members of Vestries, as were convened on the 19th. Oc- [301] tober 1797– that they have chosen by ballot, from among the Congregation, five Delegates, to represent them, in conjunction with our ministers, in the convention of the Protestant Episcopal Churches of this State. And we confidently trust that each of our sister churches will readily concur in a measure which promises to perpetuate our mutual welfare, & happy agreement; with the respect which is due to your relig-ious, & private characters,

We remain Gentlemen
Your very obt- humble servants–
for the Vestry of St. Philips Church
Keating Simons, Chairman

On motion, Resolved that three persons be appointed to repre-sent this Church in a Convention of the Protestant Episcopal Churches to be held in St. Michaels Church Charles-ton on the 17th. Instant–

Resolved– That the Delegates so to be Elected shall be & are hereby vested with full powers, give their assent to all such things as may come before the Convention which may in their opinion conduce to the Interest of the said Episcopal Churches-Provided Nevertheless that the assent of such delegates shall not bind this Congregation unless confirmed within three months thereafter- by a majority of its members–

Upon proceeding to an Election, the Revd. Mr G. Hicks Robert Barnwell & Wm. Robertson were duly Elected [302] Delegates for the above purpose–

On motion, it was Resolved– That a majority or either of

the above Delegates shall be & are hereby authorized & empowered to represent this Church subject to the foregoing restrictions—

E Barnwell Chairman—

At a meeting held at the Episcopal Church on Easter Monday the 7th. April 1806– the following gentlemen were Elected as Vestry men & Church Wardens– for the ensuing year–

Vestry Men

Robert Barnwell Qd- - J. Gibbes Barnwell Q
J. H. Cuthbert Qd- J. M. Verdier
Jacob Guerard Q Thomas Grayson Q.
Dr. Campbell Q- C- W.- E Barnwell Q & Ralph Elliott—

At a meeting of the Vestry on Monday May 26th. 1806.

Present

Robert Barnwell- John Gibbes Barnwell
James H Cuthbert Jacob Guerard
Dr. Campbell Thomas Grayson
E Barnwell C. Warden—

The Vestry having received some papers of consequence from the standing committee of the Episcopal Churches in Charleston-

Resolved. That a meeting of the members of this Church [303] be held on Monday June 9th– 1806 for the purpose of taking them into Consideration—

The Meeting was put-off untill Monday the 23 when the members of the Church having mett agreable to adjournment appointed Ed Barnwell- Chairman- and then proceeded to the consideration of the following Letter–

To the Vestry, Wardens, & other Members of the Church in Beaufort-

Gentlemen–

At a meeting of the standing committee, appointed by the late Convention of the Protestant Episcopal Churches in this state, it was unanimously, Resolved That the following resolutions of the Convention, should be printed, and forwarded to the several Churches, together with the enclosed rules; which by order of the Convention are now transmitted to you: viz–

Resolved– "That a standing Committee be appointed, to con-

"sist of four Clergymen, & five Laymen; to continue in office "untill the next annual meeting of the State Convention: which "Committee shall exercise all the powers vested in them by the "Canons made in general Conventions: Provided, That the Com- "mittee so appointed shall have no power to act in any cases, "which may require the operation of Canons, repugnant to the "Charters of any of the Episcopal Churches in the State;"

Resolved– "That the standing Committee be directed

[304]

Dr.- - - - - Edward Barnwell Church Warden

		£	s	d
1806	Cr. brought over as Verdier open'd his acco on the wrong side	£1563,,	5,,	6
	To Cash pd. sink &c Parsonage.....	13,,	18..	4
	To John Bold Junr. & Co Oil & Paint. Church	13,,	14	,,
	To Ralph Elliott.....3 Kegs white lead	5,,	5,,	
	do-.. do......12 lb lead for the caps		6,,	
	do-.. do...convention Charleston	2,,	6,,	8.
Feby....	Abram Hall. ½ years salary, singing–	11,,	13,,	4.
May	Cash pd Brister	1,.	9,,	2
August.	Abram Hall. ½ years salary....	11,,	13,,	4.
Sepr. 1	Cash pd Brister	1,,	8,,	7.
2	do. Robert Houston, President's house	13,,	10,,	11–
	do Revd. Mr. Hicks............	35,,	,,	—
	do- Estate of Ts. Talbird on acct of College	48,,	3,,	3,–
1807	do: do of Mc.Callister in full Church yard	61,,	11,,	4.
Feby.	Abram Hall ½ ys. salary.......	11,,	13,,	4
March 1.	Cash pd Brister	2,,	0,,	3–
	do- Firth boring caps painting Gates & Paint oil	16,,	5,,	8–
	do- Revd: Mr. Hicks	257,,		,, –
		£2070,,	4,,	8
	Carried Forward–			

[305]

Account — — — — — — — — — — — — — — — — — — Cr:

1806	Dr. brought over	£1504,,	6,,	11
	By Cash recd– of Mrs. Talbird 2 ys. asses. Pew–	10,,		,,
	By John Rhodes.......... do....do	10		
	By Estate John Barnwell– do....do.	10		
	By Stephen Lawrence....Interest..	11,.	4,,	—
	do......do......2 ys. ass. Pew	10,,		,,
	By John Mk: Verdier.....Interest..	14,,	14,,	
	do charg'd do already	0	0	0
	By John A Cuthbert..... 1. do....	5,,		,,
	By James Stuart.. 1. bond...... 2 ys. Interest	22,,	8	,, –
	do – do... 1. do.... do....	17,.	1,.	6.
	do– – – do........1 yr. assess...	5,,		,,—
	By Estate John Joiner...2... do...	10,,		,,—
	By Ralph Elliott. principal & Interest	30,,	1,,	8
	do- - do..........2 ys. assess....	10,,		,,—
	Philip Givens. Interest 2 bonds...	33,.	14	,, 8.
	Charles Stewart.. do... 1 year..	11,,	1,,	2
	Wm. Hutson Wigg....Pew..2 ys. assessment	10,,		,,–
	Mrs. Ann Bull..... do.... do....	10,,		,,
	Robert Houston...Int. 3 years....	16,,	16,,	—
	Michael Perriclear. Pew ass's. 1. do in full	5,,		,,
	Frederick Fraser.. bond & Intest. in full............... do- - do. Wm. Joiners Pew Tax 1 year }	102,,	6	,,8-
	Estate James Scanlan 1 bond & Int. in full	73,,	3,,	9
Sepr. 5- 1807	.do........ do. part. Prin. 2. do & do—do..–	43,,	3,,	10
	Jacob Guerard- 3 ys. assessment. Pew tax £5.	15	,,	,, –
	Estate John Joiner..1 do.–...do..	5,,		,,
	William Joiner...2 do..........	10,,		,,
	Robert Barnwell..1 do.........	5,,		,,
	Carried Forward–	£2010	2	2

[306]
"to open a correspondence with the several Churches throughout this state, which may be destitute of ministers; offering "them such assistance, as may tend to the promotion of the "spiritual interests of the said Churches:—"

Resolved— "That the standing Commitee do take proper measures, to notify to each Church in this State, the time and place "of holding the next Convention; and transmit, when printed, "the rules, as concurred in by the Convention."

Resolved. "That the several officiating ministers of the Episcopal Churches throughout the state, be earnestly requested to "visit, from time to time, or as often as circumstances may "admit, and hold divine service in, such Churches as may be "destitute of ministers."

The foregoing resolutions will, we trust, Gentlemen, be a sufficient explanation of the purposes for which the Committee has been appointed. We have it in charge, to assure you, that the rules, which, agreably to the third of these resolutions, are herewith transmitted, did not pass the Convention, without the most serious consideration; and that, whilst it has been their object, by the union of the respective Churches of this State, under the authority of these rules, to endeavour to revive among them that order and discipline which are indispensable to their existence; the most scrupulous caution has been observed, lest any privilege should be violated which may be held by any churches under [307] Charters granted by the Legislature of the State. We trust therefore, that the strictest scrutiny, into the principles on which these rules are founded, and the objects to which they are directed, will discover to you nothing, either in the one or the other, that can induce you to withhold your concurrence in their adoption. Under this impression, we entreat your early and serious attention to them; and shall anxiously wait your determination on the subject of their ratification. By the preamble it will appear, that six months, from the first of the present month, are allowed, for the determination of the Churches respecting them, to be signified to the standing Committee. In the meantime, we take the liberty to request, that such determination may be transmitted to us, within that period.

On the subject of the second of the above resolutions, we have only to observe, that, in conformity to the injunction it lays on us, we are ready to receive any communication on the subjects referred to in the said resolution.

The Clergy (who agreably to the last of the same resolutions, have been requested to visit, and perform divine service in, vacant Churches) having cheerfully acquiesced in the wish of the convention, only wait the assurance of their Brethren in the Country, that the offer of their services will be acceptable; and they will, accordingly make arrangements for carrying the resolution as far as possible, into effect.

Respectfully requesting the earliest possible [308] answer to our communication (addressed to the Chairman of the Committee–)

We remain, Gentlemen, with the sincerest wishes for both your spiritual & temporal welfare–

Your obedient humble servants

Ed Jenkins. Chairman Wm. Peircy–	Clerical Members
M. Pogson N. Bowen	standing Commitee—
Thomas Roper Wm. Doughty John Dawson Junr– Peter Smith David Alexander	Lay members standing Commitee—

P- S– It may be necessary to inform such Churches as were not represented in the late Convention held in Feby last, that it consisted of the following Delegates, from eight Parishes–

St. Philips –	Red- Dr. Jenkins, rector-	St Michaels	R. W Percy-
	Wm. Smith		N Bowen Rector
	Thomas Roper		Ths. Parker
	Keating Simons		J. Dawson Junr.
	Charles B. Cochran		D Alexander
	Robert Dewar-		T. Waring Senr–
St. Andrews–	John- S- Cripps		Wm. H. Gibbes
	Simon Magwood		R. Hazelhurst
St James Goose-creek.	Rev Mr Pogson		G. Reid
	Peter Smith		J. M. Ward
	David Deas-		J. Potter—
St Johns Berkley–	Henry Laurence –	Georgetown–	
	Peter Broughton		Samuel Wragg–
			Paul Trapier

[309]

Beaufort- -Robert Barnwell- W[m]. Robertson St. Bartholomews- Ric[d]. Singleton- John Bellinger-

The Chairman then read the following rules & regulations for the government of the Protestant Episcopal Church in the State of South Carolina

Whereas, in all societies, professing Christianity, the promotion of Religion should primarily engage their sincere attention; as being the sure and only means of rendering them acceptable to Almighty God, and calling down his blessing upon them: And,

Whereas, by general conventions of the protestant Episcopal Churches in the United States of America, a Constitution and Canons, have been formed, for the government and discipline of the same:—

Be it therefore Resolved, That the following rules be agreed to, adopted and observed, by the protestant Episcopal Churches in this State; for the local government of the same; which rules shall be considered binding upon all the protestant Episcopal Churches in this State, which shall not, within six months after the first day of March 1806, notify to the standing Committee, their dissent therefrom

Rule 1st- A stated Convention shall be held annually, in Charles-ton, on the third Monday in every February or at such time, and in such place, as shall have been determined upon by the preceeding Convention; But if a [310] sufficient number of the Churches associated, do not attend on the same day; the representatives, whether Clergy, or Laity, of any two of them assembled, shall have power to adjourn from day to day, untill a quorum is formed; which shall consist of at least seven Churches.

Rule. 2nd- Delegates shall be elected by the respective Episcopal Churches throughout the state, to represent them in the State Convention: The Delegates to be elected in such manner, time and numbers, as each Church may deem proper, to serve twelve months from the time of Election: who shall; before they are permitted to take their Seats in Convention, produce written testimonials of their Election.

Rule 3rd– The officiating Clergy of the Protestant Episcopal Churches of this State, shall be deemed, ex officio, Members of this Convention.

Rule 4th- When a sufficient number of Members have assembled, to form a Convention, they shall elect a President, from among themselves.

Rule 5th– A Secretary and Treasurer shall be annually chosen, who shall keep a true and correct journal of the proceedings, and regular accounts of any money transactions; to be annually laid before the Convention: It shall, also, be his duty to give notice to each Minister and Vestry of the time and place appointed for any extra or special Convention.

[311]

Rule 6th– A standing Commitee, consisting of such a number of Clergymen and Laymen, as the Convention may think proper, shall be annually Elected, for the purposes expressed in the Constitution and Canons; Provided the Committee so appointed, have no power to act in any cases which require the operation of any Canons repugnant to the Charters of any of the protestant Episcopal Churches of this State. Vacancies in the Commitee, caused by death, resignation, or otherwise shall be supplied by the suffrages of the remaining Members.

Rule 7th– It shall be the business of the standing Commitee, when informed by the Vestry of either of the Churches in this State, that such Church is not provided with a Minister, (in which information, the means which the Church has of supporting a Minister shall be stated) diligently to enquire for, and recommend to the Vestry, giving such information, a proper person to officiate in the said Church; and they shall report to the Convention at each annual meeting, what information of vacancies they have received, and their proceedings thereon.

Rule 8th– In all matters requiring the suffrages of the Convention, the representatives of each Church shall vote conjointly; each Church having one vote, and a majority of votes shall be decisive.

Rule 9th– The approving or receiving any Clergyman [312] into a Church, shall be vested in the vestry of the Church (or the Vestry and Church Wardens as the case may be) having authority so to do; and where there is no Vestry, or Vestry and Church Wardens, having such authority, in the Congregation that supports him, and receives the benefits of his Ministry. Provided that no Clergyman shall be admitted to the pastoral charge of any Church of this association, unless he first produces to the

Vestry, having such authority, or the Vestry and Church Wardens, as the case may be sufficient and approved testimonials of his having received full orders from a Bishop of the Protestant Episcopal Church.

Rule 10th- Wilful error in religion, or deviation from the Rubrick of the Church; charges of viciousness of life, and disorderly behaviour, may be exhibited against a Clergyman, to the state Convention; and on clear and sufficient proof thereof, by viva voce Evidence, on oath, duly administred, in the Convention, or by a commission to take such Evidence, duly executed, such Clergyman shall be excluded the Convention: and the Convention shall request of the Vestry or Congregation of the Church, in which he officiates at the time, to dismiss from the charge of their charge, for the reasons before mentioned; and also to inform the Bishop, and if there be no Bishop, the standing Commitee; which Bishop, or standing Commitee shall inform the board of Bishops of the Protestant Epis=[313]=copal Church in the United States of America, that such Clergyman is an improper person to officiate in the sacred order of Priest or Deacon, in any Protestant Episcopal Church

Rule 11th- Every Minister of the protestant Episcopal Church in this State, shall keep a Register of Births, Baptisms, Marriages and Funerals; and shall, likewise, every year, deliver in the State Convention, a fair and correct copy of the register of the Church wherein he officiates, to the President, in order that it may be recorded in the Secretary of States office, for the further safety and preservation of the same.

Rule 12th. It shall be the business of the standing Committee to call a meeting of the Convention, whenever they shall deem it necessary; and they shall report their proceedings to the succeeding Convention, to be confirmed or rescinded.

Rule 13th- The Delegates of the several Churches to the State Convention, shall, during the intervals of the Convention, be corresponding Committees, intrusted with the duty of informing the standing Committee of the situation of their respective Churches; and generally, such other things as may relate to the temporal and spiritual interests of the protestant Episcopal Churches in this State—

Rule 14th- No article, Canon, Rule, or other regulation of any general or State Convention, shall be obligatory on any Episcopal Church within this State, where the same [314] shall be found to infringe on any of its chartered rights.

Rule 15th– To the intent, that the Church in this State, may not be unrepresented in general Convention, the clerical and Lay Delegate or Delegates, who may be hereafter nominated thereto, shall on the absence of one or more of their colleagues, be empowered to nominate and appoint in place of such absent Delegate or Delegates, any citizen or citizens of this State; provided that such citizen or citizens, is, or are, a member or Members of the Episcopal Church in this State.

Rule 16th– The Book of common prayer, and administration of the Sacraments and other rites and Ceremonies of the Church, according to the use of the protestant Episcopal Church in the United States of America, shall be used in all the Churches of this association—

Rule 17th– None of the foregoing Rules shall be altered nor shall any new Rule be adopted, unless the alterations, or new Rule, or rules proposed, shall be concurred in by two thirds of the Churches in Convention; seven, at least of the Churches of the State, by their Delegates, being present

These rules were unanimously agreed to, & the Church Wardens directed to write to the standing Commitee their Concurrence thereto

Ed Barnwell Chairman

[315]

Feby. 2– 1807– The Vestry mett agreable to the publick notification

Present–

Robert Barnwell– Dr– Campbell– Jacob Guerard–
James Cuthbert Senr– Thomas Grayson– Vestry men– —
E Barnwell– C. Warden–

When they proceeded to the appointment of delegates to the State Episcopal Convention when Robert Barnwell William Robertson & Thomas Deveaux Esqrs– were duly Elected–

Resolved– That the Church Warden give a Certificate of such Election authorizing any one or more of the said Members to act for the Parish of St Helena in the Convention to be held in Charles-ton on the sixteenth instant–

A vacancy having happened in the office of C. Warden by the death of Mr Ralph E. Elliott- upon an Election Mr Sn– Deveaux was chosen in his room–

The Reverend M[r] Hicks having offered the following Books to the Vestry as a Library for the Church-
Resolved- That the Church Wardens accept the same and discount the the amount from the Church money now in his hands—

[316]

The following are the books bought of the Rev[d] M[r] Hicks

The Book of Common prayer..................	Folio	
Shephard on the... d°........................		
Wheatleys Illustration of the book of- d°.		
Jenks Meditations	2 Volumes.	
Horn on the Psalms	2.	d°-
Ket- on the Prophecies	2.	d°-
Campbell on the Miracles	2.	d°
Gilpin on the New Testament	2.	d°-
Stanhopes Epistles & Gospels	4	d°-
Jones' figurative Language		
Porteous Lectures		
Prettyman's Christian Theology,	2	d°-
Paley's Evidences	2	d°-
Watsons Tracts	6	d°
Religious- d°	12	d°
Scholar Armed.	2	d°
Cruden's Concordance		
London Cases	3-	d°
Scripture Lexicon		
Daubeney's Guide		
Nelsons Fasts & Festivals		
Seekers Lectures		
Wilsons Parochiala		
Glasses Lectures		
Ogdens Sermons		
Ogdens Antidote to Deism	2	d°
D[r] Belguys divine Benevolence		
Simeons Helps	5	
Companion to the Altar		
D[r] Craven's Discourses		
Hewletts Sermons		

[318[1]]

Dr- Edward Barnwell Church Warden– Acct

		£	s	d
1807	brought over	£2070,,	4,,	8
	To Cash pd Mulheron & Flynn act			
	College	34,,	10,,	—
	do. Mr. Paulson for schooling.			
	Farris	4,,	5,,	—
	do- -1 M bricks & freight......	4,.	4,,	—
	do– 8 C do —— do	3,,	7,.	8
June 1.	Cash pd- Brister - - - - - - - - - - -	1,.	7,.	3–
August	Abram Hall ½ ys Salary, singing	11,,	13,,	4
Octr- -	Cash pd- Brister	1,,	11,,	6
	do Abram Hall ½ ys Salary in			
	full	11,,	13,,	4–
1808	Stephen Laurence, Blacksmiths bill	1,,	10,,	4
		2144	,,7	1
	Ballance due by Edrd. Barnwell	12,.	5,.	6
	£	2156..	12.	7

[1]Page 317 is blank.

Current Cr—

1807	brought over	£2010,,	2,,	2
	Mrs. Ann Bull 1 ys. assessment Pew	5,,	,,	
	Edward Barnwell. do do 1805	5,,		,,—
	Dr. Archibald Campbell. 2 ys. do....	10.		
	John Gibbes Barnwell— 1. do...	5,,		,,–
	John Rhodes ....1 do...	5,,		
	Estate Thomas Talbird.. 1 do...	5,,		,,—
	Joseph Jonston–Interest- 1 do-.1806..	5,,	14,,	4—
	James B. Finley- 2 bonds. Int do- in full	53,,	7,,	9.
	Robert Houston ....do- - -	5,,	12,,	-
	James Bowman. 2 ys Interest in full	11,,	4,,	—
	Stephen Lawrence–1– do.........	11,,	4—	
	do do- 1 ys. assessment....	5,,	,,	
	David Campbell- 1/2- do- do. Js Stuarts pew	2,,	10,,	
	Philip Givins, Interest in part.....	11,,	4,,	-
	Joseph Johnson– do......do. 1807..	5,,	14,,	4—
	£	2156	,,12	,,7
	Balance Brought down	 12–	5..	6
	Balance Brought from acco Current in 1790	.... 33.	15.	3
	To acct- having been opened by my Father as Chh. Warden for yr. 1808 and a credit having been given by him for $47.40 on the back of a Bond of Wm Smith's to the Church; As Extr- to his Est- I acknowledge the same amt- to be due by the Estate– Edwd Barnwell Extr- Est- Col- E Barnwell	11	,, 1	,, 2

By consent of the Vestry a Note for the above balances, say Two hundred and forty four Dollars 69½/100 was taken from Edw[d] Barnwell Ex[tr] Es[t] E Barnwell Bearing In[t]. from 15th August 1815—
This Note with its Interest was paid by me on 15th Feb 1816——
Edw[d] Barnwell

[320]

March 16th– 1807. At a meeting of the Vestry & Church Wardens
Present

Robert Barnwell	Archibald Campbell
Jacob Guerard	Thomas Grayson
John G Barnwell— —	Vestry men

E[d] Barnwell & Thomas Deveaux— C. W

On motion—Resolved that the Church Wardens give public notification requesting the particular attendance of all members of the Episcopal Church on Easter Monday the 30th. of March as business of Importance will be laid before them, the Meeting will be from 10 o– clock until two– A M– The Election of Church Officers will take place on that day—

At a Meeting held at the Episcopal Church on Easter Monday the 30th– of March- 1807- the following Gentlemen were Elected as Vestry Men & Church Wardens– for the ensuing year-

Vestry Men—

Robert Barnwell	D Campbell
John M. Verdier	Thomas Grayson
John G. Barnwell	Jacob Guerard
James H. Cuthbert-	

Edward Barnwell & Thomas Deveaux—C. W

[321]

They then Elected Edward Barnwell Sen[r]. Chair–Man for the purpose of declaring who should be Church Members
On Motion– Resolved that every male white person having attained the age of twenty one years, whose profession of religion is that of the Protestant Episcopal Church of the United States of America; and who holds a Pew, or part of a Pew, paying assessment, or rent for the same, in any sum not less than four dollars p[r] Annum, shall be deemed a supporting member of this

Church; and the family of every such person be considered as belonging thereto; and the Son or Sons of such supporting Member, together with the son, or sons of any widow, belonging to this Church, paying assessment, or rent, as aforesaid, shall if resident in the family of such supporting member, or widow, being of full age, and of the Protestant Episcopal Church, be also regarded as members, and shall be entitled to vote at all Elections of this corporation.

At a meeting of the Vestry & C. Wardens- Feb^y^– 8th– 1808

Present

Robert Barnwell— J. H Cuthbert

Archibald Campbell Senr– Thomas Grayson

E Barnwell Senr. C. W–

Agreable to a notification from C^s^.ton, they proceeded to an election for delegates to the State Episcopal convention, when the Rev^d^. M^r^. Galen Hicks, Thomas Deveaux & W^m^. Robertson were duly Elected & the C. W desired to give them certificates

[322]

March 14th- 1808, At a Meeting of the Vestry & C. Wardens—

Present

Robert Barnwell- - - - - D^r^. Campbell—

Jacob Guerard– John. G. Barnwell–

E Barnwell Sen. Th^s^ Deveaux C. W-

M^r^. John Mulheron by his petition; informing us that three fourths of his Lot (N) bought of us in June 22nd– 1802, was in the pond known by the name of Wyers pond–

Resolved that fifty pounds shall be taken off the purchase money

At a meeting held at the Episcopal Church on monday april 18th. 1808 to elect vestry men and Church Wardens the following Gentlemen were Elected—

Vestry Men

Arch^d^. Campbell Tho. Grayson.

John. M. Verdier Stephen Elliott

Jacob Guerard John. G. Barnwell

Ja^s^. H. Cuthbert

Robert Barnwell & Tho. Deveaux C. W

[323]

At a meeting of the vestry & Church Wardens april 19th- 1808 the following were present and duly Qualified

Vestry	Church Wardens
James H. Cuthbert	Robert Barnwell
Thomas Grayson	Tho. Deveaux
John M. Verdier	
John G. Barnwell	

On motion resolved. that the Church wardens are hereby authorized to settle with Captn. Francis Saltus upon his paying at the rate of Five pounds ℔ anno. for the two Pews he holds in the Church for the last four years—

Resolved that the Pew rent of the present year shall be Five Pound. for each Pew. except the two small Pews of Captn. Francis Saltus, which are hereby rated at two pounds ten shillings each,—

Resolved that for the present year and until otherwise directed the mode of assessing the Pews of the Church shall be as follows, on or before the second monday after Easter monday each Pew holder shall be required forthwith to pay the sum assess'd or to give his note for the amount thereof, which shall be dated the January preceeding and made payable the January following bearing Interest from the date, which notes if not paid when they become due shall be directly put in suit for recovery

Resolved that in case the Pew holders neglect or refuse to pay such assessment or to give notes for the same [324] as above directed, that in that case on the seccond monday after the monday aforesaid. the Church Wardens shall proceed (after giving Public notice thereof) to rent for one Year from the first of april in each year the Pew of such holder thereof. and shall take a note or money for the same in the manner and on the conditions above recited, provided that should the same Pews when rented not meet the sum assess'd the Church Wardens at their discretion may purchase in such Pew or Pews on account of the Church and report the same to the vestry—

Resolved that the Church Wardens forthwith demand notes for the assessment of the Pews now due to bear Interest from april the first 1808 payable in January 1809 and if unpaid to be recovered as above directed—

Resolved that the Church Wardens demand notes to bear Interest from the first of april 1808 payable the first of January 1809 for the Interest due on the Church Bonds and should any of the Persons indebted to the Church, neglect or refuse to give such notes, in that case the Church Wardens are hereby directed forthwith to put their bonds in suit, and the said notes if unpaid when they become due shall be put in suit as above directed—

Resolved that the Church Wardens are hereby directed and authorized to liquidate the demands of the [325] Reverend M^{r}. Hicks against the Church. and to give a bond or bonds in behalf of the vestry for the amount due him up to the first day of January 1808 bearing Interest—

Resolved that the Church Wardens are hereby directed and authorized to liquidate the demands of the heirs of the Rev^{d}. m^{r}. Lewis against the Church and to settle the same either by an assignment of notes due the Church or in money as they can best arrange it—

[326]

The Church in

Date		Particulars	£	s	d
1808					
May	2	Paid Bristol for Ringing the Bell & other Services	£ 2..	10..	11
Jun	11	Paid Mr Colcock on acc debt due Graves as ℔ R. ——— ———			
		Paid do– – – – — d:— — — d– – –	70,,	,,	
Sep	1	Paid Bristol for ringing Bell &c- - -	1..	11..	6
	9	Paid Mr Colcock on acc debt due Mr Graves as ℔ receipt.	176,,	3,.	4
Dec		Paid Bristol for ringing the Bell—	1..	8	
		Ballance in R. Barnwells hands- - -	17.	18	3
		£	292..	18.	8
1809					
April		– – – – – — — £			
		Paid for revd Dr Percy's Books	3..	5..	4
		P Ballance Judgment ag Church by Mr Graves–	22,,	17.	4
August	10	Paid Mr Joyner as by Mr Walls rec on Debt to Mr Lewis $200	46	13.	4
Novr.		Paid Mr Hicks - - - - - - - - - - —	128,,	6	8
		£	201,,	2	8
		Balance due By R. B— —	63,.	0,.	6
		£	264,,	3,	2

[327]

Acc with Rot. Barnwell & Tho Deveaux Wardens

1808					
Api	28	Rec[d] of M[rs] Ann Stuart for Pew Rent of this Year £	5,.		,,
May	24	Re. of M[r] Bedon by the hands of Tho. Deveaux this Sum for rest of D[r] Stuarts Pew - - - - -	5,,	,,	
June	14	Rec from M[r] Bythwood for Leacrafts Pew - - - - - - - - - - - -	5,,	,,	
	21	Rec of M[rs] Gough on acc of Interest on her Bond—	4.	13..	4
	..	Rec of R Barnwell on acc Interest due—by Estate N Barnwell.	4,.	13,.	4
		Rec of R. Barnwell on ac. - — - - -	9..	6..	2
		Rec on acc of Interest due by M[r] Cook - - - - - - - - - - - - - - - - -	3,.	5..	4
Sep	5	Rec of M[rs] Elliott on acc Interest due by Ex W[m] Elliott- - - - - - - -	70,.	,,	
	9	Rec of M[r] Philip Givins for one bond of £160. and Interest from Jun 1809 — — — — — — —	164.	13.	4
	9	Rec two years Interest to Jun on Bond of £81- for d[o] - - - - -	11..	6..	8
			292..	18..	8.
1809					
Ap		By Balance due this day — — — —	17.	18.	3
		red one years Interest from Joseph Johnson on Bond	5..	14–	4
Jun	19	Rec[d] from Philip Givins on Bond - -	70,,	,,	
		R. from d[o] Bond in full $65 57/100	15,.	5–	6–
Oct		Ri from A Stuart on acc[t] Interest - -	8,,	19,,	
Oct-	19-	R from M[r] John Porteous on acc Int on his Bond - - - - - - - - - - - -	19..	19–	5
		rec'd from M[r] Guerard Pew rent p[d] M[r] Bullock - - - - - - - - - - -	5,,		
Oct		rec from M[rs] William Elliott acc Int[t] on Bond - - - - - - - - - - - - -	107..	6.	8
		rec of rev M[r] Cooke on acc[t] Interest -	14,,	,,	
		£	264	,,3	,, 2

[328]

At a Meeting held at the Episcopal Church on Monday March 20, 1809—

Present.	Wardens
Dr A Campbell	Rot Barnwell
Jacob Guerard	Th. Deveaux–
John M Verdier	
James H. Cuthbert	
John G Barnwell	

Resolved that the Church Wardens do authorise the Sheriff to suspend the Sale of the Lotts belonging to the Estate of Charles Capers which were sold on the last sale day and bought by C. Gabriel Capers untill the sale day in May. Provided that C. Gabriel Capers do pay the Interest due on the Bond in full with Costs and give ample security for the payment of the Principal in Six months—
Resolved that the Church Wardens be directed to raise a New acct to the Creditt of the Pew Tax and to transfer bonds to the amount of what appears to be paid on this acct up to this day. according to a statement herein made [329] and which is as follows Vitz—

1790–	Paid by Sundries on acc of Pew Tax in this year	£63..16.6
1791.	Paid by do— – d d — – – d – –	22.17.6
1793..	Paid by do	14.3–6.
1796	Paid by d	41..15..6
1801	Paid by d	59–19.6
1802	Paid by d	40..14–0
1803-	Paid by d	15..0.0
1805.	Paid by d	36.10..0
1806–	Paid by d	130..0–0
1807–	Paid by d	42..10–0
		£467..6..6–

Accordingly. Bonds for the above amount were especially assigned the Church Wardens in compliance with the above resolution.

At a Meeting held at the Episcopal Church on Easter Monday

the following persons were elected Vestry Men and Church Warden viz,

D^{r} A Campbell Jacob Guerard J. M. Verdier James H. Cuthbert Jh G– Barnwell Robt Barnwell	Vestry	John Rhodes John McKee	Wardens

Mr Rhodes being about to leave the State and Coll Robt Barnwell declining to act as a Vestry Man Thereupon

[330]

An Election was held on Monday 11 July when Mr John Rhodes was chosen a vestry Man and Coll Robt Barnwell a Church Warden. on Motion

Resolved. That all Sums hereafter rec^{d} on acc^{t}. of the Assessment of the Pews. shall constitute a separate and Distinct acc^{t}. to the Creditt of the Church—

The rev^{d} Mr Hicks having requested leave of absence on Acc^{t} of health. at a Meeting of the Vestry held July 13.

Present

Jacob Guerard J. M Verdier Dr Campbell	John G. Barnwell J. H' Cuthbert.	Rot Barnwell J. McKee	Wardens

On Motion resolved. That the rev^{d} Mr Hicks have leave of absence for Six or Eight weeks—

Resolved. That the Church Wardens give each Debtor to the Church Notice. That unless the Interest due upon their respective Bonds be paid by 1 Ja^{y} 1810 that their respective Bonds shall forthwith be placed in a Lawyers hands for recovery..

On Motion resolved that the Asessment of the present year be Five Pound payable in advance or by Note bearing an Interest from Ja^{y} 1809—

[331]

At a meeting of the Vestry held on Monday 7. Jany 1810

Present

Mr John Rhodes	Mr John M Verdier
Mr James Cuthbert	M John G. Barnwell
Mr Jacob Guerard	M^{r}. Stephen Elliott

Resolved That M[r] J M. Verdier M[r] Jacob Guerard wait upon the rev[d] M[r] Hicks and inform him that the Funds of the Church compell them to reduce his Salary to the Sum of Twelve Hundred dollars p[r] Annum. the Reduction to commence from the first of April

And Whereas a Petition was presented signed by the greater part of the Members of the Church requesting the appointment of the rev[d] John Barnwell Campble as an Assistant Minister in the Church and stating their willingness to defray the expences of his Salary. On Motion

Resolved that the said Petition be shewn M[r] Hicks stating the approbation of the Vestry. And that the abovementioned Gentlemen wait upon M[r] Campble and request his acceptance of the s[d] appointment–

[332]
The Church in acc

1810			
	Paid acc due Mr Verdier by order of Vestry - - - - - - - - - - - - - - - -	60,	10
	Paid rev^d^ Mr Hicks - - - - - - - - - - -	600–	
M.	Paid Tho Deveaux advance to Talbird- -	4.	75
	Paid rev^d^ Mr Hicks on acc Salary 1809. & Int. — — — — — — — — — — — — —	1517,.	50
	Paid d^o^ — d on acc. of Bond due - - -	666..	90
	P d — d — d — — —	569–	73
Apri. 23	P d d d	268..	69
	$	3.687–	67
	Brought down — — — — — — — — — $	3.687–	67
	Paid Mr Hicks — — — — — — — — — —	724	
	Paid Alex. Brown on acc^t^ work Parsonag Hous	15	
	P d^o^ – on acc^t^. work to the Church Steps = - - - - - - - - - - - - - -	39–	50
	P. R. Mr Hicks on acc^t^ Bond- - - - - -	152–	50
	$	4.618	67
	Paid for a Trunk for Papers — — — —	4–	

[333]

with Rob[t] Barnwell Curch Warden

1810		$	
	Re from John M. Verdier on acc[t] Interest on Bond - - - - - - - - - - - -	60..	10
	Ballance Due by R. Barnwell — — —	267–	96
	Rec. Interest on M[r] Fullers Bond & Note to April 1810 - - - - - - - - - - - -	341.	60
	Rec. from Maj Lawrence on acc of Ints' on Rich Ellis Bond - - - - - - - - -	163.	41
March	Rec[d] from Jas. Haz. Cuthbert on acc[t] Interest on Bond and Note - - - - -	425..	98
	R. fr. Th. Deveaux Pew rent for 1808 - -	23,.	10
	Rec. on acc[t] Interest on Nath Barnwells Bond - - - - - - - - - - - - - - - - - -	379..	91
	Re. on acc[t] Interest on M[r] Goughs Bond-	358,,	
	Rec. on acc Interest on D[r] Finlays Bond	187..	60
	Red on acc[t] Interest on M[r] Mulherrons Bond - - - - - - - - - - - - - - - - - -	42..	98
	Red on acc[t] Interest on M[r] Flynns Bond-	88	20
	Red on acc[t] Interest on the Bond of Es[t]. D[r] Jas. Stuart - - - - - - - - - - - -	332..	61
	Rec. Note & Interest for Pew rent for for M[rs] Bull - - - - - - - - - - - - - - -	22,	93
	Rec d d d for E Edw Barnwell - - - - - - - - - - - - - - - - - -	22	93
	Red d d d for E Nath Barnwell	22	93
	Red Pew rent for 1809– for M[r] Bull - -	21	43
	Rd P d .d d for E Edw[d] Barnwell	21	43
	Re d d d for E Nath Barnwell	21,	43
Ja;	Rd from James Bowman Int[t] on Bond	24,,	
March	Re[d] from John Porteous Interest on Bond - - - - - - - - - - - - - - - - - -	323.	18
	r from W. Smith on ac[t] Intest- - - - -	288.	60
	rec[d] from Stephen Lawrence for d. —	96,,	
	rec from Moses Fuster on acc Int on Bond - - - - - - - - - - - - - - - - - -	158..	36
	$	3.687–	67

rec^d. from Mr Boman on acc^t. Int^t- - - - -	24–	
rec^d from Mrs Elliott on acc^t. Bond - - -	700	
re. from Alex. Brown on acc^t. Interest -	207–	
	$ 4..618	67
To an Error in Carrying the Balance from former Acco^t	$ 2..	14

[324]

At a Meeting of the vestry on Tuesday 6. Feby 1710–

Present

Mr John Rhodes
M^r J M Verdier
Mr Stephen Elliott
Capt. John G Barnwell
Mr Jacob Guerard

A letter was rec^d. from the re^d John Cample accepting of the place of Assistant offered him by the Vestry. Whereupon

Resolved That the Sum of One Thousand dollars be appropriated for the Salary of Mr Cample–

Resolved That the Church Wardens Forthwith open a Subscription for the Purpose of raising the aforesaid Salary or such parts thereof thereof as can be obtained–

Resolved That the Pew rent of the Present year be Thirty Dollars.

At a Meeting on Easter Monday 22^d. April 1810. the follg Persons was duly Elected for the year ensueing.

Robert Barnwell
Stephen Elliott
Arch^d Campbell
J^s. H Cuthbert.
J. M Verdier
Jacob Guerard
Jno G. Barnwell
} Vestry

John Rhodes
John McKee
} church wardens

[335]

12 August 1810– The vestry being Called at the Request of John Rhodes Church warden, who Stated to them the propriety of

having the Pews in the Church numbered, and also to purchase a Book for the purpose of keep^{g}– the Acco^{ts} of Pew Tax, and other Acco^{ts}. more dintinctly.—
Present.

Jacob Guerard John M Verdier Stephen Elliott & John G. Barnwell	Vestrymen	John Rhodes Church warden	

They Resolved, That the Church wardens be authorised to have the Pews in the Church Numbered, and to Purchase a Book for keeping the Accounts of the Church. Such a one as they Should Judge proper for said Purpose.—

Sep^{t}. 24th– Rec^{d} from M^{rs}– Elizh. Sams one Hundred dollars on acco^{t} of Pew Taxes for Jno- B- Barnwells Pew (N°. 27)

Monday 1st– Octr 1810, The vestry having been Called together, met this day to take into Consideration the State of the Church. and the walls Surrounding the Church yard, Present—

Robert Barnwell Archibald Campbell Stephen Elliott John Mark Verdier	Vestry.	John Rhodes John McKee	C Wardens

They agreed that the walls of the Church yard Shoud be immediately repaird in such a manner as the Church wardens shoud direc^{t}. and that a Subscription shoud be Sent forward to raise money for the Building of a New Church–

[336]

Beaufort 1st—October 1810— Doc^{t}—Findley presented an order from M^{rs}. Wall late widow of the Rev^{d} Mr Lewis for \$86.93 ¾/100—the same was immediately Paid.—

————————Beaufort 14th. October 1810———

The vestry & Church wardens were call'd together this day to take into their consideration the propriety of having a Charity Sermon preached the next Sundy and making a Collection at the Church doors for the Relief of the Sufferers of the late dreadfull fire in the City of Charleston, they came to the following Resolve.

Resolved. that the Reverands. Mess[rs]– Hixt & Campbell be requested to preach a Charity Sermon next Sunday. and that. Boxes be fixed at the Church doors for the purpose of Receiving donations

Beaufort 19th. October 1810– the vestry met this day to take into Consideration the necessity there was, either to Repair the Present Church or build a new one when upon motion

Resolved That the present Church is not only unsafe but is too Small if repaired for even our present Congregation; Therefore

Resolved

That the Church Wardens open a Subscription in order to raise as much money as Possible, which when Raised shall be appropriated in such manner as to enable the vestry to use their present Funds towards Building a new church, and such a proportion of the money subscribed in Aid thereof as the vestry at any time hereafter may see fit.—

Present	Robert Barnwell	Jacob Guerard	Vestry	Jn°. Rhodes	Ch. wardens
	Arch[d]– Campbell	Jn°. M Verdier		J M[c]Kee	
	James Cuthbert	J G. Barnwell			
		Steph[h] Elliott			

[337]

Beaufort S° Carolina 2nd– Jan[y] 1811

The vestry be called together, by M[r]. Robert Barnwell, the State of their church funds

Present	Robert Barnwell	Vestry		
	John G. Barnwell		John Rhodes	C W–
	Stephen Elliott		John M[c]Kee	
	Jacob Guerard			

on motion Resolved

That the Reverend M[r] Hixt be continued as Rector of the Church on the sames as last year.—

Resolved—That the Rev[d]– M[r]– Campbell be requested to remain as assistant minister as for the last year.—

Resolved That as the vestry are unable to continue Two ministers for a longer term than the present year, that an Election shall be Held on the First monday in October next for a minister of the Church.——

Resolved That a Copy of the above Resolutions be Transmitted to the Revd. Mr Hext & Revd. Mr. Campbell

Resolved that the Church wardens endeavour to obtain the Consent of the Former Subscribers for Raising a sallary for the Revd Mr Campbell. that the Subscription shoud remain for the present year & that they obtain what other sums in addition thereto they Can—

The Church wardens did according to the foregoing resolution, furnish the Revd Mr Hext & the Revd- Mr Campbell with a Copy of the Same–

In consequence of the foregoing notification to the Revd- Mr Hext the Vestry recd the following letter from Him, dated 23rd- Jany 1811—

[338]

Beaufort 23rd- Jany 1811

Gentlemen/

Whereas it appears from your Resolves at a meeting of the 2nd Inst. that you consider yourselves unable to Continue two Clergymen for a longer time than the present year, this, together with the favorable opinion I entertain of Mr Campbells qualifications to take Charge of my flock, and of his becoming a pastor whom it might be their delight to follow, constrains me to ask your concurrance with me in the resignation of my ministry at the Close of the year.–

Shoud I request the privilege of two or three months absence, after Mr Campbells return from the northward I request that the indulgence might be granted me—

That no obstacle may remain to prevent my departure as soon as I am at liberty, I request that, as early as the first monday in october a Settlement may be made with me for my Present years Sallary, & also that you will have the goodness to furnish me with suitable Testimonials.—

Having become a Subscriber towards the Building of a Church in Beaufort, which I shall probably never have the satisfaction of beholding, I have to solicit that the Claim on me for the sum subscribed may be relinquished—

as to me the subject on which I adress you is of most important Concern, an immediate decission and answer is requested—

while thus desolving the connection between ministers and

their people ought ever to be held sacred.— My soul is overwhelmed with emotions naturally arising from the circumstance, but desirous of the things which makes for peace,—& in full hope that the ministration of a [339] a nother may tend to the benefit of the Church, and the advancement of the Redeemer's kingdom in this place, I cast my cares upon him who who Judgeth righteously & will Judge between you and me.

I am Gentlemen, with much respect
your Ob[t]. Servant
Signed Galen Hext[1]

To the Vestry and wardens
of the Episcopal Church
Beaufort—

Beaufort 19th- Feb[y] 1811.

The vestry & wardens being desired to meet this morning at 10 oClock of Business of importance. they met Accordingly Present

Robert Barnwell Jacob Guerard Archibald Campbell & Stephen Elliott	Vistry	John Rhodes Ch. warden

The Rev[d]. M[r] Hext having sent in his letter of Resignation to take place the first Jan[y]. next. the same was rec[d] and Read, but not Generally taken up, they however agreed to deliver to him Tistamoneals of his good conduct during the whole of the time he had officiated as their minister, they therefore drew them up and their Church warden delivered the same to the Rev[d]. M[r] Hext, who expressed in high terms his Gratification.

at the same meeting It was proposed & agreed to, to appoint delegates to to meet the state convention to be held in Cha[s].ton on 26th- Inst. they Accordingly appointed the Rev[d]. Jn[o]- B. Campbell to represent this Congregation—

[1]It is most unlikely that this letter was "Signed Galen Hext." The reverend gentleman's name was Hicks and he hardly signed any other. There was in the Low-Country of South Carolina a large Hext family and the clerk of the vestry and church wardens was doubtless confused by that name and insisted on giving it to the Reverend Mr. Hicks.

[340]

Beaufort 8th– april 1811

The vestry, being desired to meet to determine what shoud be done with that property sold to persons who had not Comply'd with the Conditions of the Sale, and which property has been levey'd on, and advertised by the Sheriff to be Sold this day, they met accordingly.

Present– Col°- Robt- Barnwell
Doct A– Campbell
Jacob Guerard
Stephen Elliott
&
John G Barnwell } Vestry

John Rhodes
John McKee } C W–

They came to the following Resolution

That the Church wardens be directed to attend the sales & to purchase the lotts sold formerly to Jn°- B- Barnwell & Sarah Waight if they do not sell for more than the original Cost: The Church wardens attended accordingly and purchased the lotts. N°– 144 & N°– 145 for $260 being sold under the Execution against Jn°- B- Barnwell. John Porteous Esqr bought the lot N°. [1]for $210 being sold under the Execution against Mrs– Sarah Waight. the same being above the limitation.—

[341]

April 15th– 1811—

This being Easter monday, the Congregation met and proçeed to Elect the Vestry and Church wardens for the following year, when on Casting up the votes the following Gentlemen were Elected

Col°- Robert Barnwell
Doct- A- Campbell
Jacob Guerard
James Cuthbert
Stephen Elliott
John M Verdier
John G Barnwell } Vestry–

John Rhodes
John McKee } C W–

[1]No number is given. A caret follows N°., indicating that it was the intention of the writer to interline the figures, but he neglected to do so.

Rec^d^– the following letter from Rev^d^. mr Hicks–

Beaufort June 30th – 1811

Mr John Rhodes Church- warden

Dear Sir/

My ministry with you being near its close Renders it highly necessary that I shoud obtain leave of absence for a while that I might make previous arrangements for the future support and Comfort of myself and Famaily; must therefore request that you will have the goodness to call a meeting of the vestry as early as may be convenient & solicit for me this privilege:— & should the indulgence be granted, that they will make with me such a Settlement, as under my circumstances they may deem most suitable.—

I am Dear Sir with great respect
yours sincerely
(Signed) Galen Hicks

[342]

at a meeting of the vestry on the 1st– July 1811

Present Col^o.^ Robert Barnwell, Jacob Guerard, Stephen Elliott, & John G. Barnwell } Vestry
John Rhodes & John M^c^Kee Church wardens—

An application was Rec^d^ from the Rev^d^ Mr Hicks. praying for an unlimitted leave of absence for the remainder of the year as Mr Campbell had agreed to officiate in his Stead during his absence. and also to be released from the sum he had subscribed for the Building of a new church.—

Resolved. That Mr Hicks have leave of absence for the remainder of the year. That the vestry do not consider themselves legally authorise or impowered to release mr Hicks from his subscription to the church. That the Church wardens be requested to communicate to Mr Hicks the above Resolutions— That the Church wardens be authorised and requested to liquidate the Acco^ts^ due from the Church to Mr Hicks & Give him their Bonds for the Balance which may be due—

The Church wardens did, agreeable to the foregoing resolves, deliver to Mr Hicks a Copy of them. and did liquidate his Acco^ts^ by Giving their Bonds as Church wardens for the Same amounting to– Five thousand, one Hundred & forty six dollars 26/100—

[343]

July 1st– 1811

Mr– Robert Barnwell requested to be permitted to take up Mr Thomas Fullers Bond for £200. and his note £85..10/2 with the Interest due on the Same and to give his Bond Bearing Interest, for the Same.– on motion, It was agreed that Mr Robert Barnwell be permitted to Take up Mr Thomas Fullers Bond & Note, and give his own for the same agreeable to his request—

Resolved. that the Church wardens be authorised to deliver up to mr Robert Barnwell, Thomas Fullers Bond & Note. and take his Bond for the same with what Interest might be due thereon—Mrs Bull's Bond was taken instead of Col R Barnwell's for Mr Fuller's debt—E Barnwell

[346[1]]

List of Bonds due the Episcopal Church in Beaufort 31st– March 1812

James Cuthberts Bond		$247
Richd Ellis	do	160–.
Elizh– Gough	do	180
Robert Barnwells	do	71-12
do ..... do	do	67....
do ..... do	do	337-7-10
Docr. J. E. B. Findley	do	107.
do ..... do	do	76
John Porteous	do	160–
Stephen Laurence	do	160
Alexander Brown	do	115
J. M- Verdier	do	210
James Stuart	do	160-
do....do	do	122
Charles Stuart	do	158
James Bowman	do	80
Josh- Johnsons	do	82
Nathl. Barnwell	do	189
John Cox	do	80
Wm Sams	do	160.
Ralph Elliott	do	79.
Josh– B– Cook	do	50–
William Smith	do	160- -

List of notes due the Church Viz

Name		Total
John G. Barnwell	£22	
Frederick Fraser		5.
Thomas Grayson	£5	
do .... do	5–	
do .... do	37–	47.
John M Verdiers		22
wm Robertson		27
Francis Salters		37
Est M. Perreclair	£5	
do .... do	27	32
James Grayson	37	42
do ......do	5	
Catherine Talbird		5
Stephen Elliott		5
william Joyner		5
ann Joyner		5
John Mulheron	5–	20–
Mrs- Mulheron	15	
Stephen Lawrence		5
Robert Detriville		5
Jacob Guerard Paid Mr Rhodes and inserted in his acct cast		5
James H. Cuthbert	£37.11.6	
do ..... do	5	42..11..6
John Rhodes	£28.70	

Recd. from Mr J Rhodes. late church warden the above Bonds and notes this 1st May 1812.

Edward Barnwell
church warden

[1]Pages 344 and 345 are blank.

[347]

Beaufort South Carolina
Easter Monday 30th March 1812

The Episcopal members of the Church met agreeably to advertisement and elected the following Gentlemen as Vestry and Church Wardens for the ensuing year.

Vestry	Church Wardens
Col Robt Barnwell	John Mc.Kee
Dr Archd Campbell	Edwd. Barnwell
James H Cuthbert Senr.	
Steph. Elliott	
John Rhodes	
Jacob Guerard	
Capt. John G Barnwell	

The minutes of Vestry henceforth transferred to a New Book purchased for the purpose–

Edwd Barnwell[1]

[378[2]]

Dr The Vestry or Church Wardens of

		£	s	d
1770	To Laying 175250 Bricks in Building the New Church finding them with Lime Labourers &c ..@ £15..2..6 pr	£ 2650.	15..	7
	To aditional work on Chancel pr agreement	60		
	To amount of Lumber as pr Bill	716	..0..	9
	To 900 yds plastering the inside of the Church	450–	„—	
	To 150 paving stones @ 10/.......	75	—	
1772	freight of Do from Charles Town	7..	17..	6
	To Carting Do to Church	3	—	
		£3962..	13..	10

[1]The minutes proper end here. The remaining records of the book consist of accounts and notes supplementary of the preceding minutes.

[2]Pages 348-377 are blank.

[379]

St Helena parish their acct with Hy Talbird

1770				
17 april	By your order on D Desaussure & co £	1000—		
17 august	By your ditto on ditto........	1000—		
	By my order in favr James Doharty (a pew)	160—		
	By Ballance due Henry Talbird....	1074..	6..	6
	By my order in favr– James Doharty	728..	7..	4
	£	3962..	13..	10

Beaufort April 10th 1773 Recd, of the Vestry of St Helina Parish an order of this date on the Church Warden for one Thousand seven hundred & seventy four pound Six Shillings & six pence Currency in full of the Foregoing Account and all Demands——

[389[1]]

Memorandum

May 18. 1753 Were deliver'd in the hands of the Church Wardens The Poor Rate List for the year 1752, Sub: for Rev^{r}. M^{r}. Peasely's H Rent Bond from Coll Wigg for £50. Sterling
Bond from Smith & Gordon £250: Curr^{cy} and one for £107.
Bond from Stuart & Steele £50. Sterling
A Surplice in the Chu^{r}h Delivered to J W Parsons Apr 22 1759.

[392[2]]

The Rev'd M^{r}. William Peasely.
—Sacrament Acc^{t}.——

1751.	Com^{ts}.			
Sept: 22	To Cash from . 21 .... £	22	13	——
Dec: 25	D^{o} 17	10	5	——
1752				
Mar: 29	D^{o} 18	13	——	——
May 17	D^{o} 12	7	——	——
	E. W. Recd £	.52.	18	——
Oct: 8	....D^{o}..... 19	10,	—8,	—6
Dec: 25	....D^{o}..... 21	12,	—18	,——
Apr: 22^{d}	....D^{o}..... 27	19,	—7,	—6
1753.				
	£	42.	14	,——
	left up^{d}. of the above	2,	——	——
	£	44„	14	„ ——
June: 10th..	....D^{o}..... 17	7	3	——
Oct. 7	....D^{o}..... 15	8	5	9
Dec. 25	....D^{o}..... 15	10	.——	.——
1754				
April 14	....D^{o}..... 25	16.	17	.——
June. 2..	....D^{o}..... 16	7	13	.. 9
		94	13	6

[1]Pages 380-388 are blank.
[2]Pages 390 and 391 are blank.

		£	s	d
	Cr by an overcharge Ap[l]: 14£1–.– by Sund[ys]. as ℘..Acc[t]..24 ———	25	.—	.—
	bal: Aug 5th. 1754 £	69	13	6
Sept 29th	....D[o]...... 8................	5	.—	.—
	C[r]. by Cash paid D[r]. Steele £10.–.–			
Dec[br] 25	....D[o].... 22................	15	2	.—
1755	C[r]. by Cash p[d]. W[m]. Gough £12—			
Mar: 30	D[o]——— 7................	2	1	3
	£	91	16	9
	———	22	—	.—
	£	69	16	9.

[393]

1757

January 2 Sunday — The Rev[d]. M[r]. Lewis of Prince William parish Preached & gave the Sacrament to 24 Comunicants; when was Collected £19..5 which I gave to Cap[t] John Gordon the Ch: Warden———

July 3[d]. — The Rev[d]. M[r]. Lewis preach[d]. and gave the Sacram[t]. to 26 Comunicants when was Collected £28..7..9 which I paid M[r]. Francis Stuart Ch: Warden July 4th.

July 31. The Rev[d]. M[r]. Alex: Baron Preached & gave the Sacram[t]. to 7 Comunicants when was Collected 40/—

[406[1]]

Fee's To be taken by the Clerk & Sexton

For Ringing the Bell ....0..12..6———
For Diging the Grave & filing it up &.&........——
For attendance .... 12..6
For Invitation ....1..10—0
For Carrying the Corps into y[e] Church 3..10.0

if not Carried into y[e] Church £2..0..

[1]Pages 394-405 are blank.

Church Memorandums[1]

M[r], John Delagaye sold his pew N°. 6. unto Will: Harvey Esq— — — — — — — — — —

N°. 1. Parsonage Pew
2...D[r] James Cuthbert
3..... ditto[s]....
4....Gen[l]. Stephen Bulls
5...Gen[a]. John Barnwell
6...M[r] Nath[l]. Barnwell
7—M[r]. W[m]. H: Wigg—
8..Est[te]. James Black
9...Andrew Deveaux
10...Thomas Roper
11...Est[te]. Rob[t]. Wilkinson
12...Francis Saltus
13...Capt[n]. John Joyner
14...Estate W[m]. Elliott
15...Est[te] John Grayson
16...Thomas Heyward Jun[r].
17...Est[te]. John Barnwell
18...D[r] James Stuart
19. M[rs].. Phebe Waight
20..Thomas Talbird
21..John Bull Esq[r].—
22..Est[te]. Col[l]. N. Barnwell
23.M[r]. And[w]. Aggnew
24.Gen[l]. Stephen Bull
25- -John Mark Verdier
26- -Est[te's] ..of Stone & Bell
27..Rich[d]. Fairchild
public { 28. Daniel Greene
29..Est[te]. John Delabar } ☞

N° 28 was purchased at Sherifs Sales by J. Rhodes & Edward Barnwell then Church wardens. for a publick pew–

[407]

Rights to the Pews in the Parochial Church of S[t]. Helena———[2]

Pews	
N°. 1 ---Coll: W[m]: Hazzard 2----Coll Jn°- Mullryne 3----M[r]. Amb: Reeve	East end the pulpit North side
4----Parsonage pew 5---- 6----W[m]. Harvey Esq. 7----Jones & Wilkinson	West end the pulpit North side
8----M[r]. Cha[s]. purry 9----Coll: Nath: Barnwell 10----George DelaBere	East end South side
11..—John Gordon 12---Coll: Tho[s]. Wigg 13---M[r]. And[w] Bell 14---M[r] Rowl[d]. Serjeant	West end South side

[1]These "Memorandums" were recorded from the bottom of the page, the book being turned upside down.

[2]This record was also entered on the page while the volume was turned upside down.

[408]

Augst. 5: 1751
Then settled M^{r}. M^{c}pherlin Accompt & there is due from him to Coll: Barnwell £23..18..3.
And there is this day due to M^{r}. M^{c}pherling £33.——
Sept 20th. 1753
The Ch Warden J. M. gave Jno- Linnenton an Order on Capt Gordon to the val: of £15. Curr^{y}.
Augst. 5: M^{r}. Daly p^{d}. his Fine refus^{g}. Ch' Warden £10
Aug 6,, 1759 Titles to the 3 New pews are to be made to the Proprietors, when they are Built

INDEX

www.ingramcontent.com/pod-product-compliance
Lightning Source LLC
Chambersburg PA
CBHW021853020426
42334CB00013B/312

* 9 7 8 0 8 9 3 0 8 2 9 5 6 *